Marcella Agnes Fitzgerald

Poems

Marcella Agnes Fitzgerald

Poems

ISBN/EAN: 9783741192227

Manufactured in Europe, USA, Canada, Australia, Japa

Cover: Foto ©Andreas Hilbeck / pixelio.de

Manufactured and distributed by brebook publishing software (www.brebook.com)

Marcella Agnes Fitzgerald

Poems

POEMS

BY

MARCELLA AGNES FITZGERALD

Published for the Author by
THE CATHOLIC PUBLICATION SOCIETY CO.
New York
—
1886

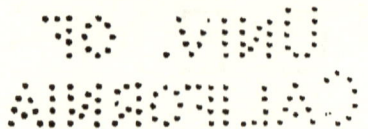

COPYRIGHT, 1886, BY
MARCELLA AGNES FITZGERALD.

TO

MY MOTHER,

AS AN OFFERING OF LOVE,

THIS VOLUME

IS

AFFECTIONATELY DEDICATED.

CONTENTS.

	PAGE
THE LORD'S PRAYER, .	13

MISCELLANEOUS.

October Pictures, .	. 21
The Voice of the Flowers,	27
Autumn Fancies, .	. 30
Death of Padre Serra, . .	31
The Women of the Revolution, .	. 38
March, . . .	43
April and May, .	. 45
The Bridal, .	48
Evening at Notre Dame.	. 51
Sunset beside the Sea, .	53
A Flower in Winter, . .	. 55
Bird Song at Midnight,	58
Gertie, . .	. 60
Easter Bells, .	61
A Magnolia Blossom,	63
Daniel O'Connell,	64
A Message from Home,	. 67
Harvest Home, .	70
The Mountain Spring,	. 72
Bridal Wishes, .	74
Columbia, .	76
A Cloud Picture, .	79
Another Year,	. 80

	PAGE
The Storm,	82
Our Dead President,	84
Donner Lake,	86
A Message to Erin,	90
A Souvenir,	92
Blind,	93
Sunset,	96
The Church of Carmelo,	97
Morning,	101
Evening,	102
Night,	103
Violets,	105
Autumn amid the Hills,	107
Bridal Stanzas,	109
The Picnic,	111
Irish Music,	116
Our Flag,	118
Onward,	121
A Spring-day Ride,	123
A Mother's Love,	127
Wild-Flowers,	129
Our Angel,	131
A Winter Day,	132
To J. A. L.,	135
Ten Years Ago,	137
The Old Adobe House,	139
To F. de C. M.,	142
Bridal Wishes.	145
Poem,	146
Gilroy Hot Springs,	149
Sonnet,	151

CONTENTS. 7

	PAGE
The Martyrs of Memphis,	152
Rain,	154
Iernian,	156
Sonnet,	159
Ireland's Appeal,	160
To Erin,	162
Unforgotten,	166
"Glimpses of the Supernatural,"	168
A Golden Wedding,	170
May-Day Memories,	174
The Centennial Ode,	176
A Memento,	184
Two Pictures,	186
To J. M.,	190
"God Bless You,"	192
The Baby Sleeps,	193
Confirmation,	194
Silver Jubilee,	196
Las Llagas,	199
Hawthorn Blossoms,	201
A Deer's Antlers,	204
Cheer Up,	206
A Memory of May,	207
To Nellie,	210
A Trinket,	211
Through Idle Hours,	212
"Golden Sands,"	214
God Cares for All,	216
The True Comforter,	218
San Diego's Centenary,	220
Thanksgiving Hymn,	224

CONTENTS.

	PAGE
Welcome to the Firemen,	225
To a Friend,	228
A Fair Spring Day,	230
To M. E. B ,	232
Waiting,	234
Greeting to the Pioneers,	235
Sunrise in Winter,	239
The Little Hat and Shoes,	241
To Annie,	243
A Token,	245
The Robin,	247
A Christian Hero,	248
Sunshine and Shadow,	251
To Fannie R.,	253
Dear Motherland,	254
In the Dawn,	257
Bridal Wishes,	258
Glory to God,	259
Bishop of Joppa,	261
Freedom,	263
At Daylight's Close,	266
Beside the Sea,	267
Amid the Pines,	269
Raising the Flag at Monterey,	272
San Carlos del Carmelo,	275
CALIFORNIA'S WELCOME TO MOST REV. P. W. RIORDAN,	281

SACRED SUBJECTS.

To the Holy Face,	295
The Most Precious Blood,	297
"Jesus Meek and Humble,"	298

CONTENTS.

	PAGE
The Rescue of the King,	300
At Benediction,	304
Our Lady of Perpetual Help,	306
The Rosary,	308
Notre Dame de France,	310
The Assumption of Our Lady,	315
"Notre Dame de Bon Secours,"	319
Telling the Beads,	322
Our Lady's Dolors,	325
Our Lady of Mount Carmel,	331
My Lady's Jewels,	334
Our Lady of Knock,	337
Lines,	340
October Roses,	343
"Hail, Full of Grace!"	345
Cause of our Joy,	346
Ave Maria,	348
Through Mary's Heart,	350
To Saint Joseph,	352
Saint Patrick's Day,	354
Saint Benedict's Day,	356
Saint Dominic,	360
Saint Thomas of Aquinas,	364
Saint Benedict Joseph Labre,	367
Saint Agnes,	370
Saint Viviana,	372
To my Guardian Angel,	375
For the Souls in Purgatory,	376
The Calla,	378
Remember the Dead,	380
A Message,	382

	PAGE
In Mission Time,	384
All Souls' Day,	390

LEGENDS AND BALLADS.

The Cross,	395
Philip's Mother	400
The Rose,	407
Legend of San Gabriel,	413
The Happiest Christmas,	416
The Haunted Dell,	421
The Poor Man's Treasures,	430
Dolores,	433
Ashes of Roses,	437
Las Lagrimas,	439
The Battle of Clavijo,	442
Little Elsie,	447
Little Gaspard's Dream,	450
The Haunted Homestead,	455
Conversion of Father Hermann,	457
"Bread upon the Waters,"	461
Maud's Hero,	471
Gertrude,	473
Dimas,	477
Homeward Bound,	481
A Christmas Legend,	487
King Alfred and the Orphan,	490
Legend of San Miguel,	495
At the General Rodeo,	499

The Lord's Prayer.

THE LORD'S PRAYER.

"Our Father, who art in Heaven,"

"OUR Father"—words of loving
    Thou hast taught our lips to frame,
Giving to earth's erring children
    The dear shelter of Thy name.
Father of the tribes that wander
    In the darkness far away,
Father of the hearts that love Thee,
    Love and serve Thee day by day;
Thou who rulest the highest heavens,
    Thou whose voice the wave commands,
Thou whose mandate called to being
    All the known and unknown lands,
Look on us with eyes of mercy,
    Let our lives Thy love still claim,
Make us, in our daily actions,
    Worthy children of Thy name.

"Hallowed be Thy name."

By the lips of every people
    Let Thy praises, Lord, be told;
All Thy glories, all Thy beauties,
    Let their eloquence unfold.

By the sound of grand hosannas
 Thrilling through cathedral aisles
When the organ's rolling pæans
 Shake the shining marble piles;
By the homage of the mighty,
 By the homage of the poor;
By the reverential worship
 Yielded while the years endure;
By the sweetest thoughts and purest
 Which Thy favored spirits frame;
By the lisping tones of childhood,
 Father, "hallowed be Thy name."

"Thy kingdom come:"

To the rich, on whom Thy blessings
 Have been showered with generous hand;
To the humble, to the noble,
 To the honored of the land;
To the pure, sweet heart of childhood,
 To the sad, worn heart of age;
To the wanderer, to the laborer,
 To the scholar, to the sage;
To the faithful who are toiling
 On their pilgrimage of pain,
Hoping, praying that their efforts,
 That their striving, be not vain;
To the souls by sorrow stricken,
 To the lips with anguish dumb,
In its bright and fadeless beauty,
 Father, let "Thy kingdom come."

"Thy will be done on earth as it is in Heaven."

Let the laws Thy love hath given,
    Lest our faltering footsteps stray,
Mould our lives and draw us closer,
    Father, to Thy heart each day.
Bind our spirits with Thy fetters;
    Let us only live and move
In the doing of Thy mandates,
    In the seeking of Thy love.
As the shining seraphs standing
    In the presence of Thy throne
Haste in joy to do Thy bidding
    When Thy will Thou makest known,
So we pray, O heavenly Father!
    That from morn till set of sun,
In our thoughts and words and actions,
    May "Thy holy will be done."

"Give us this day our daily bread."

Hearken to the sad appealing,
    Hearken to the wailing cry,
Fill the wants whose ceaseless craving
    Thou alone canst satisfy.
From the lips by famine whitened,
    From the lips by plenty fed,
Rises up the meek petition,
    Father, for our daily bread—
For the bread that sates all hunger,
    For a knowledge of Thy word,

Pure and perfect in its power
  Till the inmost heart is stirred.
Give to us the Bread of Angels,
  The dear Banquet of Thy love;
Feed us, strengthen and sustain us,
  Till we see Thy face above.

*"Forgive us our trespasses, as we forgive them that
trespass against us."*

By Thy love, which none can measure,
  By Thy pity, which all feel,
Pleading pardon for each trespass,
  Father, at Thy feet we kneel.
Pardon for the grave offences
  Which our wayward hearts have wrought,
Pardon for each word unkindly,
  For each dark, ungenerous thought:
Pardon us, and teach us, Father,
  Our forgiveness to bestow
Upon all who wrong or grieve us
  On our journey here below:
Pardon us; and as we pardon
  At Thy bidding, God of love,
May we be refreshed and strengthened
  By Thy graces from above.

"And lead us not into temptation:"

From the countless dangers waiting
  For the guileless heart of youth,
From temptations which allure us
  In the borrowed garb of truth,

From the fiend's wiles delusive,
  From his cruel spell of power,
'Neath Thy love's protecting mantle
  Shield us, Father, hour by hour.
Bid Thy angels watch around us,
  Lest the "Evil One of sin,"
Finding each heart's portal open
  And unguarded, enter in.
By Thy will divine, oh! fashion
  Every thought and word of ours,
Till they glow in deathless beauty,
  Blossoms for Thy garden bowers.

"But deliver us from evil. Amen."

Keep us from the evils round us,
  From the woes that walk by night;
From the clouds whose dreary darkness
  Fain would veil from us Thy light;
From the hatred of our foemen,
  From their malice, from their spleen,
From their venomed words of anger
  Piercing us like arrows keen.
Weak and vain our spirits' battling
  If no aid by Thee is given,
If our strength and courage spring not
  From Thy boundless wealth in Heaven.
So "deliver us from evil,"
  Humbly, Father, do we pray,
Lest our deeds, when weighed, be wanting
  In the dread accounting day.

Miscellaneous.

OCTOBER PICTURES.

LEAGUES of plain where gold and umber blend
   and merge in wondrous tinting;
Mountains east and west arising, giant warders
   proud and high;
Rivers where the white-armed plane-trees fling abroad
   their autumn banners;
Woodlands opening, in dim vistas, scenes of beauty
   to the eye;

Cottage homes in shade embowered, from whose
   lowly chimneys rising
Soar the curling smoke-wreaths softly out upon
   the frosty air,
As o'er Santa Anna's summit glows the morning sun
   in splendor,
Making all the southern valley smile in beauty rich
   and rare.

But the iron horse speeds northward, and we watch
   the shifting vision—
Hill and river, wood and mountain, and each quiet
   country home—
Till we pass the forest arches, and to westward see
   El Toro
Lifting up his wreathèd forehead proudly to the
   azure dome;

At his feet the crumbling ruins of the old adobe
    lying,
  'Neath whose roof so oft were sheltered Priest and
    Statesman, Bard and Sage,
Where the Warrior from the battle, and the rich and
    poor, were welcomed
  By the smiling lips of beauty and the reverent
    voice of age.

Onward still, the glorious sunlight painting many a
    fairy picture
  On the treeless eastern mountains, on the wooded
    western slopes,
Making brighter still the orchards, ruddier still the
    laden vineyards,
  Haloing fields where plenteous harvests crown the
    happy farmer's hopes.

Westward, half by hills encircled, we behold the calm
    Laguna ;
  Eastward, close beside the roadway, the Coyote's
    winding course—
Now a scarcely flowing streamlet, but, when winter
    storms are raging,
  Bearing all a torrent's swiftness, all a river's angry
    force.

Here the hills draw close together, until fancy loves
    to picture
  These low points by nature welded in a strong, un-
    broken chain,

Till the hand of the All-Seeing smote the jagged
  rocks asunder,
  That the springs which feed the river might send
    tribute to the main.

Once again the valley widens, stretching out in broad
    expanses
  Where the power of toil is striving, striving for the
    mastery yet,
And we see the untamed beauty of the panorama
    fading,
  With a feeling strangely blended, half of sadness
    and regret.

But the sun has veiled his splendor, and gray, rolling
    clouds of vapor
  Hide the blue skies bending o'er us, sweep o'er
    mountain-side and glen,
Till, like spectres dim and ghostlike, gleams afar the
    fair outlining
  Of the white-walled hamlet clustered on the hills of
    Almaden.

How the busy hand of labor leaves its trace on all
    around us,
  And we muse upon the progress of the swiftly pass-
    ing years!
On the changes they have witnessed, on the blessings
    they have brought us,
  Do we muse while gliding onward past the lonely
    "Hill of Tears."

And the friends whom once we cherished—how our
    hearts go out to meet them!
  Thoughts of hours we spent together, thoughts of
    days for ever fled,
As we gaze upon the cypress and the flowers that
    love has planted
  Round the silent streets and dwellings of the "City
    of the Dead."

Lo! beyond the stately poplars in their flaming
    robes of yellow,
  And the grove-like groups of foliage all in autumn
    tintings gay,
Rise to heaven the soaring spires and the stately
    domes that tell us
  We are near our goal and entering thy fair city,
    San José!

San José!—the name like magic calls to mind the
    olden Pueblo,
  With its quaint, white-walled adobes, and its quiet
    streets and lanes
Through which toiled the rude carretas, and the covered wagons bearing
  To new homes the household treasures of the Pilgrims of the Plains.

Now how changed! A mighty city stretches where
    then herds were straying,
  With its fair and lofty temples, and its halls where
    learning rules,

Where from distant homes assemble children of each
    clime and nation,
  Quaffing here in draughts that strengthen all the
    wisdom of the schools;

Streets through which the waves of traffic beat from
    early dawn till twilight,
  Lined with homes where joy abideth, and with
    palaces of trade;
And within her walls are gathered all the wealth of
    art and science,
  And the boasted powers of Progress 'neath her
    banners are arrayed.

Oh! she sits a queen of beauty 'mid her brightly bloom-
    ing gardens,
  With her far-famed Alameda leading out toward
    the west;
And she views the peerless valley that has yearly paid
    her tribute
  In the wine and oil and corn garnered from her
    fertile breast.

Lo! where once the sheltering willows lured the loi-
    tering breeze to wander,
  Now the scent of fragrant apples perfumes the Oc-
    tober air,
And a wilderness of beauty, homesteads, vineyards,
    orchards verging
  On the smooth and level roadway, greets the trav-
    eller everywhere.

City rich in wealth unbounded, rich in homes of ease
    and comfort,
  Great in all that art or nature can devise to give
    thee grace,
Royal in thy wondrous dower, in thy manifold pos-
    sessions,
  Queen by right of years of queenhood, queen by
    right of power and place !

Queen of hearts whose love, so loyal, years of change
    have left unaltered,
  Faithful still as when unclouded shone the halcyon
    days of youth,
Still we meet the same warm welcome from the smil-
    ing lips of friendship
  That are sanctified for ever by the holy chrism of
    Truth.

Blessings on thee, blessings on them, that their hearts
    and homes, rejoicing,
  Be refreshed in fullest measure by each influence
    divine !
And the fairest gifts and graces, and the rarest, sweet-
    est pleasures,
  Dwell within thee, flow around them, is the wish
    that we would twine.

THE VOICE OF THE FLOWERS.

A SOUVENIR, SEPTEMBER 12, 1871.

WHILE through the night, with far-reëchoing
    tramp,
  The iron charger sped,
By the pale lamplight in the crowded car
  Thy floral gift I read.

For the sweet flowers thy loving hands had twined
  Held each within its heart
A lesson pure and holy there enshrined,
  In fragrance to impart:

A lesson written in its glorious dyes
  By the great Master's hand—
A lesson beautiful to mortal eyes—
  For all to understand.

I clasped the Laurestina's snowy bloom—
  "A token," sweet, from thee;
Pansies and Rosemary whose pleading said:
  "I pray remember me."

The green leaves of the Violet, promise-fraught,
  "I will be faithful still";
The Lilac whispering of a love which yields
  In all things to God's will.

The Oleander ripe with blushes spake
    Its cautioning words : "Beware !
When round thy path the waves of evil break,
    Shun thou the tempter's snare."

The Lavender with fragrance-giving breath
    Sang softly thus : " Believe
Not all thou hearest ; words, though sweet, may be
    Attuned but to deceive."

The Aster said : " Seek thou in quiet ways
    The beautiful in life,
Where the clear stream of calm contentment flows
    Unchecked by worldly strife."

"There," sighed the queenly Rose, " in some fair
    bower,
    How sweet my task would be
To guard in guileless purity and trust
    The blush of modesty !"

The fragrant Vervain spoke of noble hearts
    That wake to Beauty's feast
When blossoms tremble on the dewy lawn,
    And Spring treads through the east ;

Of hearts that feel the joys which Nature gives
    In measure deep and grand,
But, filled with joy, feel too the thorns which wound
    The lover's outstretched hand.

In robes of purple and of orange dight,
    The gay Lantana smiled—
Emblem of rigor, yet in outward garb
    Fair as earth's fairest child.

The Immortelle, pale as though washed in tears,
    Spoke of remembrance deep
And strong as life, although the loved have sunk
    Into their last, long sleep.

The Cypress whispered: "Dread not death; it brings
    To true hearts sweet release";
And the Palm sang its proud, triumphal hymn
    Of victory and peace—

Of victory o'er passions and o'er woes
    Upon this earthly shore,
Of peace eternal in the realms of bliss
    When life's short fight is o'er.

Thus while the glittering stars of night looked down
    O'er forest, field, and dell,
The spirits of the blossoms sang to me
    From out each perfumed cell.

And treasured in the depths of my true heart
    I keep the happy hours
Spent with thee when the sunset's golden light
    Illumed the garden bowers,

And, resting 'neath the tall Acacia's shade,
    We heard a wild bird trill
A song full of the endless peace and joy
    Which thy dear home doth fill.

AUTUMN FANCIES.

LO! the Autumn's thousand torches
  Have been lighted in the wood,
Where the poison vine is dripping
  With the summer's reddest blood,
And the glades are brown and barren
  Where of yore the wild oats stood.

In the marsh amid the willows
  White and purple asters shine,
And the golden-rod is lifting
  Chalices of amber wine—
A libation to the goddess
  By the ancients deemed divine.

And the shadows of life's autumn
  Gather round us thick and fast,
Youth's bright joys like summer's leaflets
  Flutter downward on the blast,
And the sunny skies of friendship
  By drear clouds are overcast.

But God grant that through life's autumn
  Flowers of Faith and Hope may bloom,
And the golden light of Charity
  Its darkest hours illume,
Till each moment in perfection
  Glows with love's celestial bloom!

DEATH OF PADRE SERRA.

AUGUST 28, 1784.

SOLEMN and sweet the mighty waters sang
    Throughout that August day,
Filling with billowy waves of sound the air
    Round quiet Monterey,

Till all the gorges of the wooded hills
    Sent back their tones' deep strain,
And pine and cypress blended in one voice
    Their answer to the main.

Veiled in the azure hue the summer weaves
    With subtle golden dyes,
The untamed scene in its weird beauty seemed
    Drawn nearer to the skies:

The forest's fragrance drifted down the slopes,
    As though an Angel's hand
Had touched the boughs in passing, and had flung
    Their freshness o'er the land;

And all the pulsing echoes of the waves
    Seemed but the beating wings
Of seraphs waiting till a precious soul
    Would burst earth's fetterings.

For in the Mission, worn with days of pain,
    And toil, and journeyings long,
Good Padre Serra heard, in accents clear,
    The dear Death-Angel's song,

And saw his flaming sword divide life's clouds,
    And with its glorious ray
Illume the path whose course doth upward lead
    To realms of fadeless day.

But o'er his spirit fell no shade of dread,
    No fear of death's grim power:
The love which lit his pathway during life
    Sustained him in that hour.

Prayerful and patient as his wont, he marked
    The moments gliding past;
Ah! those who looked upon him little deemed
    That day on earth his last.

Upon that morning Canizares came,
    A hero tried and true,
Fresh from the dangers of the sounding deep,
    And glories of Peru.

He had been one of that heroic band
    Who, fifteen years before,
With Padre Serra lifted first the cross
    On California's shore.

Since then his vessel traversed distant seas,
    Strange winds his flag had blown,
And he had drifted through the breathless calm
    Of the fierce torrid zone.

DEATH OF PADRE SERRA.

Now, after all his wanderings, once again
    His ship at anchor lay
Where the rare golden sunlight of the west
    Shone bright o'er Monterey.

Thence he had hastened, all his heart aglow,
    To fair Carmelo's hall,
Eager to hear from lips prayer-sanctified
    Love's benediction fall.

And Padre Serra welcomed him with joy,
    Rising to clasp his hand,
And give him cordial welcome o'er and o'er
    To the wild western land;

Questioning of every voyage he had made,
    The countries he had seen,
And all the deeds whose kindling glories filled
    The years that came between;

Then gently said: "Dear friend, I truly bless
    The hand of the Most High,
Which led thee here that I might see thy face
    Once more before I die.

"For it is sweet to know the friend of years
    Will bear me to my rest,
And kindly place the holy churchyard clay
    Above my pulseless breast."

Turning to Father Francis, 'mid the tears
    Of those who gathered round—
The poor expression of a woe and grief
    Whose fulness knew no bound—

He said: "I crave one little boon of thee,
    Too small to be denied:
Lay me to rest, when I have passed away,
    By Padre Crespi's side."

Checking the sobs that quivered in his voice,
    Spoke Canizares then:
"Thy mission is not all accomplished yet
    Among the sons of men.

"In the drear darkness of the pagan night
    Thousands are born and die;
For the baptismal waters' healing grace
    The wailing infants cry;

"They wait thy coming: shall they wait in vain?
    Courage, my noble friend!
Christ will restore thee to us; this cannot—
    This cannot be the end."

But Padre Serra only calmly smiled
    At Canizares' zeal:
His soul had foretaste of the boundless joy
    God's chosen servants feel.

And while his words prophetic filled with pain
    Each loving listener's breast,
He rose and sought the pallet in his cell,
    Saying, "I go to rest."

The moments fled; then Father Francis sought
    The holy cell once more,
To find that Padre Serra slept for aye,
    His earthly trials o'er.

DEATH OF PADRE SERRA.

As a child slumbering on his mother's breast,
    Peaceful and calm he lay ;
But at the angel's call his soul had fled
    Its tenement of clay.

Upon his pulseless breast his gentle hands
    Still clasped the cross he bore
Since first, a novice 'mid Saint Francis' sons,
    The garb of gray he wore.

Upon his face, no longer marked with care,
    A glow of heavenly light,
As though the throne of Calvary's Lamb had shone
    Upon his failing sight ;

As though his closing ears had caught the sound
    Flung from seraphic lyres,
The strains of victory and of triumph sung
    By heaven's exultant choirs ;

As though he saw the guerdon which would crown
    His labors here below—
Each Mission planted 'mid the pagan tribes,
    A gem of purest glow.

  .   .   .   .   .

Then over all the tranquil summer scene
    Tolled forth the funeral-bell ;
It thundered o'er the waves of Monterey,
    The valley of Carmel.

The sailor, in his vessel on the bay,
    Bent low and signed the cross ;
From hut and hamlet rose the wail which told
    How bitter was the loss!

Far as on fleeing winds the knell was borne,
    All bade their labors end,
And thronging sought the Mission walls once more
    To gaze upon their friend ;

To gaze upon their father and their friend,
    Their teacher true and wise,
Whose loving hand had guided them along
    The pathway to the skies.

The children gathered, from the shadowy nooks,
    The fragrant wild-wood flowers,
Whose blushing beauty filled with fairy life
    The lonely forest bowers ;

Sweet flowers that treasured in their painted cells
    The dew-drop's pearly tear—
Meet offering for these simple, trusting hearts
    To lay upon his bier.

Soldier and mariner and neophyte
    Thronged through the Mission's hall
Till twilight over all the golden west
    Her purple robes let fall.

Then, while the solemn voice of chant and prayer
    Blent with the ocean's roar,
In sad procession to the lighted church
    His sainted form they bore.

And there they laid him : tapers shone around,
    Soldiers kept guard beside,
While Mission and Presidio ceaselessly
    Poured in their living tide.

And through the watches of that summer night,
    Upon the balmy air
Rose, like a column of celestial light,
    The people's fervent prayer,

As round about the holy dead they pressed,
    Touching his robe, his hand,
Calling him saint and father, as they wept
    His loss unto the land ;

Their wail—it seems to linger even yet
    Upon the breezes' swell,
Sung by the pines, and murmured evermore
    Around thy shrine, Carmel !

1871.

THE WOMEN OF THE REVOLUTION.

WHEN our nation yields her homage
   To her heroes true and bold,
To the *men* who won her freedom,
   Let her trace in shining gold,
On the column she has lifted
   To commemorate their fame,
Names of mothers, wives, and sisters
   Who *alike* our reverence claim.

True, they went not forth to battle
   When along the startled air
Beat the drum's far-reaching summons,
   Rang the bugle's shrilly blare;
When the cannon's tones of thunder
   Shook the listening earth around,
And the crash of charging squadrons
   Echoed from the trembling ground—

Nay, not there they won their laurels,
   But amid a sterner strife:
In the constant toil and trouble
   Of the daily cares of life.
Through the years of bitter warfare
   When, with dauntless heart and hand,
Against hordes of arméd foemen
   Our forefathers made their stand.

THE WOMEN OF THE REVOLUTION. 39

As we turn the pages telling
  The sad history of these years,
Can we fathom half the suffering,
  Half the heartache and the fears,
Of that band of valiant women?
  Ah! we ne'er can realize
All they bore with martyr firmness
  For the freedom that we prize.

When the call "To Arms" resounded,
  Tearfully but bravely they
At the altar of their country
  Their most cherished gave away:
Husband, father, son, or lover
  Hastened forth to do and dare,
Crowned with many a tender blessing,
  Sped by many a fervent prayer.

All whose hands could wield a weapon
  Marched to join the Patriot band:
Oh! the woe and desolation
  In the homes of our young land.
But the mothers of our nation
  Faltered not, though hard the way,
As they wrought amid their households,
  Hopefully, from day to day;

Seldom resting from their labors,
  In the field or at the loom,
Planning, caring, working ever,
  In the time of snow or bloom;

For the stores thus closely garnered
  Must be shared with generous hand :
Food and raiment must be furnished
  For the soldiers of the land.

Could they dwell content and happy
  When from many an icy gorge
Swept the winds in mad derision
  Round the huts of Valley Forge?
When they thought upon their dear ones
  Bearing hunger, want, and cold,
Language fails to paint the anguish
  Of their agony untold.

We who shrink from thoughts of hardship,
  We who shudder if the breeze
Comes to us at moments laden
  With the cool breath of the seas,
We whose love depicts these women,
  Dainty ladies, fair and grand,
Robed in rich and quaint attire,
  Jewels upon brow and hand,

Queens by right of wealth and beauty—
  Lo! with reverent voice we pause
To thank God, who gave such champions
  Unto Freedom's holy cause,
When all ranks, as one united,
  Worked against the common foe,
And a patriotic fervor
  Fired all spirits with its glow.

Far and wide the tide of battle
  Swept with its destructive force,
Blotting many a sunny landscape
  With fell ruin in its course;
And though thousands sank to perish,
  Women, faithful at their post,
Lifted up their hands to Heaven,
  Pleading for the Patriot host.

Oh! their bosoms proudly kindled
  At each tale of victory won,
Though perchance their joy was darkened
  By the loss of sire or son;
Though, to many, Peace returning
  Her clear light o'er earth to shed,
Would behold them fondly strewing
  Memory's roses o'er their dead.

Yet they murmured not, repined not,
  But nursed hope when hope seemed vain,
Looking up to Him whose power
  Could alone their hearts sustain
Through those dreary years of trial,
  Days of danger, nights of gloom.
Surely light from Heaven was lent them
  These dark moments to illume.

Brave, true-hearted, noble women!
  When we pledge our heroes great,
Warriors famed on fields of battle,
  Helmsmen of the ship of state,

First upon the roll of honor
  We will place your cherished name,
Praying that our Nation's daughters
  May prove worthy of your fame;

That the trust you held so nobly,
  Love of God and Fatherland,
May for ever light with glory
  Every household of our land;
And your virtues, priceless jewels,
  Our best heritage shall be,
Mothers of a glorious Nation!
  Pride and glory of the Free!

MARCH.

HARK! to that trumpet sounding from the walls
    That circle the great palace of the Year;
And mark! as with a crash the drawbridge falls,
    The gallant warrior, March, comes riding here—

Brave, princely March, the New Year's haughtiest son,
    Though doomed, like his late brothers, soon to die;
He lifts his white plume proudly to the sun,
    And fills with shouts of triumph earth and sky.

The laughing brooklets lift their voice in joy,
    The wild-birds carol forth a pæan sweet,
And Nature lays her gifts which never cloy,
    Her floral incense, at the conqueror's feet.

Fair as the fairest lily gleams his brow,
    And, as the spring's first roses glow his cheeks,
At times his voice is tender, soft, and low;
    But, roused to wrath, in thunder-tones he speaks,

And waves his sword, so flashing, cold, and keen—
    His sword wrought by an artisan of old
In the far North, its diamond hilt's bright sheen
    Torn from the treasures of the Ice-King bold.

How shines his shield, rich with the armorer's art,
  With rarest emeralds set in blazing gold !
While, draped with careless grace across his heart,
  A flower-wreathed mantle falls in many a fold.

On the tall mountains, 'mid the forest glades,
  By winding river and by murmuring sea,
Each morn will gleam his trusty followers' blades,
  And his white banners flutter fair and free.

On, March! glad March! thou warrior of the Year;
  On with thy martial strains, thy ringing mirth!
And Viva! viva! hark the sounding cheer
  That thunders upward from the awakening earth.

APRIL AND MAY.

THE fairest daughter of the year,
    The beautiful, the bright,
Sweet April, with her sunny smiles
    And eyes of laughing light—

Sweet April, queen of birds and flowers,
    Has passed from earth away,
And left her wealth of fields and bowers
    To her fair sister May.

She came to us when storm-torn scenes
    Marked where proud March had trod;
The wild-birds circling round her sang,
    The flowers smiled from the sod.

The leaves from out their sheltering buds
    Burst forth to greet their queen,
And woo her steps to tarry long
    In each glad sylvan scene.

The lilies, emblems of the soul
    That knows no stain of sin,
Flung open wide their golden hearts,
    That she might gaze within.

The roses, parting ruby lips,
    Poured forth their tales of love;
And through the gloaming, in the wood,
    Was heard the plaintive dove.

In dimpling waves of grass and flowers
  We knew her mantle's fold ;
The goldfinch and the oriole lit
  Her groves like lamps of gold.

And in the murmurings of the leaves,
  The brooklet's babbling voice,
And whispering of the balmy breeze,
  She bade the earth rejoice.

But she is dead. And yet no voice
  Is hushed o'er her to grieve,
No wailings thrill the fragrant bowers
  Which she was forced to leave.

For o'er the hills in beauty clad,
  And through the smiling plain,
With ringing glee and melody
  Comes May's exulting train.

She treads the scenes her sister trod,
  'Mid bird-notes warbled clear ;
The welcomes from uncounted hearts
  Are sounding in her ear,

The while with reverent hand she culls
  The flowers from hill and wold,
And breaks upon fair April's tomb
  Her cup and wand of gold.

A denser shadow clothes the woods,
  But threads of silver run
No more amid the emerald robes
  By April's fingers spun.

And April's grass and April's flowers
  In whitening swaths are rolled,
While May is flinging o'er the hills
  Her amber and her gold.

Oh! she is fair and young and bright,
  But she will bear away
From earth the wealth her sister gave
  To beautify her sway.

Already on her snowy brow
  Mark how the blossoms pale;
The fragrance of her balmy breath
  Scarce trembles on the gale.

And soon, alas! amid the groves
  The birds will warble clear
A requiem o'er those sisters fair,
  Those darlings of the year.

THE BRIDAL.

SWEET perfumes from the hearts of flowers
    Throb out upon the summer air,
And heavenward soar, commingling with
    The incense of the voice of prayer.

For through the heavy, odorous calm
    The tapers gleam upon the shrine,
And angel-hosts bend low to view
    The mystery of Love Divine,

Bearing rich blessings from on high
    With which to crown the youthful pair
Who in His presence vow to-day
    Their mutual path through life to share ;

To crown the fair young bride, who stands
    With downcast eye and blushing cheek,
With all of love and hope and bliss
    The human heart on earth can seek.

For she is passing from the path
    Her girlish feet in glee hath pressed,
And childish joys and childish aims
    No longer reign within her breast.

But in the Future's valleys wait
    With welcoming smiles the angels good,
Whose care shall lead her day by day
    To pure and perfect womanhood.

THE BRIDAL. 49

For her may come no hours of grief,
  No dreary shadow mar her life,
Blest in her noble husband's love,
  Thrice happy as his honored wife.

So now within her childhood's home,
  With him whose love her heart hath won,
She answers to the solemn words
  Which blend their lives and souls in one.

The rite is o'er; loved ones throng round;
  Fond words for future weal are said,
While from the pictured walls look down
  The faces of the cherished dead,

As though in their mute smile they gave
  The blessings which their lips would frame—
The blessings which a hundred hearts
  Twine round the bride and bridegroom's name,

As forth amid their friends they move,
  While praise in lavish strain is poured,
And lead the way where viands fair
  Weigh down the groaning festal board.

Fast flows the bowl by pleasure crowned,
  The toast and jest go circling by,
And music lends its spell of power
  In chorus swelling deep and high.

Forth from the feast once more they pass,
  To linger in the colonnades,
Or wander where the wild-bird's notes
  Make glad the forest's opening glades;

Or listen to some voice of song
  Whose clear notes mock the lark's sweet glee,
Or murmur o'er a lover's vows
  Where whispering winds breathe low and free;

Till on the evening's fragrant breeze
  The swelling music wooes once more
The wanderers to the banquet-hall,
  And bids them tread the dancing-floor.

Still as the white-winged hours speed by,
  And star-lamps light the fields of blue,
Fond wishes for the happy pair
  Once and again all hearts renew.

God bless them in their mutual love!
  God grant them hope! God grant them bliss,
The foretaste of eternal joys
  Which crown a better world than this!

And may their bridal day be still
  An omen of their future way,
As happy in its speeding hours,
  As cloudless in its sunny ray!

EVENING AT NOTRE DAME.

ANOTHER day has written out its record
   Of good and ill upon the book of life,
And evening's pitying angel shuts the volume
   Upon the story of earth's toil and strife:

Another day—a day of summer beauty—
   Laid with its kindred in their dreamless rest,
Where amethystine lines with amber blending
   Bound the bright realms of cloudland on the west.

Above the mountains, robed in twilight's purple,
   The stars come forth in beauty one by one,
Glorious as spirits of earth's sainted martyrs,
   Bright as the fadeless splendor they have won.

Beyond the convent's fragrance-breathing garden,
   Beyond the shadow of its quiet wall,
The tides of life, like summer ocean's breaking
   On shell-strewn beaches, softly rise and fall.

Mellowed by distance comes the dying murmur
   Of noisy bustle from the busy mart;
But here is peace—God's peace, deep and eternal,
   In this his chamber of the city's heart.

Yes, here is peace—such peace as floods the spirit
   When morning sets day's golden gates ajar,
And grateful earth looks up from dews refreshing,
   And earliest bird-notes hail the morning star;

Peace on each face and in each throbbing bosom,
    As, gathering now in the soft twilight haze
Around Our Lady's shrine, with hearts uplifted,
    Sweet voices carol a glad hymn of praise;

And, blending with the anthem to our Mother,
    Our pleading wish for blessings bright and fair
On those whose love has wooed our wandering spirits
    Back to this tender atmosphere of prayer;

Has won us back unto the convent's shelter,
    Eager as children wearied wandering far,
To lay awhile before the pitying Saviour
    Our portion of earth's turmoil, strife, and jar;

To quaff from founts of heavenly consolation
    Strength for the present, healing for the past,
And grace to walk in firmest faith unflinching·
    Where'er the future of our lives be cast.

'Tis silence now; the last faint, silvery echo
    Of song dies out upon the calm of night,
But the bright stars, in soft midsummer glory,
    Are eloquent of lands of heavenly light.

    SAN JOSÉ, July 1, 1870.

SUNSET BESIDE THE SEA.

THE autumn's banner floated o'er the hills
  Beside the sounding sea,
Where up the hollow courses of the streams
  It sent its summons free,
Claiming the tribute from the fertile land
  Its waves had drawn for years,
The crystal waters from the hidden caves
  Where fall the wood-nymph's tears;

Wooing with sighs their laggard steps to leave
  The shadows cool and green,
Where laughing Spring and smiling Summer wrought
  To weave a leafy screen.
And forth they came at evening's quiet hour,
  Answering the ocean's call,
While all around the sunset's signal-fires
  Burned on the mountains' wall.

And westward, lo! in answering colors bright,
  Borne landward by the swell,
The golden garments of the god of light
  Drift rose-wreathed where they fell,
Forming a chain of splendor all along
  The wide, far-reaching west,
Seeming to mortal eyes as if they veiled
  The Islands of the Blest.

Gazing I mused: "Oh! if such glory shone
  When first the freshening gale
Blew aromatic fragrance from these shores
  To fill Cabrillo's sail;

Or when Viscayno with his valiant men
    Sailed northward o'er the main,
And to the wondering natives of this land
    Displayed the flag of Spain,

" As from afar with awe-struck eyes they gazed,
    And saw him kneel to pray
Where 'neath the spreading oak the Mass was said
    At storied Monterey—
What wonder, then, Hispania's gallant sons
    Deemed that unto their sight
Opened a land whose riches manifold
    Would rival Ophir's light?—

" A land whose praises to his sovereign king
    Viscayno's letters bore :
Praise of its forests dense, its mountains grand,
    Its fair and tranquil shore."
But while I mused a sudden blaze of light
    Shot o'er the ocean's breast,
Marking with crimson where October's sun
    Had slowly sunk to rest.

High flamed the clouds, as though the pirate Drake
    Had started from his grave,
And with the glow of burning galleons lit
    The broad Pacific's wave ;
Till Twilight in her matchless beauty came
    With eyes of starry ray,
And tenderly her treasured violets flung
    Upon the grave of Day.

OCTOBER, 1874.

A FLOWER IN WINTER.

HOPE IN WOE.

A WEEPING mother came to kneel
    Beside her first-born's tomb.
'Twas when the dreary winter hours
    Had veiled the earth with gloom:
The fields around were waste and wild,
    No sunbeams lit the land,
And far away, with sullen din,
    The breakers shook the strand.
She knelt beside her darling's grave,
    And bitter tears fell fast,
As, rushing o'er her spirit, came
    Fond memories of the past—
Fond memories of the far-off days
    That all unclouded flew,
Each blended with some thought of him,
    Her son so good, so true.
Though other children claimed her love
    And in her home had part,
None, none could fill the first-born's place
    Within the mother's heart.
And—bitter woe to her—he died
    Far, far from home's bright charms;
Not hers to soothe his parting hours,
    Enfolded in her arms.

He left her when the spring-day light
    Shone fair o'er vale and hill,
And, ere a single blossom died,
    They brought him, cold and still,
Shrouded and coffined for the grave,
    His fair face maimed and torn :
The memory of that awful hour
    Her soul for years had borne.

Now, while with trembling lips she poured
    To God her earnest prayer
For strength through all life's coming days
    Her heavy cross to bear,
She marked, amid the summer's wreck
    That strewed her darling's tomb,
A radiant, golden-tinted flower
    That smiled in fullest bloom—
A blossom from Spring's floral crown,
    Unmarred by wind or frost,
As fair as when the zephyrs bland
    Its shining petals tossed.
It seemed an emblem of the life
    Of him who slept below;
Bright as his memory in her heart
    It bloomed 'mid winter's woe,
And cheered her with the soothing power
    That sorrow's wounds can heal,
As pierced into her inmost soul
    That wild-flower's mute appeal :
"The God who through the wintry hours
    Protects my fragile head,
And bids me keep, through sun and showers,
    My watch above the dead,

Forgets not faithful hearts that turn
   To him in trust and love :
He leads them through the shadowy vale
   To his bright home above ;
He sends his angel-hosts to guard
   And guide our steps the while :
Each cloud of sorrow only veils
   The glory of his smile."

BIRD-SONG AT MIDNIGHT.

THE summer's dreamy beauty.
   Lay over all the west,
And night into completeness
   Rounded the Sabbath's rest,

When o'er the slumbering valley,
   The last sweet hours of May,
I watched the bright moon gliding
   Calmly upon her way.

Far off the noisy murmurs
   Of life had sunk and died,
As when from sounding beaches
   Rolls back the ebbing tide.

The leafy trees above me
   Moved to no zephyr's sigh;
Peace on the earth around me,
   Peace in the cloudless sky.

The perfume of the roses
   And woodbine filled the air;
The great, warm heart of Nature
   Grew eloquent of prayer.

It seemed an hour when only
   Sweet thoughts of Heaven could thrill,
When at the fount of mercy
   The heart might quaff its fill;

BIRD-SONG AT MIDNIGHT.

An hour when earth was yielding
   Its homage, fresh and free,
In loveliness and fragrance,
   Father of light! to thee.

When, lo! the breathless silence
   A strain harmonious stirred,
And through the air went floating
   The sweet song of a bird;

As though the music dwelling
   Within the lark's meek breast,
Amid such tranquil beauty
   Had burst the bonds of rest,

And from its heart o'erflowing
   The melody outrang;
In accents clear and joyous
   The midnight warbler sang.

Glory and love and worship
   Seemed blended in each tone—
Glory and love and worship
   To God, and God alone.

And ere the last note trembled
   Its mate caught up the strain,
And in the night's deep silence
   Sang once, and yet again.

While faintly sweet the echoes
   Would fain each note prolong,
May's latest hour of beauty
   Went out in light and song.

GERTIE.

A LITTLE fay whose golden tresses twine
    In clustering rings above her forehead white,
O'ershadowing eyes whose dark and lustrous cells
    Imprison rays of soft and tender light;
Round cheeks on which the rose's tint is laid,
And rosebud lips for kisses only made;

Wee hands that cling in fond and close embrace,
    And baby-tones whose gentle accents fill
Her happy home with music, baby-words
    Whose echoes linger in my memory still,
As oft I muse upon the smiling grace
And perfect beauty of her winsome face.

Close sheltered in the arms of truest love,
    Knowing no shadow on her sunny way,
She seems an angel lent us from above,
    A sunbeam sent to brighten with its ray
The flowers of love, buds of celestial birth,
Whose beauty cheers the pilgrim upon earth.

Dear Baby Gertie! May the angels keep
    All tears of sorrow from her loving eyes,
And bright the clear, unclouded sunlight sweep
    Across her path from Joy's soft summer skies,
Till the sweet promise of her youth shall be
Blessed and perfected, O my God, by thee!

EASTER BELLS.

OVER the breast of the budding earth,
    The verdant meadows aglow with bloom,
Over the woodlands whose waving boughs
Are casting shadows of vernal gloom,
    Ring out sweet bells with a joyous chime,
    Hailing the dawn of the Easter time!

Waken the echoes slumbering far
In rock-ribbed glens of the mighty hills,
Till the laughing streamlets dance with joy
At the musical call of their vibrant thrills;
    Breathe to the hurrying wind and wave
    That Love has triumphed over the grave!

Echo the songs that the angels sing
In the shining courts of Heaven to-day,
The alleluias glad that ring,
The hymn of praise, the glorious lay
    That tells to the world its woes have fled,
    For its Saviour has risen from the dead.

Kindle the sunshine of hope and love
That lurks in the depths of the human breast
Bid the pilgrim turn to his home above,
The only haven of peace and rest,
    Purchased for him by the Precious Blood
    Shed for man on the Holy Rood.

O bells, sweet bells! again, again
Fling your musical message across the land,
Till its people's voices from mount and glen
Soar up to Heaven in chorus grand,
    While the tidings of joy o'er earth are spread:
    "Lo! Christ is risen from the dead."

A MAGNOLIA BLOSSOM.

A FAIR white bloom from convent garden brought,
   Fragrant and dewy in its perfect glow,
Pure as some Alpine peak's untrodden snow,
Or beauty of a child's unsullied thought,
Is this rare gem by God's own fingers wrought.
'Mid scenes of peace and love its chalice bright
Uplifted basked within the sun's warm light,
Till every petal glowed, with splendor fraught.
O sweet, symbolic flower! thy words of cheer
An angel-whisper speaketh to the heart
When, fainting 'neath the burdens of each day,
Gloomy despair contending for the sway,
We hear thee softly murmur: "Persevere!
He wins the crown who nobly does his part."

DANIEL O'CONNELL.

O MOTHER of saints and heroes!
   Arise in thy grace to-day,
And speak to the hearts of thy children
   Wherever their footsteps stray.

Oh! speak with a mother's fervor
   Who tells of the great deeds done,
For the sake of her love and honor,
   By a true and dauntless son,

Till their patriot souls shall kindle
   With many an answering thrill,
As memory calls up the accents
   That thundered from Tara's hill:

The voice that over the Curragh
   Swept clear as a trumpet-blast,
And fired the hearts of the people
   At the Rath of Mullaghmast—

The voice of the Liberator,
   Sounding sweet as silvery chimes,
Dispelling the gloom and the darkness
   And horror of penal times.

His eloquence won for thee, Erin,
   That thy valiant sons might stand
In the light of the Faith of their fathers
   Once more in their native land.

Oh! great was the burdening anguish,
  Most cruel the thorny crown,
And galling and heavy the fetters
  With which tyrants weighed thee down.

They martyred thy priests and bishops,
  Laid altar and abbey low,
And thy children's pastors and teachers
  Were marked as a common foe.

The sword of the persecutor
  Still dripped in his bloody hand
When O'Connell was sent unto thee
  To comfort his fallen land.

Oh! never before—nay, never—
  Was such glorious victory won,
Without ruin and battle carnage,
  As that which crowned thy son

When with words of such burning power—
  Words echoing far and wide—
He roused in the hearts of his people
  Their national love and pride;

When, not as a pleading nation,
  But as strong men demand their own,
He taught them to claim their freedom
  And rights from the British throne.

What blessings of untold merit
  He labored to win for thee—
For thee and thy exiled children
  Afar by each distant sea!

For wherever the flag of England
  Had marked the earth for its own,
Lo! there was Emancipation
  To the sons of the true Faith known.

He stood to the last unflinching
  And firm in thy cherished cause,
And laid at thy feet, O Mother,
  The corpse of the penal laws!

For this do thy children owe him
  Love fervent and strong and deep;
For this in our hearts' recesses
  Most sacred his name we keep.

And over the earth's expanses,
  Wherever thy children stray,
Their voices are raised to honor
  O'Connell's natal day.

For now, in the light of the freedom
  His thrilling eloquence won,
We know, O Mother of heroes!
  The worth of thy noble son.

And while others fresh wreaths of laurel
  For his mausoleum twine,
Take thou from the golden westland
  This spray of moss for his shrine.

AUGUST, 1875.

A MESSAGE FROM HOME.

OH! the human heart turns backward, with a longing deep and tender,
  As the evening shadows gather closer, closer round
  life's way,
Longing for the scenes of childhood which beheld
youth's sunny glory,
  As the cross of years and suffering groweth heavier
  day by day.

Little marvel, then, that, standing in the softened sunset splendors
  Of a life whose fleeting moments, on their heavenward journey, told
That the diamond milestone marking her last quarter-
century's dawning
  Had been passed with buoyant spirit and with
  courage true and bold—

Little marvel that her fancy, turning from the present,
lingered
  On the scenes round Newtownbarry, on her old
  home o'er the sea,
Picturing oft, in loving language, joys that 'neath its
roof-tree blessed her
  In the merry, merry hours of her girlhood's cloudless glee.

Fourscore years had sown their tear-drops and their
    smiles around her pathway;
  Love and pleasure, death and grieving, flung their
    largesse o'er her life;
Pain and suffering held and bound her with their
    keenest pangs of anguish,
  When Death's angel came to call her from earth's
    haunts with trouble rife.

And across the sounding ocean came a loving mes-
    sage speeding,
  Bearing to her sweetest greeting with a shamrock
    green and bright—
A shamrock that was nurtured by the suns and dews
    of Erin
  On the soil of Newtownbarry, where her eyes first
    saw the light;

The shamrock, precious ever to the exiled child of
    Ireland,
  Sacred since Saint Patrick blessed it with the touch
    of his right hand
When he taught the wondrous mystery of the Trinity,
    revealing
  Its meaning to the people by this floweret of the land.

Gentle hands received the token, tear-dimmed eyes
    gazed on it fondly,
  Tremblingly low accents murmured: "She who
    would have loved it best,
In the true home of the spirit, where the pure of soul
    dwell ever
  In the splendor of the Trinity, has found her long-
    ed-for rest."

Oh! the heart so true and faithful never more would
    thrill with rapture,
  And the sealed lids open never, though the sham-
    rock was so near;
For it found her lying calmly in death's stern and
    awful beauty,
  With her nearest and her dearest weeping by her
    silent bier.

Sweet home-token! tender message! blending with
    the solemn summons
  Which had called her where Faith merges into
    everlasting love,
And in Heaven's perpetual summer the redeemed, in
    joy celestial,
  Join the angels' song of worship sounding ever-
    more above.

HARVEST HOME.

NOT when October 'neath the red leaves lieth,
    And chill November bids the wild winds roam,
But in the fullest flush of summer glory,
    We sing our Harvest Home.

September smiles on fields o'er which the sickle
    Has sped its glittering course ;
On white straw billows flung in mad upheaval
    Before the threshers' force ;

Upon broad vineyards where the purpling clusters
    Drag down the weighted vine ;
On orchards where, in gold and ruby blending,
    The fragrant apples shine,

While vale and hill vibrate with ceaseless echo
    As freighted cars speed past,
Bearing to distant lands the harvest garnered
    From seed the sowers cast.

For this, in many a hymn of adoration
    And thanks to God above,
Soars upward like a cloud of fragrant incense
    Our people's grateful love.

For peace in California's golden border,
    For plenty in her fields,
For all the mercies of his hand which ever
    Her wayward children shields ;

For all the good gifts sent so freely to us,
  By joyous heart and tongue
Most gratefully unto the bounteous Giver
  Our Harvest Home is sung.

SEPTEMBER, 1880.

THE MOUNTAIN SPRING.

FRESH from the balmy air of upland meads,
    Beside the spring we checked our panting steeds—
Beside the spring, a crystal jewel pressed
Upon the green folds o'er the mountain's breast,
Where, with tall branches lifted to the skies,
Prone on the earth a giant oak-tree lies;
But generous Nature still its life maintains,
And pours the quickening sap through all its veins,
Bidding it from its summer foliage fling
A wealth of shadow o'er the lonely spring,
To shade its waters from the noontide heat
And bless the wanderer to this calm retreat.

A quiet spot, but oh! how bright and fair :
The mountains rising through the sunlit air,
The clustering trees beside the winding stream,
Where the first blossoms of the spring-time gleam
Amid the waving grasses there that cling,
Where the blithe robin plumes his glossy wing,
And the light-footed zephyrs speeding by
Leave not this solitude without a sigh ;
For 'tis a spot in which to linger long,
Cheered by the music of the wild-birds' song,
And joying in the beauties which the hand
Of the great Master scatters o'er the land.

Lo! from the rugged headlands rising round,
The eye may trace the valley's widest bound,
And see afar within the distant west
The opposing mountain lift its plumèd crest,
And proud El Toro midway to the skies ;
Or northward where the low Laguna lies,
And the Coyote in some long-past day
Cut through the hills a pathway to the bay;
Or southward mark, within the sun's warm fires,
Lifted in air the city's soaring spires,
And by the white-armed plane-trees, gaunt and gray,
Trace through the vale the Llaga's winding way,
Where in the May time, bright with birds and flowers,
We trod with rose-crowned Pleasure through her bowers,
While far below us wave in emerald sheen
The fields and forests fair of San Martin.
But ere the shadows of the evening fell
We bade the cool spring of the mount farewell,
And, through the wondrous beauty of the day,
Across the valley sped our homeward way ;
But tender memories of that scene will bring,
'Mid winter frosts, foreshadowings of the spring.

BRIDAL WISHES.

A SINGER in the olden time
   Sang sweetly, "Love is lord of all."
And still men own Love's power sublime
   In cottage or in palace hall.
His smile illumes earth's wildest scene;
   He mounts the very throne of kings,
And round the warrior's valiant heart
   He dares to fold his shining wings.
Love! dearest of the poet's themes,
   The wandering troubadour's gay song,
The minstrel's fairest, brightest dreams,
   To thee, and thee alone, belong.

Glad ruler of the realms of youth,
   Of hearts whose hours are always May,
Of spirits whose sweet bond of truth
   Was knit beneath thy gentle sway,
Thy flame, which sheds such fervid light
   When wooers strike the tuneful lyre,
Burns not in wedded bliss less bright,
   But shines with calmer, holier fire—
The tender glow, the lambent beam,
   That haloes these blest hours of life,
And bids a heaven-sent glory stream
   Around the husband and the wife.

Such glory may your future fill,
  With purest joys, O Cousins mine!
And balm and fragrance sweet distill
  Around your sacred household shrine,
As o'er life's fair and pleasant way
  Onward and upward still you move,
Companioned through youth's sunny day
  By the dear angels Hope and Love.
Be yours the strong and perfect faith
  That time and care alike survives,
And, victors o'er grief's shadowy wraith,
  Dwell wedded lovers all your lives.

COLUMBIA.

Mother of heroes! on thy noble brow
    Another year has set
Its seal of promise, and our hearts rejoice
    To find thee glorious yet.

Ay! fair as when our great forefathers hailed
    Thy birth with glad accord,
And, freely as wine floweth at a feast,
    Their blood to guard thee poured;

When through the din and smoke of battle-storms
    They bore thy colors on,
And foremost on thy roll of honor graved
    The name of Washington—

The name thy sons by every sea and shore
    In reverent honor shrine,
Which even lisping childhood learns to name
    As synonym of thine;

First of thy warriors, an illustrious band,
    Whose names shall honored be
Where'er thy sway extends, where'er are heard
    The anthems of the free,

Through all the length and breadth of thy domain,
    Columbia! peerless queen!
From where the Orient laughs in morning light
    To the West's sunset sheen.

For State by State unto thy banner drew
  The sons of every zone,
And brightest jewel of thy starry crown
  Was given our land, our own!—

Fair California, throned beside the sea
  In regal beauty grand,
Flinging abroad her glittering treasure-stores
  With a most generous hand.

Fairest of all the daughters of thy house,
  And true as she is fair,
Lo! how her sons assemble at her call,
  Thy glorious feast to share.

They come with banners dancing on the breeze,
  Their songs are of the free,
And ever and anon the cannon's tones
  Go thundering to the sea.

At the full fount of Liberty to-day
  Their spirits quaff their fill,
And at thy knee, Columbia, they swear
  To wish and work thy will.

For, oh! no laggards in their love are they,
  But ready at thy call
To bear thy starry flag o'er land and sea,
  To guard thee or to fall.

But oh! God grant that never, nevermore
  Thy shores with blood be dyed,
But gentle Peace and Liberty combine
  To bless thy country wide.

May no returning birthday on thy face
    Behold the trace of tears,
But find thee still as beautifully grand
    Through all the coming years;

Teaching thy children reverence for the past,
    Courage for days to be,
And that the power to guard thy rights be found
    In one word—Unity.

So shall thy reign for evermore extend,
    If but their true hearts hold,
In holy trust, the sacred charge bequeathed
    By thy brave chiefs of old.

A CLOUD-PICTURE.

Down sank the sun, and in his stead there came
   Clouds shining like a city all aflame;
High blazed the roofs of lofty spire and dome,
Red glowed the embers of each lowly home.
Upon a distant upland far unrolled
A monarch's tents and army rich with gold—
Hosts of a victor looking proudly down
Upon the ruin of the burning town,
Where dim, black shadows drifting to and fro
Seemed bands that forth to waste and pillage go.
A shaft of light, lance-like and tipped with blood,
Struck where the army of the conqueror stood ;
A flash, a blaze, and then—O vision dire !—
The tents were wrapped in sheets of living fire,
As though, when joying in triumphant flame,
Avenging hosts upon the victors came.
Their mingling bands were swiftly swept away,
And hidden by dense clouds of leaden gray;
And as the picture faded from my sight,
Came twilight softly ushering in the night.

ANOTHER YEAR.

ANOTHER year, grown old and worn and weary,
    His burden down has cast,
Sealed with his blood the volume he has written,
    And laid it with the past;

Another year whose gifts of peace and plenty
    Our fair, wide land have blessed,
Another year whose fleeting hours have brought us
    Nearer our home and rest;

Another year whose crown of precious moments
    Can nevermore be ours,
Save those which shine in virtue's holy records
    And bloom as heavenly flowers;

Another year—a year whose tears have fallen
    On graves whose red mounds hide
The forms we loved, our hearts most cherished darlings,
    Who in life's morning died;

Another year—well if each cross it brought us
    Has been in patience borne,
Lest they arise as witnesses against us
    In the dread Judgment morn.

ANOTHER YEAR.

Another year—the good old year has perished,
    And the new comes apace,
Pity and joy and hope, in tender blending,
    Imprinted on his face.

Another year—bright angel-hands are twining
    A wreath with which to crown
His infant brow, the glad New Year whose glories
    The Old Year's woes shall drown.

Another year—oh! may its dawn be joyous
    To all the sons of earth,
And gentle Peace and holy Concord linger
    Beside each household hearth.

May Love eternal smooth life's rugged pathway,
    And Hope reign in each breast,
Till, earthly turmoil o'er, Faith's guerdon crown them—
    The New Year of the Blest.

THE STORM.

THE King of the icy North
   Once summoned his hordes in glee—
Once summoned and sent them forth
   To raid upon land and sea.
They swept on their course of death
   Through the fields that so late were fair,
And chilled with their freezing breath
   The blossoms found springing there.

With a wild, far-ringing shout
   They tore from the old oak's clasp
The garland of summer leaves
   Still fluttering within its grasp;
A volume of wrath they poured
   In the voice of the mountain pines,
And smote a discordant chord
   On the harp of the clinging vines.

Then out to the sea they passed,
   And the mariner's cheek grew pale
At the crash of the falling mast
   And the flap of the wind-torn sail,
As down to the south they sped,
   And roused from their tranquil rest
The sprites of the mist whose bed
   Lies under the ocean's breast.

Then, mounting the skies once more,
   Back, back on the whirlwind's wing
They came with the tempest's roar
   To the home of the fierce Storm-King,

And told of the ruin wild
  In the paths which their steps pursued,
The wasted fields where they passed,
  The snow on the hill-tops strewed.

Then the Storm-King laughed aloud,
  And his hoarse, loud notes of glee
Rolled out of the thunder-cloud
  And echoed along the sea;
The hills to their great hearts shook
  With a thrill as of sudden fear,
And the echoes awaked from sleep
  And answered: "O King, we hear!"

Then the lance of the lightning leaped
  From the sheath of the blackest cloud,
And the winds in their anger shrieked
  Till the crest of the wood was bowed;
While pitiless, drear, and cold
  Was the fall of the driving rain,
Till the writing of ruin shone
  On the desolate, sodden plain.

But the sun with his shining wand
  The clouds from his pathway flung,
And over the east in light
  The bow of fair promise hung.
Then the Angel of Hope sang clear:
  "In patience await. We bring
In the wake of the wasting storm
  All blessings to crown the spring."

OUR DEAD PRESIDENT.

WEEP for the fallen one who lies
   In still and calm repose,
Death's seal upon the loving eyes
   That will no more unclose,
Though round him throng with reverent tread
A people mourning for their dead.

Weep for the Nation's Chief who fell
   When life was in its prime—
Not in the battle's maddening swell,
   But by the hand of Crime,
When Peace, in bridal robes arrayed,
The fortunes of our country swayed.

The noble heart no more will thrill
   At Duty's bugle-call;
The ready hand, the earnest will,
   That wrought for one and all,
Are resting now, their life's work done,
Their goal attained, their victory won.

The ruler of the fairest land
   On which the bright sun shines,
Each State of all its star-crowned band
   A wreath of memory twines—
A wreath gemmed with affection's tear—
To lay upon the hero's bier.

OUR DEAD PRESIDENT.

The flag he served above him floats
   In sombre symbols dressed ;
The voice of Joy has hushed its notes
   And will not mar his rest ;
But many a sad and bitter moan
Waketh the echoes with its tone.

From lake to gulf, from sea to sea,
   The mournful murmur swells,
The drums' low roll of agony,
   The solemn toll of bells,
As o'er our murdered chieftain's sleep
Our watch and ward we fondly keep.

But deeper, darker, heavier woe
   One gentle heart must bear,
Love's links dissevered by this blow
   That bids her spirit share
The sudden blight, the midnight gloom,
The awful shadow of the tomb.

We mourn the widow's lonely lot,
   The orphan's hapless fate ;
And, oh! by whom can be forgot
   The soul so desolate—
The aged mother, whose last years
Are darkened by this grief, these tears?

To each dear mourner true hearts yield
   A meed of sympathy.
God's love be still their strength and shield
   Through all the years to be!
God keep them in his sweet control
And soothe each sorrow-stricken soul!

DONNER LAKE.

LIKE a gem in rarest setting, or a poet's dream of beauty,
   Or that haven which a pilgrim pictures in his thoughts of rest,
Is the lake which lies encircled by the fairest, sweetest blossoms,
   Sentinelled by giant pine-trees near the tall Sierra's crest.

O'er its waves of crystal clearness lightly dance the mountain zephyrs,
   And across the fringing grasses come the timid deer to drink,
While the song birds carol gaily many a joyous glee and anthem,
   Resting on the branches bending downward to the water's brink.

Looking on it in the glory of the summer's fairest moments,
   Who would deem its echoes ever heard the wild, despairing cry
Of that little band of heroes who had toiled through many dangers,
   By its margin, then so lonely, there to famish and to die ;

When those lofty pines were writhing in the storm-
    king's fierce embraces,
  And the winter's snow had drifted, forming barriers
    broad and deep,
While the craggy heights beyond it, in their weird and
    grim outlining,
  To the travellers' straining vision seemed an ogre's
    castle-keep.

Here they rested, worn and weary, the bright visions
    which allured them
  Veiled behind the cloud whose darkness, low and
    dense, obscured their way ;
The wide vales of peace and plenty which their eager
    fancy painted
  Lying still so far beyond them at the western gates
    of day.

Who can paint the dreary picture of those sadly
    lengthening hours,
  When the moments, sorrow-freighted, slowly drag-
    ged their iron chain,
While across the tortured spirits of the sufferers came
    the haunting
  Memories of the homes whose comforts rose before
    them in their pain ?

Pictures of the happy evenings spent around the blaz-
    ing hearthside,
  Or when mirth and music cheered them round the
    joyous festal board,

Came to mock them 'mid the gnawing of the fearful
    pangs of hunger,
  Or when o'er the echoing mountains loud and fierce
    the tempest roared.

But from out the gloomy shadows which o'erhang
    that distant period
  Shine the names of valiant women, glorious hero-
    ines, who wrought
Marvels for their starving children, and, with words
    of hope and cheering,
Courage to the fainting spirits of their hapless com-
    rades brought.

Valiant women! noble mothers! Give to them a
    deathless glory,
  Laurels brighter than the warrior bringeth from
    the battle-field.
Write their names in fadeless letters on our land's his-
    toric records,
  Who, though facing death and danger, to despair
    would never yield.

They have passed unto their guerdon, and, O chil-
    dren loved so fondly!
  Let no cloud obscure the brightness of their mem-
    ory through the years;
Cherish it with fond affection, teach your children to
    revere it,
  Keep it green with the bedewing of your love's sin-
    cerest tears.

How the grand old pines of Donner seem to breathe
    the story over,
  As their murmurings sound like echoes of the pray-
    ers heard long ago,
Sighing still as though in pity for the anguish which
    they witnessed,
  For the heart-break and the sorrow, for the agony
    and woe!

Lake of weird, romantic beauty! for the sake of
    friends who bravely
  Quaffed the chalice of affliction by thy waters at
    that time,
For their sake, true friends and cherished, do I dare
    to make this offering,
  To thy beauties and thy memories, of this simple
    wreath of rhyme.

A MESSAGE TO ERIN.

FROM this bright realm of Occidental beauty,
    Laved by the waters of the sunset sea,
With hearts o'erflowing with true, filial fondness,
    We send our greeting, Erin, unto thee—

Mother of hero sons, whose hearts, undaunted,
    For thee have faced the battle's desperate shock,
And poured their blood upon thy fields of carnage,
    Or bowed their heads upon the fatal block.

How many hearts for thee have throbbed and broken,
    How many prayers for thee have rent the skies,
How many bursts of agony unspoken
    From hearts that longed again to see thee rise!

How many bards, with love for thee o'erflowing,
    Have sung thy beauties in undying strains,
Though with each note of harp and voice was blended
    The sullen clanking of their galling chains!

Erin, our Queen, though crownless, we salute thee!
    And mourn with thee thy fallen, saddened state,
Praying that, in the years the future veileth,
    Bright days for thee and for thy children wait,

When, Gedeon-like, our chosen band of brothers,
    Their spirits freed from thoughts of earthly gain,
Shall strike the shackles from thy suffering people,
    And crown thy regal forehead once again;

When, clannish hate and civil strife forgotten,
   And hands close clasped in unity and love,
Unto our island home once more returning,
   We hail fair Peace and Freedom's banished dove;

When, not as now, on this thy yearly festal,
   Our strains of joy are blent with falling tears,
But when in fullest glory on our vision
   Dawneth thy future bright through coming years;

When the All-Father, moved by prayers to pity,
   Shall drive the tyrant brood from out thy land,
And, freed and purified by Heaven's ordaining,
   Dear Mother Erin, thou again wilt stand.

A SOUVENIR.

I CLASP a crystal vase of winter flowers,
  Of fragrant, golden jonquils sweet as fair,
Breathing of chivalry and love returned,
  And dark-blue violets whose beauty bear
    The tender wishes faithful spirits twine,
    The message of thy gentle heart to mine.

A perfect gift, a souvenir to prize,
  A bright memento through succeeding days
Of one whose pathway lies 'neath cloudless skies
  Lit by the splendor of love's golden rays—
    A thought of thee, whose aim through life has been
    To gladden by kind deeds the hearts of men;

Lending thy aid, thy words of gentle cheer,
  Thy smile's clear sunshine chasing sorrow's gloom,
Thy presence as the violets' perfume dear,
  Thy spirit's worth as golden as this bloom
    Which wafted once from winter's emerald sod
    Its incense to the very Throne of God.

Thus while the rain-clouds rest on hill and vale,
  Showering their precious freight along the lea,
I gaze upon these gems from Flora's crown,
  And, gazing, weave sweet dreams, beloved, of thee:
    Sweet dreams, fond hopes, that all thy future know
    In full perfection Love's and Friendship's glow.

BLIND.

AS one who, wandering through the woods alone
    When evening hours grow late,
And, filing past the twilight's purple throne,
    The stars come forth in state,

Hears o'er some tendrilled harp of tangled vines
    The zephyr's fingers play,
And fancies in the moaning strain he hears
    The voice of one astray;

Pausing to listen with bewildered brain,
    Deeming it some poor child,
Like the lost babes of childhood's well-loved tale
    Related in the wild;

Then calls, to hear no answer to his voice
    Save echo's ringing tone,
Or the low cry of some awakened bird
    Blent with the wind-harp's moan;

While round about him ever denser grows
    The shadows of the leaves,
The showers of darkness from the garner floors
    Where Night unbinds the sheaves;

Then wanders on as through an unknown world,
    The starlight's silvery ray
Piercing the darkness like an angel's wand
    To guide him on his way—

So do I wander through the world alone,
    Saddened in heart and mind ;
Earth brings no comfort to my bleeding heart,
    For I, for I—am blind.

I tread where scenes of occidental light
    Their vistas fair unfurl,
Where genii at the foot of Nature's throne
    Their brightest offerings hurl.

To me the murmurs of the tide of life
    Seem wind-harps heard afar,
And my soul turns in weariness away
    From noontide's heat and jar ;

But the bright stars, whose glories poets sing,
    Look down on me at night ;
Through the Egyptian darkness of my soul
    They send their shafts of light,

Kindling upon the altar of my heart
    Their soft, celestial fires,
Stirring within me by their holy glow
    A flood of sweet desires.

And earth unveils before me in those hours
    Her gems of field and flood,
The rare, bright blossoms of the spring-time's crown
    She scattered in the wood :

The blooms o'er which my listless footsteps press
    While wandering on the wold,
The cowslip in her robes of purple state,
    The violet's cup of gold,

Frail, fairy blossoms flecked with creamy white,
 Reflecting March-day skies,
And gilias locking in their purple cells
 Heart-secrets from all eyes.

She shows me fairy grots by hillsides far
 Where fern-leaves cluster green,
And ruby-throated humming-birds astir
 In all their glorious sheen.

And bird-songs that I listened to all day
 Come back to me again,
Filling with their soft music, glad and sweet,
 The chambers of my brain.

The blended voices of the day arise
 In chorus deep and grand—
The heart-thanksgiving by the millions poured
 Throughout this golden land.

And with them may my poor weak strains arise,
 Not in repining tone,
But grateful for the gifts which generous hands
 Around my path have thrown.

SUNSET.

THE Day-God paused on our western hills,
    Where Evening waits in a tender glow,
And took from her fingers a crystal cup
    To pledge his love for the vale below.

The cup was crowned to its golden rim
    With wine of a beautiful amber hue,
Pressed from the vintage of cloudland shores,
    And beaded with tears of the morning dew.

He held it aloft while it glowed and gleamed
    'Neath the burning glance of his fiery eyes,
And the azure arch of the heavens caught up
    And mirrored it back in a thousand dyes.

He quaffed the draught to the valley fair
    As it calmly lay in its peace and rest,
And proudly yielded to Evening's sway
    The garden-spot of the glorious West.

Then, with murmured phrases of love and praise,
    Her regal forehead he fondly kissed;
When lo! at her blushes the amber clouds
    Took the tenderer tints of the amethyst.

And he passed away while the rosy glow
    Like an arch of glory the blue vault spanned,
And Evening, flushed with her monarch's kiss,
    Raised her starry sceptre above the land.

PADRE JUNIPERO'S MONUMENT.

THE CHURCH OF CARMELO.

THERE are songs of deathless glory twined to
crown the brows of heroes
With the laurels love and reverence as a meed of
honor yield
To the gallant knights and leaders who have borne a
stainless banner
For earth's noblest cause and purest over many a
battle-field.

There are lofty marble columns builded in commemo-
ration
Of the works their hands completed and the victories they won,
Telling in a deathless language to the swift succeeding ages
All the hearts now cold and pulseless to uplift our
race have done.

But our land's first Saint and Hero—he whose name
will shine for ever
First on California's records, foremost by a right
divine;
He whose fervent zeal enkindled in her wilds the light
celestial
Of God's holy Faith, and builded many a fair and
lofty shrine;

He, the pure, the true, the fearless follower of the
    great Saint Francis,
  With a spirit as devoted and seraphic as his own,
Our sainted Padre Serra, who within our Father's
    kingdom
  Ranketh now the tribes he rescued round about the
    Maker's throne—

Must *he* sleep, unknown, unhonored, where the wind
    its dirge is breathing,
  And the waves are breaking, breaking on the beach
    with thund'rous swell,
Where the tear-drops of the Winter and the Summer's
    smile of pity
  Fall on broken arch and column of the Mission of
    Carmel?

Must the shrine that holds such treasure as his pre-
    cious body perish?
  Nay; let saving hands extended bid it rise in grace
    once more,
And its bells give daily greeting at the joyous hours
    of Ave
  To the echoing hills around it and the lone, surf-
    beaten shore.

It was there his heart was centred with his neophytes
    around him,
  Teaching them to pray and labor by example as by
    word;
In the fields he toiled amidst them, while his gentle
    voice, uplifted,
  Sang the holy hymns whose cadence e'en the rudest
    bosoms stirred.

There he rested from his journeys—rest which shames
    our weak repining,
  With the history of its ceaseless thought, its fond,
    paternal care,
For the children of our country, wooed and won
    from pagan darkness,
  And called the light and glory of God's tender love
    to share.

California's fairest valleys by his presence have been
    hallowed,
  For he walked, as angel guarded, fearless through
    the trackless land,
Winning from each wild and fastness its rude race,
    who heard in wonder
  Meek Junipero's voice of pleading and obeyed his
    sweet command:

"Come to God, whose hand hath made you to his
    image and his likeness ;
  Come to him whose love, my children, is unmea-
    sured and untold ;
Come to him who died to save you, and the mantle of
    his mercy,
  And his love sweet and consuming, will your souls
    in joy enfold."

How the zeal which fired his bosom lit and glorified
    his features,
  Trembled in his voice and echoed in each hearer's
    kindling heart!
Till the present seemed to vanish, and in glad, en-
    raptured vision
  They beheld the shining kingdom wherein they
    might claim a part.

One who shared his toils and dangers, one who watched his latest moments,
  Paints for us the anguished sorrow, overwhelming and deep,
Of the broken-hearted Indians, as in agony they clustered
  Round the form of their apostle wrapped in death's unwaking sleep.

Lo! a hundred years have numbered countless changes in their passage
  Since the day the Saviour called him home to everlasting rest;
But his hallowed memory lingers with us, ever fresh and glorious,
  And we deem that spot as holy which his **sainted** presence blessed.

Therefore should all grateful spirits aid to **raise** in pristine beauty
  The fair church within whose shadow sleeps our Pioneer and Saint,
For to him are all indebted; 'twas his dauntless **zeal** and courage
  Won our land's rude sons from evil to religion's **sweet** restraint.

MORNING.

BENEATH star-gemmed arches glowing
  In the Orient's gorgeous land,
Rose-hued robes about her flowing,
  Diamond dew-drops on her wand,
In with merry, joyous air
Entereth Morning, sweetly fair.

Bright her lustrous eyes are glancing,
  Round her flits a fairy train,
Onward moves she 'mid their dancing
  Over ocean, hill, and plain,
Kissing Night's dark frown away,
Softly ushering in the Day.

EVENING.

Drawing wide the crimson curtains
    From the sunset's golden dome,
See above the western mountains
    Star-browed Evening softly come,
While her purple robe's rich glow
Trails along the hills below.

With her great voice, deep and holy,
    Bidding earthly cares depart,
Giving both to high and lowly
    Peace and rest of brain and heart,
Passing on with footsteps light
Yields she to the dark queen Night.

NIGHT.

THE last faint flush of the eventide
    Fades out from the western hills,
And the farewell notes of the song-birds come
    With a quiver of " Good-night " trills.

The dark-robed shadows with timid steps
    Glide out of the gorges deep
Where, shunning the gaze of the fervid noon,
    They have lain in a dreamless sleep.

How they cluster in groups 'neath the woodland
    shades,
    Or flit o'er the valley's breast,
But pause awe-struck where yon crimson line
    Still brightens the glowing west,

Till over the Coast Range's crested heights
    Hangs the beautiful Evening's shield—
A silver star in its radiance bright
    On a peerless azure field !

Then with swifter footsteps the shades flit by
    In chase of the flying light,
And starry banners in many a fold
    Float over the towers of Night.

While, soft as the stir of an angel's wing
    As it sweeps through the realms of air,
Down through the hush of the solemn hours
    Comes a balm like the breath of prayer,

As through the fragrance of grateful hearts,
    Upraised with the fading light,
Was soaring up to the gates of Heaven
    And flooding the heart of Night.

For Night brings rest to the weary brain,
    Glad rest to the hands that toil,
And sleep shuts out each scene of strife,
    Of grief, and of wild turmoil.

Then welcome, Night, with thy radiant brow
    And its soothing charm untold!
Welcome the boons that thy presence brings,
    And the blessings thy pure hands hold!

In the silent hours of thy reign, O Night!
    Speak to each listening heart
Of the Saviour's kingdom of love and light
    Where his servants alone have part;

That, rising with higher and holier aims,
    And strengthened for earthly strife,
They may onward press o'er the narrow way
    To the halls of eternal life.

VIOLETS.

BLUE-EYED violets, fragrant and sweet and tender,
  Earliest gift of the generous hand of Spring,
Fresh and sweet, and with diamond dew-drops glittering
  Brushed in haste from the beautiful Morning's wing.

Emblems meet of a loving and faithful spirit,
  "I will be constant," and never forget, they say;
Like a woman's heart which treasures some precious memory
  To fling its halo over life's shadowy way.

Blue-eyed violets, emblems of fadeless friendship,
  Ye waken again the dreams of the buried past,
Of hours which caught from rose-red lips' sweet smiling
  A summer glory too fair and too bright to last;

The hours when Twilight her dewy violets scattered
  In rich profusion over our Western land,
When the balmy air was heavy with garden odors,
  And queenly Hesper uplifted her shining wand;

Calm, dreamy hours, when heart unto heart replying
  Quaffed the full chalice of Hope by Friendship crowned,
When the weary discord of earth, into silence dying,
  Lent the charm of rest to the stillness that reigned around.

Dear friend, who trod with me through the summer gloaming,
  Emblemed by violets, constant and leal and true,
May the present be fair as the glow of these spring-day blossoms,
  And the future hold naught but the brightest of gifts for you.

God bless you, sweet friend! May the fragrance of good deeds surround you,
  And heavenward soar as the breath of the violets rise,
And angels keep watch till our Heavenly Father shall call you
  Home to his love and his rest in the beautiful skies!

AUTUMN AMID THE HILLS.

I ROAMED to-day where the summer's wreath
  Lay trampled down 'mid the mountain heath,
And with balsamic breath the fresh breeze sweeps
Where the tall pines tower on the rocky steeps.
Far, far below by the river's side
I saw the maples stand crimson-dyed,
Like torches lit by the Autumn's hand,
To brighten the glens of our Western land.

'Twas a fair, wild scene. From the shadowy glooms
Peered timidly forth a few frail blooms,
And the branching ferns 'neath the old oaks spread
A carpet green for the wanderer's tread;
While rich zauschnerias in beauty stood
Gemming the hills with their hearts' best blood,
And the sweet pink blossoms of eglantine
Poured their wealth of perfume on Autumn's shrine,
While over the dead leaves, drifted low,
Glistened symphoricarp's shining snow.
Northward far on the loftiest hill
I marked the trace of the Fire-King still,
Where the gloomy pall over nature cast
Showed that his train in their wrath had passed.

Beyond the river the mountains old
Rose, wrapped in their mantles of cloth of gold,
Clasped by the laurel's fadeless green
And broidered with many a dark ravine,

Their firm feet planted in pride below
Where the sycamores gleam with a golden glow,
And the honeysuckle's trailing vine
Delights o'er the moss-grown rocks to twine,
Drooping low o'er the waterless bed
Of the river, that looks to the sky overhead
With a pleading cry for the gladsome rain
That will speed it forth to the sounding main—
That will speed it forth with its message free,
The mountain's greeting unto the sea.

'Twas a fair, wild scene. Yet a stillness lay
Like a shadow of death o'er the lovely day:
No sound arose in the solemn hush
Save the quail's light flutter from bush to bush,
Or the jay's swift flight as he lightly sped
To feast on the holly-berries red;
And now and then was the silence stirred
By the musical twitter of some wee bird,
That waked a longing to hear again
Each echo answer in glade and glen.

How changed these wilds since the bright Spring days
When blossoms brightened their tangled maze,
And in accents thrilling and sweet and clear
The linnets sang in the thickets near;
When the mountain streams with a leaping bound
Answered the river's murmuring sound!
Now, veiled in a silence sad and drear,
They wait the death of the passing year;
They wait till the Autumn has passed away,
And chill old Winter resigned his sway,
When joyous Spring over hill and glen
Will come to their fairy haunts again.

BRIDAL STANZAS.

WHILE Spring by the Occident's rivers
    Still lingers in beauty and pride,
We bring our heart-blossoms of friendship,
    Of love, and of joy to the bride.

And we heard in the leafy old woodlands,
    Where the shadows fall dusky and dim,
The wild-birds, with musical cadence,
    As they sang for her bridal this hymn:

"Crown her chalice of life with the roses
    Spring twined for the coming of May,
And fill with the nectar of pleasure,
    Clear, sparkling, and pure in its ray;

"That her lips may not taste of the fennel
    Which embitters the red wine of life,
But from fountains of peace, whose o'erflowing
    Shall banish all sorrow and strife,

"While she walks in youth's bowering garden,
    The marital ring on her hand—
The symbol of union unending,
    Love's honoring token and band.

"And we crave for our darling a future
    As bright as the blossoms of spring,
As glad as the skylark's clear anthems
    When mounting aloft on the wing.

"Let Friendship and Truth stand beside her,
   To guard and protect as of yore,
And Love be the helmsman to guide her
   Life's bark to the angelic shore;

"While Charity, Heaven-sent maiden,
   And Faith in her beauty divine,
And Hope with her carol of cheering,
   Fresh joys for her voyage will twine,

"As she leaves the bright shores of her childhood
   Her girlhood's glad, blossoming bowers,
To lean on the husband whose loving
   Shall strengthen and cheer through all hours.

"And we pray that the storm-clouds of sorrow
   May never their spirits enfold,
But their lives' tides be calm as our rivers'
   Asleep on their sands' drifted gold;

"That the angels of love who watch o'er them
   May bless with beneficent hand,
And with honor and virtue united
   Their names be revered through the land;

"That when Azrael's warning shall summon
   Them home when his Master has willed,
He may find no life-duty left waiting,
   No mission of love unfulfilled."

MAY 2, 1870.

THE PICNIC.

THROUGH many a scene where Flora ruled,
    Or Ceres blessed the smiling plain,
We followed on with merry hearts,
    And joyous Pleasure led our train.

The blithe lark carolled overhead
    His morning anthem, sweet and clear;
Soft breezes stirred the blossoming copse,
    And flung its fragrance far and near.

Around us, fair as poet's dream,
    The queen of valleys spread her charms,
While peace and plenty, joy and hope,
    Seemed guarding her from rude alarms.

We passed the stream whose May-day voice
    Scarce waked an echo on its course,
Though round it lay in ruin piled
    Mementoes of its wintry force.

Then left the broad domain of man,
    The city, town, and hamlet fair,
To wander 'mid the mighty hills
    Where lofty pine-trees tower in air;

Where all of beautiful or bright
    That owns the sway of Nature's hand
Makes Saratoga's lone dell seem
    A garden-spot in Fairyland.

There blossoms bright with tropic glow,
  And humming-birds of gorgeous dyes,
Mocked the brown linnet's modest plumes,
  And foliage born 'neath Northern skies.

Tall, branching ferns and clustering moss
  Draped the rude rocks that lined the dell,
Or leaned above the dark abyss
  Where, white with foam, the waters fell.

And wild-flowers, with their beauteous hearts
  Athrob with May's warm light and glow,
Drooped where the mineral water dropped
  Into the deep-hewn rock below.

Amid the waving grass that spread
  Its carpet 'neath the spreading trees,
The timid white forget-me-not
  Seemed whispering to the passing breeze.

There was a beauty in the air,
  A wondrous sense of calm and rest,
A power to soothe the weary mind
  And still the tumult of the breast.

But how can my weak words portray
  The rapturous feelings of delight
Which swelled in every gazer's heart
  When burst that vision on our sight,

As the good genius of the hour,
  Robed fairylike in forest green,
Guided us to the charmèd bower
  Beside the cascade's sparkling sheen,

And with the witchery of her smile,
  And birdlike notes so sweet and gay,
Made every passing moment seem
  A rosebud in the lap of May?

And there where from the blooming bowers
  Soft perfumes loaded every gale,
And where admiring eyes might rest
  Upon the snowy Bridal Veil,

They spread the princely banquet forth
  With many a dainty viand stored,
And wines whose sparkling ray might well
  Have graced a monarch's festal board.

And so with feast and song and dance
  On rosy pinions sped the day,
And hearts beat high when noble deeds
  Or love of country fired the lay.

Friendship with brow serene was there,
  And Love, whose sceptre swayed the throng,
And cheered the mazes of the dance
  Or lent his pathos to the song.

Who owned his power? Oh! answer, ye
  Who trod that far, sky-soaring ridge,
Or paused where fell the rippling brook
  Across the road beneath the bridge.

What wealth of wild-flowers from the hills,
  What treasured blooms from cliff and bank,
We twined with fern-leaves culled where fell
  The spray on mosses dark and dank;

And leaves whose fadeless emerald sheen
  Had decked the red Madrona's crest,
And sprays of fragrant eglantine,
  And laurels from the mountain's breast!

So wandered we through Nature's bowers
  Till far the lengthening shadows lay,
Like warning spectres that proclaimed
  The closing of that merry day.

Then homeward from that beauteous scene
  With care-free hearts we turned once more;
While rang the wild-bird's sunset-song,
  Commingling with the torrent's roar:

Homeward while pale-browed Evening trod
  In shadowy robes across the land,
And in the watch-towers of the sky
  The stars, like guardians, took their stand:

Homeward beneath the drooping plumes
  Of many an old oak's storm-worn crest,
While through the shrubbery light and shade
  Played like weird spirits of unrest:

Home! and within its lighted halls,
  Where music's swell rose on the air,
Where soon amid the merry dance
  Light-hearted trod the young and fair.

With song and glee the night sped on
  Till midnight's witching hour had fled,
And Time's relentless monitor
  Proclaimed the day of joy was dead.

Dead, but its beauties long shall live
 Enshrined 'mid memory's treasures rare,
In after-years to cheer the heart
 And banish thoughts of grief and care.

Then, blithe companions of those hours,
 The merriest hours that crowned the May,
Pledge we once more our parting toast :
 " The host and hostess of the day ! "

IRISH MUSIC.

I HEARD a voice along the strand
  And echoing o'er the sea,
A strain of music deep and grand
  That sang, beloved, of thee—
    Of thee, dear land.

It whispered of the days of old
  When thou wert young and fair,
When richest gems and gleaming gold
  Were shining in thy hair
    And on thy mantle's fold.

It sang the deeds of noble knights
  In thy heroic days;
And all that heart or ear delights
  It murmured in thy praise,
    Whose wrong no lover rights.

I listened till I seemed to hear
  The low, melodious call
Of streamlets flowing pure and clear
  'Mid mountains, green and tall,
    Where browse the timid deer.

I heard the tramp of armèd men,
  And marked them pass along,
While out of many a fairy glen
  Arose the wild war-song,
    Till far beyond my ken

There rose the sound of combat dire,
   Of deadly mortal strife.
O souls of many a patriot sire!
   Ye kindle into life
      Our hearts with fond desire.

How grandly, sweetly sound thy strains,
   Dear music of our land,
While she upon her fertile plains
   Weeps 'mid her captive band,
      And lists the clank of chains.

O voice of music! speak once more
   Of Erin's hope and pride,
Of those who the green banner bore
   O'er fields of carnage wide,
      And blessed the Irish shore.

For dearer than thy notes of glee
   We love the fervent lays
That breathe of bright days yet to be,
   And chant our Mother's praise,
      The fair gem of the sea.

MOSSY WOODLAND, Aug. 23, 1881.

OUR FLAG.

WHEN first out of chaos and darkness arose,
    By God's potent word, this fair world which we view,
When the bounds of streams, rivers, and oceans he set,
    And painted the skies such an exquisite blue,

Then he made day and night, and commanded the stars—
    Fair lilies of light in the sky-fields that bloom,
Sleepless guardians of earth o'er the wide stretching zones—
    The darkness of night with their rays to illume.

And lo! as a herald of dawning he spread
    O'er the gates of the Orient a warm crimson glow,
That broadens and brightens as Morning comes forth,
    One jewel of light on her forehead of snow.

And so when our country, by tyrants oppressed,
    Quaffed the chalice of woe by the far eastern sea,
Our forefathers rose in their courage and vowed
    That the land of their love should be joyous and free.

And as symbol of Hope, on a field azure blue,
    Lo! the stars of the heavens in beauty they set:
With the crimson of dawning and snow of the morn
    They fashioned the banner that waves o'er us yet—

The banner we love, the dear " Flag of the Free,"
That is flinging its folds to the soft breeze to-day
From the North to the South, from the East to the West,
Where Freedom rejoicing holds jubilant sway.

'Twas their beacon in darkness, their herald of dawn,
Their light of a morning whose midday should see
The homes which they held as the pulse of their heart
From the bonds of the tyrant for ever set free.

How nobly they struggled! God rest those who fell
In the battles for freedom! Their memory we'll hold
Enshrined in our souls, while a grateful land writes
Their names on her annals in letters of gold.

Bright Flag of our country! how proudly it waved
In the front of the conflict, exulting and high,
When the angry strife echoed o'er mountain and shore,
And our brave sires went forth pledged to conquer or die.

And they conquered! The foot of the spoiler no more
Leaves its blight on the green of our fair Western land :
He was driven from America's beautiful shore
By her sons, earth's most gallant and valorous band.

Dear Flag of the Free ! With what rapture we hail
Thy light as it burns on our watch-towers to-day !
May thy stars never pale, but shine on evermore,
Illumining our path with their silvery ray !

May the years as they pass see thy splendors increase,
    And the land thy smile blesses still prosper and grow,
While the hearts of her children, rejoicing in peace,
    Keep the fire on the altar of Freedom aglow!

God bless thee, dear Flag! May thy folds ever wave
    Over scenes where no hatred nor rancor may dwell,
But where Faith, Hope, and Love lend their graces divine,
    And the glad voice of Plenty her sweet carols swell.

Float, float o'er our homes, O loved Flag of the Free!
    Through the winter's wild tempest, the light of the spring,
Through the summer's soft glow, and when autumn will steal,
    Thy crimson o'er forest and woodland to fling.

Float, float o'er our homes through the glad hours of life,
    Fill our hearts with fond thoughts of our noble and brave;
And when death comes at last may the Stars and the Stripes
    Be stirred by the breeze that steals over each grave!

JULY 4, 1881.

ONWARD.

UP and onward, idle dreamer!
   There is work for all to do:
Lo! the fields around are whitening,
   And the harvesters are few.

There are fields where Wrong is trampling
   On the seeds of Truth and Right,
There are fields where hunger crushes
   With the iron wheel of might.

There are scenes where sin and wassail
   Hold enslaved the priceless soul,
Where the mind is bowed and broken
   By its bondage to the bowl.

There are duties waiting on thee,
   There are tasks thou shouldst fulfil,
In the pathway traced before thee
   By thy Heavenly Master's will.

Wounded hearts demand thy caring:
   Whisper words of kindly cheer,
Lift the Cross from aching shoulders,
   Breathe of hope to those who fear.

"Onward! upward!" be thy motto;
　Take thy place amidst the band
Of the toilers in the harvest,
　Pilgrims to the Better Land.

Not through idle, aimless dreaming,
　Not through murmuring or despair,
Lies the path which leads us upward
　To the great white Throne of prayer.

A SPRING-DAY RIDE.

LET us check awhile our chargers
    Here upon the mountain's height,
While we look along the valley
    Bathèd in the May-day light—
While we look along the valley
    With its leagues of brilliant blooms,
And their gorgeous tints contrasting
    With the wheat-fields' emerald plumes;
On the shorn and whitening meadows,
    On the barley's bearded lips,
And white cottages whose roses
    Veil them in a sweet eclipse.

Down upon the vale's broad bosom,
    'Mid its thousand trees and flowers,
See the villages encircled
    By their orchards' waving bowers.
There the Llagas windeth slowly
    Down unto the willowy glades,
And far northward spreads the forest
    With its wild, gloom-haunted shades.
Eastward lies Lake Tequisquita,
    First to greet the morning star;
Thence the Pajaro windeth seaward
    Through the western mountains far.
Is it not a lovely picture?
    How its beauties stir the heart!
But what language can portray it?
    And it mocks the power of art.

On! we may no longer tarry,
  For the way is long to trace
Ere we reach the wondrous fountain—
  Gentle Health's abiding-place.
Now our roadway windeth upward
  Round the hillsides stern and steep;
Down beneath us in the cañons
  See the vernal shadows sleep;
Here thy smiling vale, Las Osos,
  Winds 'twixt many a sheltering slope,
Where the waving grain-fields' promise
  Bids the sturdy farmer hope.

Now we leave where man is master,
  Greeting Nature's reign once more,
Where the river's crystal waters
  Murmur by its flowery shore;
Here where trees like giant warders
  Seem to guard the rugged way;
Where beneath the waters flashing
  We can mark the fish at play;
Where the ceanothus blossoms
  And the laurel's arms are spread,
And the tasselled plane-tree mingles
  With the maple overhead;
Where the hills rise towering o'er us
  In their grandeur rude and wild,
And the heart that loves their beauty
  Turns to Him whose hand has piled
Up those monuments majestic,
  That a lesson they might teach,
Bidding man look up for ever
  To the heavens no care may reach;

And the pine-trees, grand and gloomy,
  Chant for us a solemn song,
As beneath their swaying branches
  We are swiftly borne along.
Joy! at last we near the summit,
  And the longed-for goal is won,
As above us, all unclouded,
  Shines the glorious noonday sun.
And we rest beside the fountain
  Where of yore the savage came
With his wild, weird incantation
  To the mystic god of flame;
And when midnight shadows rested
  On each rugged, tree-crowned hill,
Here he culled the herbs whose magic
  Was a balm for every ill.

And may we not, wiser pilgrims,
  Pausing thus beside the spring,
Raise our souls in mute thanksgiving
  To our Maker and our King,
Whose hand raised this wondrous fountain
  From the great earth's throbbing heart,
Gave it powers strange and wondrous,
  Far exceeding human art,
That the wearied and the drooping,
  And the sick and those that pine,
Here might come and win fresh vigor
  From this pure, health-giving mine—
Here might come and win fresh vigor
  From the mountain breeze that sweeps,
Laden with the balmy odors
  Of the wild-flowers on the steeps,

Where, beyond the jar and trouble
  Of the busy world afar,
They may look unto a future
  Lighted by Hope's silvery star?

A MOTHER'S LOVE.

IT is not like youth's affections,
   Blooming early, fading soon,
Or the love that poet-lovers
   Sing in sonnets 'neath the moon.

It is holier, deeper, stronger
   Than all other ties of earth:
'Tis the strong guard of existence
   From the moment of our birth;

'Tis the light that cheers our childhood
   With its fond, benignant ray;
'Tis the power that scatters blessings
   Ever round our youthful way;

'Tis the charm that strengthens manhood
   When the inmost soul is stirred
By the fury of the passions,
   And the tempter's voice is heard.

Other loves will fade and falter,
   Other friends will flee our path
When the demon of Misfortune
   'Whelms us in a sea of wrath.

But a mother's love unflinching
   Passes through each fiery test;
Day succeeding day but finds it
   Glowing brighter in her breast.

Day succeeding day she raises
   Unto Heaven her earnest prayer
That the future of her children
   May be free from sin and care.

Mother! What a charm lies hidden
   In the sound of that dear name
Since the smiling baby-lisper
   First its syllables could frame!

Mother!—earliest, sweetest murmur
   Fashioned by the infant's lips;
Mother!—last word man will falter
   When death holds life in eclipse.

'Tis the true heart's dearest watchword,
   As her love is still its stay;
'Tis the figure given to mortals
   Of our Father's gentle sway.

WILD FLOWERS.

WITH their green robes folded round them,
    And bright chalices dew-filled,
They are standing in the meadows
    Where the lark's sweet songs are trilled.

They are clustering on the hillside,
    They are blushing in the glen,
They are smiling in the forest's shade
    And 'mid the haunts of men.

They are springing by the roadside,
    Spite of trampling feet and dust—
Fragile emblems of our being,
    Of our human hope and trust.

I have marvelled at their beauty,
    Gazing on them day by day,
Marking meek-eyed blossoms open,
    Brighten, bless, and pass away.

Looking thus with love upon them,
    I have learned their story well;
'Tis the same, the same for ever,
    That the sweet wild-flow'rets tell,

Teaching all the self-same lesson
    Ere they pass from earth away:
"Mortal, life is swiftly speeding,
    And death comes at close of day.

"Do thy duty to thy neighbor,
　Give thy worship to thy God;
He will lead thee, blest and happy,
　Where the just before thee trod.

"Feed the hungry, clothe the naked,
　Bid want-darkened homes grow bright,
Cheer the mourner sitting lonely,
　Make the laborer's burden light.

"There are duties waiting on thee,
　There are tasks that must be done;
Speed thee, for the day is closing,
　And the mountains near the sun.

"Speed thee, for life's spring is passing,
　And God's service must not wait,
If thy hands would clasp the guerdon
　Waiting thee beyond Heaven's gate."

Thus great Nature's poet-teachers
　Plead with mortals day by day,
Mingling still their mute appealing
　With the wild-bird's warbled lay.

Thus from hillside and from valley,
　And from forest glade and glen,
Still the sweet flowers lift their voices
　Hourly to the sons of men;

Waking longings for the beauty
　Of the land beyond the skies,
Glimpses of whose charms are mirrored
　In the blossom's lifted eyes.

OUR ANGEL.

ANNIE MARGARET.

ERE one short summer faded,
   Ere one short year had told
Its chaplet of the crownèd months,
   Her little heart grew cold.

Marked by the chrism of suffering,
   We saw our darling wait
In meek, unmurmuring patience
   Beside the Pearly Gate,

Until the pitying Saviour
   Undid pain's cruel band,
And angels bore her through the morn
   To Heaven's unclouded land;

There, 'midst its shining mansions,
   To join their bands who sing
For ever and for evermore
   Hosannas to the King.

And there in fadeless beauty,
   While here on earth we roam,
Our angel babe is waiting
   Her loved ones' coming home.

A WINTER DAY.

GREAT waves of sunlight all our land are flooding—
   Our glorious land, so verdant and so fair,
Where peaceful labor o'er the scene is brooding,
   And bird-songs burden all the balmy air,

As if in prayer yon oaks their arms are lifting,
   Their long gray tresses floating on the breeze;
Across the skies white clouds are slowly drifting,
   And comes at times the voice of distant seas.

From north to south, yea, to the bounds of vision,
   We gaze on naught but beauty's perfect lines—
Vales that recall the fabled fields Elysian,
   And dells that echo to the singing pines.

Storm-swept, but scathless, Santa Anna towers
   With the proud monarchs of our eastern heights;
And westward, redwood forests, home of flowers
   And ferns and birds, awaken new delights.

The lofty mountain-sides are deeply rifted
   With lovely glens where fairies might abide,
Where through the long, long summer days lie **drifted**
   The sweet wild blooms above the stream's clear **tide.**

And, nestling calmly on the valley's bosom,
   The quiet village slumbers in the sun—
A tiny germ that yet shall bud and blossom
   When Art and Labor have their triumph won.

A WINTER DAY.

Behold how, through the clear, still air ascending,
   Blue wreaths of smoke from many hearths arise,
Higher and higher, till their vapory blending
   Is lost amid the azure of the skies,

Like incense rising from the sacred altar
   Of homes where Peace and Plenty ever reign ;
For who is there with trembling tongue can falter
   Of want-born woe upon our Western plain,

While toil can wrest from out the valley's bosom
   The farmer's wealth, the sheaves of golden grain,
And the great orchards burst from bud to blossom
   With promise of the autumn's glittering gain ?

Toil, honest toil—the meed is worth the winning,
   The joys that only honest labors bring ;
Toil and be hopeful with the year's beginning,
   And its glad promise of a glorious spring.

All, all is peaceful as a poet's dreaming,
   This peerless day so wondrous bright and mild ;
And yet beneath this emerald banner streaming
   We hail the King in other lands so wild.

No sound of discord comes to mar the quiet,
   The holy quiet, of this winter scene,
Save when the chattering blackbirds' merry riot
   Disturbs the woodland solitudes serene,

Or where the hungry rooks in clouds assemble
   To scold and wrangle o'er the new-turned sod.
But hark ! hark how the air is all a-tremble
   With the glad hymn the lark outpours to God.

Grant, Heavenly Father, that within our valley
    No ruder strains may in the future rise ;
That never here may wake War's dreaded rally,
    Nor battle-smoke bedim these azure skies ;

And that, within the New Year spread before us,
    Our feet may tread the path thy Saints have trod,
And thy bright angels watching ever o'er us
    Lead us in safety to thy home, O God !

TO I. A. L.

IF to uplift to heights of purer feeling
    Where scenes of beauty thrill the gazer's sight,
Heaven's rays that linger still on earth revealing,
    Be the true artist's dream, the poet's right,
Well hast thou proved thyself lord of that art
That wakes the mystic lyre—the human heart.

No picture on thy shining canvas glowing,
    No scene thy pen's inspired power portrays,
But mirrors Truth's celestial fountain flowing
    With sparkling waves to gladden earth's drear ways,
Telling, in numbers thrilling and sublime,
Tales of the past, tales of the present time.

Thy muse hath lured us to Italian waters
    Where sunny Naples rules her fair dominion,
Or shown Spain's valleys, red with Moorish slaughter
    Following the flight of thy swift fancy's pinion :
The wealth of courts, the low moan of the dying,
And the sad prodigal in silence sighing. ·

Thus guided through the mazes of transition,
    Our spirits bowed beneath the spell divine ;
Amid the grandeur of the Recognition
    See ! Right triumphant over Error shine,
And like the echo of exultant song
The pæans of the victory prolong.

Not here the guerdon of such faithful labor,
    Save in sweet gratitude; but, soaring higher,
The fragrance of thy good works for thy neighbor
    Will shine illumined with celestial fire,
Within whose deathless radiance behold
Thy name upon Fame's shining scroll enrolled.

TEN YEARS AGO.

DO I forget this week ten years ago?
    Nay, dearest, I remember,
Clearly as yesterday, the light and glow
    Of that far-off September:

How shone the landscape 'neath the subtle dyes,
    The gold and azure of the summer's weaving,
The rounded capes that cut the valley's sea,
    And on the hills the pine harp's note of grieving;

The white-armed plane-trees, in the mirage blue,
    Like giant spectres seemed to bend and quiver,
Held in the deep and voiceless Sabbath calm
    Upon the margin of the sun-dried river;

And on the eastern slope a guardian fair—
    The cross-crowned chapel in its holy quiet,
Standing within "God's Acre," where the dead
    Slept sweetly in their dreamless slumber by it.

And there we parted. Memory loves to dwell
    On that last parting, though the wound is aching
Freshly as when the cherished dreams of youth
    Fled in the fond farewell that thou wert taking.

I look around on hill and valley now:
    Thy name to me is linked with all their beauty;
Dwells not a vision of their charms with thee
    Amid thy tranquil life of love and duty?

For through each lovely scene our feet have trod,
   As side by side in bright spring-tides we wandered
Where floral treasures o'er the vale were flung,
   Or dark oak isles the blooming billows sundered.

No more they seem the same, the glad, the free,
   Although no beauty with the years departed ;
Earth is unchanged—only to human hearts
   Comes grief when those who loved for life are parted ;

Parted to tread through different ways below
   Our paths of life, which to one goal are tending :
For all our hopes are centred in that home
   Whose summer never knows a dreary ending.

All unforgotten are the years that rest
   Beyond that week within that far September
And those that lie between that hour and this :
   All thoughts of thee most fondly I remember.

    SEPTEMBER 10, 1875.

THE OLD ADOBE HOUSE.

DARK and desolate, drear and still,
　　Under the shade of the rocky hill,
Years have passed since its builders trod
The flowery green of the valley sod:
Years have passed since its old walls rang
To the merry strains by glad voices sang,
When genial pleasure and social mirth
Sat in the glow of its lighted hearth,
And hospitality's open hand
Welcomed the wanderers from every land.
Now the moss of age on its walls is gray;
It has owned the power of thy touch, Decay;
And, dark and desolate, drear and cold,
It is crumbling fast to the valley mould.

Yet, could its old walls find a tongue
To echo the strains that within them rung,
What tales it might tell of the poet's lay,
Of the warrior resting after the fray!
What tales of the dreams that at night would come
To the weary exiles from friends and home,
Sick of their search after wealth untold
In the darksome caves of the yellow gold!—
For rest and shelter were ne'er denied
When sought in that home by the lone hillside.
Perchance they would breathe of the words of prayer
That throbbed each eve through the balmy air,
When angels the azure archway trod
To bear them up to the Throne of God.

Or the old oak-trees that above it lean,
Twining through summer their leafy screen,
Might whisper, in accents soft and low,
Some sweet love-tale of the long-ago—
Some silvery echo, faint and far,
Heard here when the light of the evening-star
Shone softly down on the tranquil scene,
On the silent vale and the forest green ;
When earnest lover and blushing maid
Walked to and fro in the vernal shade—
For here hearts quickened and eyes burned bright,
And Cupid ruled with his rod of might,
And the bridal feast in that home has been spread
Where Ruin now keeps her vigil dread.

Ay, Ruin rules in the homestead gray
Where the road winds southward to Monterey,
And proud El Toro in silence towers
A sentinel over this vale of ours—
A sentinel grim over glen and wold,
Over broad plains wrapped in their cloth of gold,
Over forests where wild, weird harpings swell
When the breeze strikes the lyre of the Moronel,
Where the flitting shadows dance and play,
And the sad dove moans at the close of day ;
And his echoes answer with trumpet-blast
When the fire-fed steed with a neigh sweeps past
On its pathway which bindeth mart to mart
With an iron band through the valley's heart.

Dark and desolate, drear and cold,
And crumbling fast to its native mould,
The old house stands in its ruin grim ;
But it has memories time cannot dim—

Memories whose treasured halos crown
The lonely home by the hillside brown ;
Memories whose golden links are cast
To bind the present unto the past :
A chain by a grateful genius wrought
Of many a tender and kindly thought,
Of deeds whose blessings will with us stay
Though the generous doers have passed away
And sleep where the tangled grasses wave
And the wild-flowers droop o'er each silent grave.

TO F. DE C. M.

"WAVERLEY."

I CLOSE the Poet's volume, but my fancy
    Doth still the theme pursue ;
Before me shine the pictures which the Author
    In matchless beauty drew.

Around me rise no more our Western mountains,
    No more our vales extend ;
But down through rushing glens the leaping torrents
    From Scotia's hills descend.

The sound of waves in wintry anger breaking
    Upon these shores of gold
Seem but the echo of stern battle's thunders
    O'er fields of carnage rolled.

I hear the angry clash of crossing sabres,
    I mark the arrow's flight,
The charging lancers, and the deaf'ning clamor
    Of cries that cheer the fight.

Yonder the setting sun's last ray just touches
    The claymore's dripping blade,
As the fierce forces of the victors follow
    The vanquished down the glade.

Or, as the winds wail through the leafless branches,
    I seem to hear the cry,
The bitter coronach, of grief ascending
    Towards the evening sky—

Such strains as filled the air with keenest anguish
    Beside Loch Katrine's wave
When Rob Roy's Helen raised the notes of sorrow
    For Rob, her captured brave.

Now from the fields of carnage shifts the vision :
    I see the bright lamps shine
In old baronial halls, their lights reflected
    From golden cups of wine,

Where lordly knights and stately dames are feasting,
    While sweetly to the ear
Are borne the minstrel's songs of love and conquest
    To Scottish hearts most dear.

The picture changes. Spreading now before me
    I see the good green wood
Beneath whose boughs so often were assembled
    The band of Robin Hood—

Bold men, who made their lances hold their tenure,
    But whom the author draws
As heroes still, despite the daily breaking
    Of England's royal laws.

No more to ruin and to ivy given
    Proud Leicester's castle lies,
But hall and lake and lawn with pomp are glowing
    To please his monarch's eyes ;

While he, false-hearted, stooping for her favor
 And kneeling to her grace,
Must in his heart be haunted by the murder
 And wrong of Cumnor Place.

So through the wild and wondrous realms of fancy
 I follow, musing still
Upon the Poet whose skilled hand hath left us
 These gems of heath and hill.

And while his power the present charms and pleases,
 I bless thy generous hand,
And pray thy hours with pleasure may be freighted
 While journeying through the land.

BRIDAL WISHES.

ANGELS of love and duty
 Upon their path attend,
In perfect bliss uniting
 Their spirits till the end.

And Peace, sweet household darling,
 Their guardian spirit be,
With gentle influence moulding
 Their lives through days of glee.

And, Faith, when sorrow's billows
 Around about them roll,
Keep thou in fadeless beauty
 Thy taper in each soul,

Till, crowned with life's best blessings,
 Home, happiness, and love,
Their lives may mirror back the light
 Of cloudless realms above.

POEM.

THE decades of the years are thrice told o'er
    In blessings manifold
Since first Columbia as a daughter hailed
    Our cherished " Land of Gold ":

Our land, which on the broad Pacific's shore
    Arose the first-born State;
Our land, whose name is known throughout the world
    As beautiful and great.

Hers was no long probationary term
    Of Territorial school,
But, like Minerva from the brow of Jove,
    She sprang full-armed to rule ·

Armed with the power of her untold wealth,
    Glories of hill and lea,
A queen of beauty, love and light, and song,
    Enthroned beside the sea.

Her mighty mountains' giant hearts are veined
    With glittering yellow ore:
The proud commercial navies of the world
    Bring tribute to her shore.

Her valleys in their fertile beauty vie
    With the Elysian Fields ;
Her vineyards, pouring out their purple blood,
    Wine of Olympus yields.

But not alone of treasures such as these
    Is California's boast;
Nay, dearer far she holds the valiant men
    Who first explored her coast;

Who broke the seal that held with magic power
    Her hidden wealth so long,
And sped its golden current o'er the world,
    A torrent deep and strong.

Theirs was no journey of luxurious ease
    Who dared the toils and pains
Of the long journey round the stormy cape,
    Or roadway o'er the plains.

The Rocky Mountains' rugged barrier frowned
    Defiance on their way,
The wild Sierra's terrors vainly strove
    To keep their hosts at bay.

Though many perished in the dark defiles
    Or 'neath the ocean's waves;
Though the wide prairies' billowy hillocks marked
    The pilgrims' lonely graves;

Though Darien's fever slew with burning breath,
    Still fearlessly they came,
And on the annals of our country traced
    In noble deeds each name.

From the primeval wilderness they gave
    Our star to crown thy brow,
Mother of Heroes! and with them we hail
    Thy glorious Birthday now.

With them we hail thee, as their children should,
  With them thy name we breathe;
"Twas they first taught our childish lips and hearts
  Love's flowers for thee to wreathe,

And bade us honor the great men who stood
  In battle for thy cause,
And the wise statesmen who so well have framed
  Thy grand, thy matchless laws.

And while above us floats the dear old flag,
  The banner of the free,
With joyous lips and loyal hearts we pledge
  Fidelity to thee;

Vowing to love thee with unfaltering love,
  Our Mother dear and fair,
And make thy weal through all the future hours
  Our every thought and care;

To walk with honor in the paths of right
  Our great forefathers trod,
And serve untiringly with hand and heart
  Our Country and our God.

GILROY HOT SPRINGS.

HIGH up upon the mountain's breast
    A nook of wondrous beauty lies,
A temple of the goddess Rest,
    Arched by the cloudless summer skies—

A temple of the goddess Rest,
    A shrine where Health her goblet fills,
And pledges with unfailing zest
    The pilgrims to the leafy hills.

Through all its shadowy aisles there floats
    The music of the wild birds' song,
And echo treasures up its notes
    In cadence tremulous but strong.

Close hidden by the sheltering trees,
    The laughing brooklet winds and falls;
Answering the calling of the breeze,
    . Glides swiftly down the rocky walls.

All sounds that Nature's lone haunts fill
    Rise on the air, and faint, and fail;
And comes at times in accents shrill
    The quaint "Que es eso?" of the quail.

Here Spring her rarest garlands twines,
    And Summer lingers, loath to part,
Till all the murmurings of the pines
    Seem moanings from her breaking heart.

The fern its fairy forest rears
  Along the hills in brightest green,
And blushingly the wild rose dares
  On many a rugged height be seen.

The Virgin's Bower bending swings
  Its snowy blossoms o'er the way,
A bridal-wreath to which still clings
  The fragrance of the perished May.

Here the glad blood responsive leaps
  Along the veins with quickening thrills,
When wakes the joyous breeze that sweeps
  The wind-harp of the mighty hills—

The wind-harp of the hills, which takes
  The voicing of that solemn strain
Sung where the great waves rise and break
  Upon the boundaries of the main,

As though some echoes lingered here
  Of Winter's message fierce and free,
Sent up, on wings of storm and fear,
  From the broad bosom of the sea.

O fair, wild spot with beauty crowned!
  Long tower thy voiceful oaks and pines,
Where, guardians of thy charmèd bound,
  They quaff the morning's dewy wines.

Long may their shadows fall to bless
  The weary ones that seek their shade,
A blessing like a love-caress
  Upon their heated foreheads laid!

SONNET.

TO A.

A SUMMER day in languid beauty died;
  Night came with glittering jewels on her brow;
No breezes swept the fragrance from the bough
Impearled with starry jasmine blooms, or hied
Eager to kiss the agave's crown of pride
'Mid humbler blossoms in the garden near,
Cleaving the air to seek a loftier sphere
O'er which to fling its fragrance far and wide;
Lingering together while each silvery star
On cloudless azure in deep brilliance shone,
Mingling with music's notes floating afar,
Bearing sweet promise in its tender tone:
Earnestly beautiful the "Gates Ajar"
Thrilled from thy heart and made the hour its own.

THE MARTYRS OF MEMPHIS.

TWINE ye bright and fadeless laurels
   For our martyrs one and all,
But the brightest and the fairest
   For the Daughters of De Paul—
For the pure and valiant Sisters
   Who, obeying God's behest,
Dared the plague, with all its terrors,
   In the suffering South and West.

When the weakest fell to perish,
   And the strongest fled away,
They remained to soothe the dying
   And beside the dead to pray—
Ministers of heavenly comfort,
   Angels lent to earth awhile,
With their loving care to brighten
   Scenes of sorrow, pain, and guile.

Never steel-girt heroes leading
   Armèd cohorts to the front,
Cheered by sounds of martial music
   To the onset's dreaded brunt—
Never in their fiery bosoms
   Thrilled such courage pure and grand
As hath nerved to deeds heroic
   These meek daughters of our land.

For the warriors sought their guerdon
   In the world's applause and praise,
In the wild, tumultuous cheering
   When along the public ways

Thronged the people glad and eager,
  Crying: "Welcome! welcome home!
Welcome! welcome to the victors!"
  Thrilling to the azure dome.

But the Daughters of Saint Vincent
  Sought no fleeting earthly meed,
As they bent above the sufferers
  In their hour of sorest need;
When they saw the Plague-King smiting
  Old and young around their way,
Following in our dear Lord's footsteps,
  Nobly wrought they day by day.

And while pain-wrung lips in anguish
  One fond, grateful prayer could frame,
Did their dying accents falter
  Blessings on the Sisters' name—
Blessings on their lives whose guerdon
  In a heavenly land is won;
There the angel-hosts have borne them,
  There the Saviour says: "Well done!".*

Faithful servants of the Saviour,
  Valiant soldiers of the Cross,
O'er their graves a mourning nation
  Bitterly laments her loss;
And when her true heart will number
  The brave ones she loves the best,
Reverently her love will cherish
  The pure Martyrs of the West.

* "Sisters of Charity, with their usual unselfishness, watched beside the sick and ministered to the dying; fearless of death, though death spared them not."—H. B.

RAIN.

SATING all the thirsty meadows,
   Weeping o'er the fallen leaves,
Dancing on the cottage roof-tree,
   Leaping downward from the eaves—
All day long the glad rain-spirits
   Sang their songs so blithe and free,
And the wild Pacific's surges
   Echoed back their notes of glee:

"Welcome us from out the regions
   Which the hazy mist enshrouds,
For we bring you, sons of mortals,
   The best vintage of the clouds:
All the treasures we have garnered
   Through the season's shade and shine—
Plenty for the barren valleys,
   Life-blood for the drooping vine,
Dainty hues for fairy blossoms,
   Crimson for the rose's cheek,
Songs of joy, all songs excelling
   Which the earth's great heart shall speak;
Quelling all the bitter murmurings
   That along the calm air thrills,
Pouring out the oil of gladness
   On our young land's thousand hills."

Thus the rain-drops sang their anthems
  O'er the vale's autumnal woe,
While the winter crowned the mountains
  With a bridal-wreath of snow ;
And a voice of warm thanksgiving
  Swept along the western plain,
Thanking God, o'er all his bounties,
  For the blessing of the rain.

IERNIAN.

HO! brothers by mountain and moorland,
   Bold brothers by river and sea,
Are ye true to the oath that ye plighted
   When ye vowed our fair land should be free?

Have ye cherished her love as a mother's
   Is cherished by children most dear?
Have ye walked in the paths that our fathers
   Trod aye without faltering or fear,

While they sang in bold strains their glad anthems
   Far-sounding, exultant, and free—
The praise of our own Mother Erin,
   Discrowned, but still Queen of the Sea?

Have ye stanched all your red feuds, O brothers?
   Linked in friendship each clan unto clan,
That when Ireland shall summon her children
   They will answer her call to a man?

For no blessings can rest on our armies,
   No foemen before us will yield,
Till all hatred and rancor are vanquished
   And *Union* is graved on our shield.

Have ye proved that the patriot pulses
   Which throbbed through the hearts of our sires
Still quicken your soul into action
   With the glow of their heroic fires?

For ye know on the brow of the valiant
  Shall the crown of the victor descend,
And a nation's thanksgiving will hallow
  His name who is true to the end.

But woe to the traitor who, turning
  Away from the teachings of old,
Shall barter his high hopes of freedom
  For chains that are burnished with gold.

To him will come days full of sorrow,
  And nights that are drear with unrest,
For the curse of a down-trodden nation
  Shall press its dead weight on his breast.

But to you who are faithful the children
  Of Erin cry out o'er the waves;
Oh! the sharp, sullen clank of their fetters
  Might waken the dead in their graves!

They call upon you, O my brothers!
  By the rights you have sworn to regain;
They plead by their long years of anguish,
  Fraught with pestilence, famine, and pain.

Then answer them quickly and truly;
  Let the blue skies re-echo the cheer
That will ring from their hearts when they hear that
  The day of deliverance is near.

God hasten the day when our banner's
  Green folds will float free on the air,
And joy's smiling power will have banished
  The memory of years of despair;

When the heather-crowned hills of Ierne
   Will answer exulting and free
To the praise of our own beauteous Mother,
   Crowned by freedom as Queen of the Sea!

SONNET.

MAY blessings rest upon thy youthful head,
And Pleasure walk beside thee ; hand-in-hand
Repose and Peace thy guardian spirits stand ;
Youth's genial charm around thy pathway spread,
And friends be true where'er thy footsteps tread ;
No heart-frosts ever chill life's sunny glow,
No heavy cross thy portion here below ;
Each day new graces o'er thy spirit shed,
Making thy future as a flower that blooms
Under the fervid glow of southern skies,
Rich in its wealth of beauty and perfumes :
Peerless in all that charms thy Maker's eyes,
Holiest of blossoms from the vernal glooms,
Yet—sweetest grace !—its beauty never dies.

IRELAND'S APPEAL.

DECEMBER, 1879.

I CALL upon you, my children—
   I call, and oh! not in vain
Shall the winds of the winter bear you
   The wail of your Mother's pain.

For, given of the generous bounty
   Of the land which you now call home,
In the hour of my direst anguish
   Came over the ocean's foam

Brave ships that were richly laden,
   And out of whose stores were fed
The stricken ones o'er whose anguish
   My heart in wild woe had bled.

O ye whom my old arms sheltered
   And clasped to my loving breast!
Think of your sorrowing Mother
   In the Island of the West.

For again o'er the hills of Mayo,
   In the chilly, sweeping blast,
With her train of ghastly horrors
   Has the spectre Famine passed.

All up through that desolate border
   They shrink from her step's swift fall,
And soon will her court hold revel
   In the cabins of Donegal.

Ye who are housed in comfort,
  Who are clothed and served and fed,
Think of the poor and the naked
  Who hunger and cry for bread.

Think of the cold, bleak winter,
  The pitiless, falling rain,
Of the famine-stricken gathering
  Round the fireless hearth in vain :

For the turf in the bog lies sodden,
  And little for warmth remains,
Save the fever whose kindling torches
  Are firing the sufferers' veins.

When music is thrilling around you,
  And your homes are bright with cheer
In the light of the New Year's dawning,
  Think of my children here.

God, who has blessed your harvests
  And given you gold in store,
Who led you, my cherished exiles,
  To a fair and plenteous shore—

God move your hearts to pity
  The wants of your brethren here,
And speed to their darkened dwellings
  The aid which will bring them cheer :

The aid which will win you blessings
  An hundred thousand fold,
And open to you the City
  Whose streets are paved with gold !

TO ERIN,

SORROWING FOR HER PRIEST, PATRIOT, AND ORATOR,
REV. THOMAS N. BURKE, O.P.

O ERIN, Mother Erin, dark is thy day of sorrow!
   Thy bravest and thy noblest, thy truest and thy best,
He who from Heaven's own fountains such burning words could borrow
   To paint thy ancient glory, lies dead upon thy breast.

For thee he lived and labored, for thee his voice was lifted
   In deep, soul-stirring accents, in thunder-tones of might.
Whene'er he spoke, as vapor by the swift north wind is drifted,
   Fled the darkening clouds of ignorance and dawned the welcome light.

How our eager spirits kindled 'neath his words of fervid power
   When he told with patriot rapture thy joys of long ago;
Or, turning to the present, robbed of all thy priceless dower,
   He pictured thee, Beloved, in thy agony and woe.

Oh! his stirring strains of eloquence have rung the
  wide earth over,
  Where'er thy exiled children have pitched their
    tents, and long
They will bear within their bosoms, like the fond
  words of a lover,
  The warm, impassioned breathings that have thrilled
    them as a song.

Better far than earthly guerdon, than gold or laurels
  crowning
  The proud brow of the conqueror, the hero, or the
    sage,
Is the faithful love they gave him when from False-
  hood's forehead frowning
  He rent the veil and taught men thy true place on
    History's page.

In thy cause he never faltered, his courage was un-
  daunted;
  His fidelity was proven in a thousand trying ways;
He fought the vulture Famine and its countless train
  that haunted
  Thy mountains and thy valleys for so many dreary
    days.

He fought the vulture Famine—yea, his latest breath
  was given
  For the sake of thy dear children, the wan babies
    at thy knee;
He heard their voices calling, even as thy great
  Apostle
  Heard the wailing of thy infants, and he gave his
    life for thee.

The Angel stilled his gentle heart, with purest fervor
    glowing ;
  He died as heroes love to die, his ready lance in
    rest.
No wonder that such sorrow all the earth is over-
    flowing
  With sighing and with mourning for the Priest so
    loved and blessed.

True child of great Saint Dominic, whose sons, white-
    robed and glorious,
  Watered with their blood thy valleys in the sad
    days long ago,
Lo ! they stand before the Saviour with their martyr
    palms, victorious,
  Giving greeting to their brother who so well defied
    thy foe—

Giving greeting to their brother, Priest, Patriot, and
    Hero,
  Crowned alike with earthly homage and the glory
    of the just,
With thy love, warm and undying, with thy gratitude
    endearing,
  Yielding back to Him who gave it his life's most
    precious trust.

Wail ! wail ! O Mother Erin ! above thy lion-hearted,
  Thy son whose mind was lofty as the eagle's soar-
    ing flight,
Whose lips unto thy children wise counsel e'er im-
    parted,
  And urged them ever onward in the paths of truth
    and right.

Faith, Hope, and gentle Charity will watch above his
    slumber:
  In his life a living mirror of Faith and Hope we see,
While in the cause of Charity we vainly strive to
    number
  All the labors that he fondly wrought, dear Mother-
    land, for thee.

Sweet is the rest God-given to thy laborer on his mis-
    sion,
  Thy true and faithful Shepherd of the Master's
    precious fold ;
And blessed his glorious guerdon, the beatific vision
  Of the Saviour 'tis his happy lot in Heaven to be-
    hold.

Mother of noble children ! O sorrowing Queen of
    Sorrow !
  Another name is added to thy roll of saints to-day,
Another son is pleading that for thee a near to-mor-
    row
  May usher in the dawning of a brighter, happier
    day

UNFORGOTTEN.

IN fading leaves and blossoms,
  'Neath bright autumnal skies,
The memories of past moments
  Again before me rise.
Thy presence lingers near me
  In each familiar spot;
Though many miles divide us,
  Thou hast not been forgot.

When Spring with fragrant blossoms
  Comes smiling down the vale,
When Summer's golden mantle
  Floats on the languid gale,
Where through fay-haunted cañons
  The rippling streamlets glide,
I muse on bygone moments
  When thou wert by my side.

Each lowly hillside blossom
  With pearly tears bedewed,
The fern-leaves' fairy tracery
  O'er rocky barriers strewed,
The pine's low voice of grieving,
  The poplar's whispering leaves,
Are eloquent of rambles
  Through balmy Sabbath eves.

And when the winds come rushing
  From Winter's icy throne,
And far in rustling eddies
  The fallen leaves are blown,
As in the olden chimney
  I watch the red flames glow,
I dream of winter evenings
  Lost in the long-ago.

I know the hopes we cherish
  Tend to the same bright goal—
The land where grief or parting
  May never reach the soul;
And though long miles divide us,
  Whatever be my lot,
Through all my life I'll cherish
  Thy sweet "Forget-me-not."

"GLIMPSES OF THE SUPERNATURAL."

LEGENDS o'er which to dream
  When all the golden west,
Forest and hill and stream,
  In twilight beauty drest,
Fragrant with breath of flowers,
  A dream of beauty lies,
Watching through passing hours
  Her star-illumined skies;

When all we hold most dear
  Lies nearer to the heart,
When care and toil and fear
  On hastening wings depart,
As from their shining bowers
  Bright angel-hosts descend,
And with mysterious powers
  The past and present blend.

Thought-pictures then each tale
  These glowing pages hold,
Of faith which ne'er can fail,
  Of courage true and bold,
Of grace whose plenteous showers
  On trusting spirits fall,
And with its strengthening dowers
  Life's cunning foes forestall.

God bless the hand that traced
These pictures pure and quaint,
Before our vision placed
Each well-belovèd Saint!
Be his the perfect peace
The faithful laborer knows
When toil shall find release
In Heaven's serene repose.

CONGRATULATORY ADDRESS

TO MR. AND MRS. MARTIN MURPHY ON THE FIFTIETH ANNIVERSARY OF THEIR BRIDAL DAY, JULY 18, 1881.

SHINE, O golden light of Summer!
   Over hill and vale to-day;
Breezes, bring the sweetest fragrance
   From the blossoms round your way;
And, ye green and leafy woodlands,
   Fling your waving shadows wide,
As we bring our joyous greeting
   To the bridegroom and the bride:

Unto you whose faithful spirits
   Keep the flame of love aglow
With the same pure, tender radiance
   As when, fifty years ago,
In the quaint Canadian city
   By the far Atlantic shore,
You, when life was in its morning,
   Pledged your vows for evermore—

Vows that still, through sun or shadow,
   You have kept a sacred trust,
Walking in the pathway trodden
   By the gentle and the just.

Blessings on you, joy and blessings
  From the hearts of all to-day—
Blessings grand and sweet and lasting
  Crown you with their shining ray!

Oh! it is not cold lip-homage,
  Which even strangers may command,
But with love through life cemented,
  Loyal clasp of loyal hand,
Do we bring our words of greeting,
  Do we vainly strive to tell,
While our accents weakly falter
  All the joy we feel so well;

Do we pray for blessings on you—
  May the blessings you have sown
Freely in the lives of others,
  Bear sweet fruitage in your own.
Blessings on you! Calm and peaceful
  May your future moments be,
Gliding onward, fair and tranquil,
  As when rivers near the sea.

Looking backward through the vistas
  Of the past half-century, lo!
We behold your hours illumined
  By love's clear and perfect glow—
Love whose flame made bright your dwelling
  Where the tall Canadian pines
Dare the Winter's fiercest tempests,
  Quaff the Summer's rosiest wines;

Love whose angel wended with you
  To Missouri's fertile vales;
Love which nerved you on your journey
  Over lonely hills and dales,
When, your course still westward holding,
  'Neath the blue, o'erarching dome
Here you hailed the blue Pacific
  With its crest of sparkling foam.

And when all these wilds were joyous
  In their untamed beauty's glow,
Here you pitched your tent and rested
  Six-and-thirty years ago.
Here you toiled with earnest spirit,
  Willing heart, and generous hand;
Here your names are linked for ever
  With the history of our land.

Many a weary, footsore pilgrim,
  Toiling through the trackless West,
Found beneath your sheltering roof-tree
  Welcome, comfort, food, and rest.
Many a grateful heart remembers,
  Many a grateful voice has told,
Of your deeds of gracious kindness—
  Memories sweet for us to hold.

And though God has set his milestones—
  Graves of dear ones—round your way,
Lo! they are as angels pointing
  On to realms of endless day.

God has blessed your faithful union;
  May those blessings never cease,
And the hours of life's ripe autumn
  See them daily still increase!

Blessings on you! Friends and kindred
  The sweet chorus gladly swell,
With your children, and their children,
  Loved so fondly and so well.
Blessings on you! May our Father,
  From his treasure-house on high,
Shower his choicest graces on you,
  Naught your hearts desire deny;

Bless you in your garnered treasures,
  In your children's lives and fame,
In the thoughts that friends and kindred
  Twine around your cherished name,
In the pleasures that await you,
  In the good deeds you have done,
Till love's golden years are ended
  And your lives' last victory won!

MAY-DAY MEMORIES.

OH! blithely, blithely rose that morn,
   That laughing morn in May!
And wooed us forth with willing feet
   O'er hill and dale to stray,
To gather flowers, and dance, and sing
   Throughout the livelong day.

And forth a merry, care-free band
   Of boys and girls we went;
The freshening breezes of the spring
   Blew o'er the hills of Kent,
And quick, electric thrills of joy
   Through all my being sent.

Where thick and white the hawthorn bloomed,
   And cowslip bells were seen,
We raised the pole with blossoms wreathed,
   And crowned our sweet May Queen.
Then followed music's ringing notes
   And dancing on the green.

Oh! there was many a bright-eyed girl,
   And many a rosy lad,
And all were blithe as blithe could be:
   No face looked grieved or sad;
Age smiled on youth, and 'neath that smile
   Youth grew more bright and glad.

Oh! many a long and weary year
  Has passed by since that day,
When in my heart of hearts I crowned
  One maiden Queen of May—
A blue-eyed, bright-haired, laughing sprite
  Who stole my heart away.

I was just then an amorous youth
  Whose willing muse could 'plain,
In accents full of sweet desire,
  Love's pleasurable pain
Which burned in crimson on my cheeks
  And throbbed within my brain.

I told her of my love that day,
  And, coy though she would be,
She owned, with many a timid blush,
  Her heart's pure love for me—
Love, woman's love, whose depths are still
  As soundless as the sea.

Oh! life's full cup of joy was filled
  Unto the brim that day;
Love crowned with perfect light the eve
  That closed the dawn of May—
A light that from my inmost soul
  Can never pass away.

THE CENTENNIAL ODE.

1784-1884.

WHY do we gather here to-day,
Where westward, stretching far away,
The great Pacific's waters smile
Round frowning cape and verdant isle,
And with reverberating tone
Along the sounding beach make moan,
That with its ceaseless echo thrills
The bosom of the mighty hills?

Why meet we here, 'mid summer's bloom?
To lay our laurels on the tomb
Of him who light on darkness shed,
And to Faith's living fountain led
The countless tribes who trod of yore
In savage pride our golden shore.
We come with reverent hearts to prove
Our depths of gratitude and love
To him, the earnest, true, and brave,
Who sleeps in yonder hallowed grave.

Who was he? In immortal speech
What lessons doth his lifetime teach?
As the most precious jewels glow
Deep hidden in earth's caves below,
So from the humbler walks of life
He sprang a warrior for the strife
Which valiant hosts for ever wage

Against the demons' tireless rage.
Majorca's Isle, whose sunny clime
Dreams in perpetual summer-time,
Nursed his first hours, and marked with joy
The lofty spirit of the boy ;
The purity of heart and soul ;
The feelings held in sweet control;
Each thought that fired his youthful breast
By heavenly love alone possessed ;
The love whose power, while yet a child
And life a cloudless vista smiled,
Urged him to lay, as offering meet,
That life before his Saviour's feet,
Pledging his loyalty and love
To the great King who rules above.
He in the convent's shelter found
True peace and healing for each wound ;
There from each grand, inspired page
He conned the lore of Saint and Sage,
And Science hastened to impart
Her treasures to his longing heart.
There learned he, 'neath love's gentle sway,
Who best commands must first obey,
Who other souls would safely guide
Must cleanse his own of wrath and pride,
And he who other lives would rule
With humble will his own must school ;
There won that knowledge, strength, and power,
His stay and shield in many an hour
When toil and danger, want and pain
Oppressed, and earthly hope seemed vain.

   A soldier dreams of laurels earned
When the fierce battle's tide has turned,

And, thundering o'er the trampled plain,
The cheers of victory ring amain ;
Then, 'mid the echoing acclaim,
Hears praise for valor crown his name ;
Rejoicing feels that fame will bring
To him proud honors from his king.
So to the young Franciscan came
A vision of celestial fame ;
A longing all his thoughts possessed
To labor in the savage West,
And to its hapless children bear
The joys that Christian nations share—
The gifts of Faith and Hope and Love,
The triple key of Heaven above.

A heart like his, so fired with zeal
For God's dear cause, so prompt to feel
For others' woes, so swift to aid
Weak souls by suffering dismayed,
Bled for the children of the wild,
By pagan rites debased, defiled.
For them he prayed, for them he wept,
And many a fast and vigil kept,
And with his chosen friends, who claim
Our country's fairest wreath of Fame,
In love's impatience, fond and sweet,
Waited the coming hour to greet
When, on the missionary field,
They too the arms of Christ might wield.

Fair Cadiz sitteth by the sea,
A queen in power and majesty.
The throbbing waves her shores that greet
Bring the world's commerce to her feet.

What treasures through her port have passed,
As East and West their tribute cast,
In gold and pearls and raiment rare,
Before her in profusion fair!
But never galleon bore such freight
Of priceless value through her gate
As when, toward the sunset world,
Sped forth a ship with sails unfurled,
Bearing to fields of labor new
Brave hearts and noble, strong and true;
For with that band of heroes came
Padre Junipero, whose name,
A golden nimbus, crowns our land
With deathless glory, pure and grand.
With him sailed, too, the friends of years—
Crespi, Palou, Verger: who hears
That roll of honor called, nor feels
Within his heart a sense of pride,
Nor yields the homage ne'er denied
To those whom Fame reveals
As worthy of the loftiest place,
The proudest honors of our race,
Knows naught of gratitude or love;
His thoughts can never soar above
   The grovelling cares of earth.
For daring toils of land and deep,
They waked this fair land from her sleep
   Ere Freedom's hour of birth.

. Oh! vainly would the Muse essay
To tell the dangers of the way,
When, driven by storms, by calms oppressed,
By woes of famine sore distressed,

Till nine-and-ninety days passed o'er,
They landed on the Mexic shore.
For nineteen years her valleys heard
Their voices preach God's holy word,
Until the hour so long delayed—
The hour for which Junipero prayed
From childhood's tender glow—
Came with his monarch's mandate: " Go
To California's lonely wild ;
There labor for the forest's child,
And lift him from his savage state
To Christian knowledge true and great "—
Thrice welcome message, heard in tears
Of joy too deep for speech ; the years
Of waiting vanished as a dream,
A shadow on life's hurrying stream.

 He came. The desert wild and lone,
The mountains stern and high,
The sombre pall of silence thrown
In awe o'er earth and sky,
The barren wastes of drifting sand,
The cactus with its arm èd band,
The burning thirst, the fiery heat,
The rugged rocks that pierced his feet,
The thousand dangers of each day,
Barred not our sainted Father's way.
For his the heart of warrior-mould,
The zeal that never groweth cold ;
Sickness and suffering, pain and want,
Hunger and warfare—naught could daunt
The heart whose only thought and aim
Was but to glorify God's name.

He viewed our country's beauty first
　In summer's fervid glow ;
And as upon his vision burst
　Its charms, in accents slow,
In accents solemn, slow, and grand,
Rose heavenward from his faithful band
Such heartfelt hymns of praise and love
As echo in God's courts above.

O ye who mark the spreading plain,
A billowy sea of golden grain,
And, as the time of harvest nears,
Dream of the wealth of ripening ears—
The glorious product of the soil,
The hundredfold reward of toil—
Can ye not fancy how he felt
When first upon our shores he knelt,
And all its wealth of land and wave
As tribute to his Maker gave?
And—offering dearer far than all—
He gave the tribes he came to call
　Beneath the Cross to dwell :
The harvest ripening for his hand,
The field where his devoted band
　Labored so long and well.

Words fail, and fancy's busy thought
Compasseth not the works he wrought
In California, peopled then
By tribes of wild and warlike men.
But, fifteen years of patient toil,
And lo! as flowerets of the soil

Rose nine fair missions, from whose towers
The sweet chimes told the passing hours,
Calling to labor or to prayer
The Indians dwelling 'neath his care.

Oh! not in idleness and ease
Were won his victories by these seas.
For savage hate too oft repaid
With blood and fire the blessings laid
Before them by the generous hand
Of the Apostle of our land.
Nor easy was the task to train
Wild dwellers of the hill and plain
In peaceful arts to win by toil
The plenteous harvests of the soil.
Only the strong, unfaltering love,
The wisdom given him from above,
The deep humility of heart
Which made them of his life a part,
And nerved him and his priests to share
The trials they were called to bear,
Could e'er have won in such short space
The homage of the Indian race.
And he was loved. Thy hills, Carmel,
Seem yet to echo the wild swell
Of agony and grief and woe
Heard here one hundred years ago
When the Apostle of the West
Entered into eternal rest.
What lamentations filled the air
When, reft of his paternal care,
An orphaned band, they gathered near
To strew sweet flowers upon his bier,

To kiss his hand, his robe, his cross,
Wailing with bitter tears their loss—
A cry of heartfelt agony
Which echoing rang from sea to sea,
Bearing the burden of its pain
Unto the farthest shores of Spain.

O faithful shepherd of the flock,
O priest both wise and brave,
Whose hand earth's secrets did unlock
Beside the Western wave,
Around thy holy tomb to-day
Another people bend to pray.
Blending with those whose sires of yore
Trod with thee first this golden shore
And heard thy burning words of love,
The hearts of all with ardor move.
'Tis theirs to reap the harvest sown
  By thee in faith and trust.
They to the listening world make known
  Thy name, O great and just!
For thine shall be a deathless fame,
To which the years shall add acclaim;
Within our land its light shall glow
While mountains stand and rivers flow,
And the deep tones of wind and wave
Sing ceaseless dirges round thy grave.

A MEMENTO.

SHE sent me a violet deeply blue,
   And a daisy white and pure,
The emblems meet of a stainless life
   And a love that will endure;
They had drunk the showers
Through the winter's hours,
   And answered the sun's soft smile
Where the green hills keep
Watch over the deep,
   Broad bay for many a mile.

I looked in the daisy's face so white,
   And the violet's eyes of blue,
And said: "Dear flowers, you were nursed to life
   O'er a heart as pure and true
As e'er sank to rest
In earth's tranquil breast
   When youth was fair and bright,
And the future gleamed
With the rays that streamed
   From love's illuming light.

"Ye have watched her rest through starlit hours
   And noontide's fervid ray,
Through the purple glow of twilight's reign
   And the dawning cold and gray;

Your fragrance has been freely shed
Where our darling lies in her lowly bed
  'Mid the scenes she loved so well;
Ye have heard the wild bird's carol ring
In that favored haunt of the beauteous spring
  When the buds and blossoms swell."

And I laid the fairy blooms away
  With the tokens I love the best,
A sweet memento evermore
  Of our dear one's dreamless rest—
A sweet memento evermore
Of one who passed to the shining shore,
  Where the spotless of soul abide
In the glorious light of our Father's face,
And the shining rivers of love and grace
  Flow on in a boundless tide.

TWO PICTURES.

THE PAST.

FAR away in that far country where the sons of
    France first labored,
  Where their names, brave saints and martyrs, with
    a haloing glory dwell,
And the great Saint Lawrence rushes down its myriad
    miles triumphant
  To the ocean, where its waters join the wild Atlan-
    tic's swell,
Stood a home beneath whose roof-tree dwelt the an-
    gels Love and Friendship—
  A dear home where Death had never entered with
    his mien of woe,
But the laughing tones of children waked the echoes,
    clear and ringing,
  With the ceaseless mirth and music which from
    childish hearts o'erflow.

Of that home the artist Memory loves to paint a shin-
    ing picture.
  Ah! I gaze with love and yearning on her ever-
    varying dyes,
As I trace the fields and meadows, with the waving
    woods beyond them,
  'Neath the swiftly-changing glory of the early
    spring-day skies.

And she shows the evening hours when around the
    blazing hearthside
  All were met in genial converse at the closing of the
    day ;
While fond parents, proud and joyous, smiled upon
    the group around them,
  Thinking ne'er was home so happy, never parents
    blessed as they.

How the great logs blazed and sparkled, leaping up
    in crimson radiance,
  As the youthful watchers listened to some won-
    drous fairy-tale—
Such quaint legends as have echoed in the hearts and
    homes of Erin,
  Crowning with a magic interest lonely cairn and
    haunted vale.
Then the evening prayers ascended, incense sweet
    from hearts unsullied,
  Thanks and praise celestial blending, upward borne
    by angels bright,
Till the calm and peace descending from the treasures
    of our Father
  Seemed to rest upon all spirits as they softly said :
    " Good-night."

THE PRESENT.

Now the present paints a picture of that home once
    bright and joyous,
  Shows the change the years, in passing on their on-
    ward journey, wrought :

Still it stands amid its meadows, fair as when the smiling children
    Flowers of spring and summer's berries to its welcoming portals brought—
Still it stands amid its meadows, with the rare October sunlight
    Flooding all the land around it with the autumn's gorgeous dyes;
But no more the echoes waken to the sound of carefree laughter,
    For a cloud of woe and sadness on that olden dwelling lies.

The children, men and women now, no longer cross its threshold;
    Dwellers they in realms far sundered—one where Walla Walla flows,
One amid Ontario's beauties, one on Michigan's fair borders,
    And one where California's brightest valley shines and glows;
Two still linger where the Storm-King holds high revel when the winter
    Wraps the wide Canadian country in a winding-sheet of snow;
Two, the nearest and the dearest, have laid down life's weary burden,
    Bade farewell to all they cherished, all who loved them here below—
Two who walked, in sun or shadow, with pure souls and hearts uplifted
    To the Saviour who so loved them that he gave to them to bear

Some small portion of his burden in the pain he bade
    them suffer,
  Drawing them from earth to enter still more closely
    in his care.

And their parents, prayerful, patient, by the Christian's hope supported,
  Dwell beneath the sheltering roof-tree that once
    saw so much of bliss,
In the calm and peaceful beauty of a ripe old age beholding
  Through death's angel-guarded portal shine a
    brighter world than this.
Blessed Faith! whose rays inspiring cheer us in our
    hours of sorrow,
  Showing us that death and parting are but transitory things,
To that home, and hearts it shelters, bear a boundless
    wealth of comfort,
  Strength and graces from the treasures of the wondrous King of Kings.

TO J. M.

LO! within the precious volume
   Which thy love hath sent to me
I have gathered many blossoms
   Fraught with tender thoughts of thee—

Blossoms which, like dewy violets
   In their foliage hidden deep,
Yield to passing winds the fragrance
   That their perfumed bosoms keep:

Dreams of days when golden summer
   Knew no wearying round of toil,
When in ceaseless calm the seasons
   Blessed the owners of the soil;

Ere across the tall Sierras
   Came the pioneers of old,
Here to win as shining guerdon
   California's wealth untold.

California's fertile valleys,
   California's cloudless skies,
California's voiceful rivers
   Wooed to deeds of high emprise.

In her wild, imperious beauty
   There was much the heart to move,
And the bravest still are winners,
   Be the object land or love.

Years have passed since first thy footsteps
  Pressed the smiling western slope;
Vanished now are all the dangers
  'Gainst which thou wert called to cope.

Thou art victor; time has blessed thee,
  All best joys of life are thine;
Yet not more than I could wish thee
  In this heart-wreath which I twine.

May thy future still be happy
  As the sunny days gone by,
And no cloud of sorrow ever
  Mar the azure of thy sky!

GOD BLESS YOU.

"God bless you!" 'Twas a simple prayer,
   And yet it reached God's throne
As surely as the ringing psalm
   Blent with the organ's tone.

"God bless you!" 'Twas the grateful prayer
   Of lips by mercy fed,
The prayer of one whose hands had grown
   Too weak to earn his bread;

A prayer for blessings from the store
   Whose wealth can never fail,
Though earth should crumble into dust
   And starry skies grow pale.

Then listen to the pleading tones
   Of those in want who live,
And from their grateful pleasure learn
   How bless'd it is to give.

THE BABY SLEEPS.

THE baby sleeps, his silken lashes sweeping
    The rounded beauty of each velvet cheek,
Veiling the lustrous eyes whose tender glances
    So well the infant's guileless love could speak;
O'er his white brow dark, clustering tresses rest,
And his wee hands lie lightly on his breast.

Just one short month ago he came from Heaven,
    Bringing its sunshine in his smiling face,
And day by day he drew each fond heart nearer
    By his sweet purity and childish grace.
How well beloved he was they feel alone
Whose mother-heart such treasures dear have known.

The baby sleeps the sleep that knows no waking;
    The luminous eyes will never more unclose;
The stainless soul will ne'er by earth be tarnished,
    Nor the young heart be wrung by sorrow's throes:
For, 'mid the shining ministers of grace,
He looks to-day upon our Father's face.

The baby sleeps, but, robed in radiant splendor
    Amid the glory of celestial light,
He joins the strains of rapturous worship sounding
    Where Jesus' presence maketh all things bright.
There baby Wilfrid, angel Wilfrid, hears
No more the mourning of this vale of tears.

CONFIRMATION.

THEY knelt before the altar,
    A white-robed, white-crowned throng,
Pure-hearted children lifted
    Anear the angels' song.

They knelt before the altar,
    And from the Bishop's hand
Received the sign which sealed them
    True soldiers of Christ's band—

True soldiers of that legion
    Which battles, day by day,
Against the world's corruption,
    Against the demon's sway,

Against the grovelling passions
    Which in the flesh find place,
And lead the senses captive
    Far from the throne of grace.

Dear lambs whom the One Shepherd
    Has gathered to his fold,
Pure-hearted, happy children,
    Beneath the Cross enrolled;

Signed with the sacred chrism,
    Sealed with the Saviour's sign,
Enlightened by the beauty
    Of the sevenfold gifts divine.

Sweet subjects of the Spirit,
  Whose wisdom, thought, and power
To each he freely giveth,
  A rare, a priceless dower—

A priceless dower to aid them
  Along life's rugged way,
Sustaining, strengthening, cheering
  Their young hearts day by day.

For many are the trials
  That on their footsteps wait,
The unbeliever's scoffing,
  The bigot's words of hate,

The malice of the demons
  Who seek to vent their spleen
Upon the humble followers
  Of the "lowly Nazarene."

But, strengthened by the Spirit
  To tread religion's ways,
Their lives in virtuous actions
  Shall sing their Maker's praise.

SILVER JUBILEE

OF THE MOST REV. JOSEPH S. ALEMANY, D.D.

SON of Saint Dominic! blessed be the hour
   When first our shores thy favored footsteps pressed,
True shepherd, seeking with unswerving love
   Thy scattered flock within the golden West—

The flock that wandered far without a fold,
   For whom no Pastor's hand the Banquet spread,
Or to the ever-flowing fount of grace
   The sinner, thirsting for God's mercy, led.

The holy seed Saint Francis' sons had sown
   Seemed whelmed beneath the evil tide which swept
Across the land when, drawn from every zone,
   Votaries of Mammon here their orgies kept.

There was no home to shield the sick or poor,
   No shelter for the orphan's head was found;
Only from Missions lying far apart
   Was heard at morn and eve the church-bell's sound.

Wide-spread the whitening harvest to thy hand,
   Heavy the labor, and the laborers few;
But, strong in Faith's divinest love and trust,
   Thou didst the work the Master bade thee do.

And blessings crowned thee with the passing years :
  Unclouded shines thy Silver Jubilee
Where, symbol of our Faith, the Cross keeps watch
  O'er spire and dome beside the sounding sea.

From every altar through the land to-day
  Prayers of thanksgiving for thy past arise,
Prayers that thy future hours may ever be
  Fraught with the glorious riches of the skies ;

Prayers of the orphans sheltered by thy care,
  Prayers of the poor thy pitying love hath fed,
Prayers of repentant sinners by thy hand
  Back to the path of truth and virtue led ;

Prayers from the city's throbbing heart that rise,
  Prayers that are echoed far by hill and plain :
From rich and poor, from high and low alike,
  Ascends for thee love's glad and grateful strain.

For never father with paternal care
  More tenderly his children's wants supplied
Than thou hast guarded from the ways of ill
  For five-and-twenty years thy household wide.

The lofty temples builded to His name
  Whose law is love and mercy, who is just,
The stately halls where gracious learning reigns,
  Bear witness thou hast well fulfilled thy trust.

But not alone by monuments like these,
  O faithful Pastor ! are thy labors told ;
The spirits thou hast strengthened in the faith,
  The legions 'neath the holy Cross enrolled,

The bright soul-treasures precious beyond price,
  Crown-jewels given into thy Maker's hand—
The hearts of those who love thee and to-day
  Arise to call thee blessèd in the land.

Joining with those who speak their love to thee,
  Thy distant children waft their wishes too—
Wishes that every coming year to thee
  In peace and bliss its glories may renew.

No words can tell the gratitude we feel,
  The debt we owe thee love alone can pay;
But joy for thee, and endless peace and bliss
  For all thy future, we can fondly pray.

And oh! God keep thee in his holy care,
  And leave thee to the children of thy fold,
That they may hail thee as their Father still
  When Time shall sound thy Jubilee of Gold.

JUNE 30, 1875.

LAS LLAGAS DE SAN FRANCISCO.

THERE are buds of beauty swelling
  Into being on its brink,
Where the clematis is clambering,
  And the pale rose bends to drink,
And the giant plane-trees o'er it
  Their white fingers interlink.

Down upon its verdant margin,
  Where the blithe larks build and sing,
Spreads the greenest and the softest
  Velvet carpet of the spring;
And the first-born of the song-birds
  There essay their flight to wing.

From the summits of the mountains
  Wafts of fragrance drift adown
When the breezes stir the leaflets
  Of their foreheads' laurel crown,
While the babbling of the streamlets
  Fain all other tones would drown.

Tracing it from out its fastness
  To the valley broad and fair,
Can we wonder, 'mid its beauties,
  That some pious missionaire
Gave to it the name of reverence
  Which its charmèd windings bear?

"The Stigmata of Saint Francis"—
  Name of holiness sublime,
Like a blessing on its waters,
  Like a halo for all time,
Like a beacon 'mid the darkness
  Of this world of woe and crime.

Thus the children of St. Francis,
  When religion's glory streamed
O'er this country and the darkness
  Within which its people dreamed,
Set the seal of Love Eternal
  On the land they had redeemed;

Giving names of saints and martyrs
  To each stream that murmurs by,
To the hills whose cloud-veiled summits
  Seem to rest against the sky,
Making each a silent teacher
  Of the Lord who rules on high.

HAWTHORN BLOSSOMS.

O HAWTHORN blossoms, white as snow!
   From brow and brain to-day
Your beauty drives with magic power
   Pain's cruel band away.

Sweet wizards of the April hours,
   From out your pearly cells,
Upon the soft, still air of noon,
   A strain of music wells:

Low whispers of the western vale
   Where, by the breezes kissed,
Ye revelled in the sun's warm glow,
   And quaffed the sea-born mist,

And quaffed the beaded draughts of dew
   Borne inland from the sea,
And heard beneath your spreading shade
   The children's merry glee—

The winsome, bright-eyed girls and boys
   Whose rose-embowered home
Was free from care as winds that sweep
   The cloudless summer dome.

Oh! far beyond the present's hour,
   On airy wings of light,
Ye bear my fancy floating far
   Across the ocean bright,

Across the sounding waves that beat
  Beyond the mountains tall,
O'er plain, and waste, and peopled towns,
  To Erin's sea-girt wall.

There, when the golden year is young
  And twilight's hour is born,
The fairies trip their mystic dance
  Around the snowy thorn.

Full many a legend of our land
  Around the tree is twined,
And deep in fond and loving hearts
  Its name for ever shrined.

For wandering exiles 'neath its shade
  Have spent their care-free hours,
And watched with childhood's curious gaze
  Its wondrous wealth of flowers;

Have seen its emerald foliage gleam,
  Its blooms like drifted snow,
And, brightly shining amid all,
  Its berries' crimson glow—

Blending like homes where haply reigns
  The power of love and truth,
The fruit of age with manhood's prime
  And the pure hours of youth.

O hawthorn blossoms, white as snow!
  Fair emblems, truly meet,
Of Hope, whose smile o'er darkened days
  Has shed a radiance sweet.

Around her life whose dear hand culled
  This wand of light for me,
May Hope pour forth her choicest gifts
  In measure full and free.

May gentle Love and Peace combine
  To bless her future hours,
And earth reflect in tender hues
  The light of heavenly bowers!

A DEER'S ANTLERS.

(RECEIVED FROM B. T. M.)

THOU timid ranger of the wild,
   Whose flying feet the mosses spurned
On heights where day's last embers burned
Or morning's rosy splendors smiled,

How oft thy stately front has shone
   At dawn upon the ferny hills,
   Or gleamed reflected in the rills
That murmur down through cañons lone.

There, when the noonday heats oppressed,
   And, save the insect's droning hum,
   The mighty solitudes were dumb,
How sweet it was to lie at rest

Where flowers their fragrance freely shed,
   And the tall brackens' nodding plumes.
   Made denser still the vernal glooms
Around the mountain monarch's bed!

Thus didst thou on the trackless waste
   Dwell 'mid all things both fair and free,
   Hearing afar the moaning sea
Roar hoarsely when by tempest chased,

Or from the echoing hills around
   The challenge answered back again,
   As though defiance to the main
Was given in the thunderous sound.

Oh! bright the Spring day's fadeless sheen,
   And Summer's fadeless beauties smile
   Around thy haunts for many a mile
Where waving groves are ever green.

But never in their sylvan shade
   Thy graceful form again shall move,
   Thy swiftly bounding speed to prove,
Where thou so oft of yore hast played.

No more upon the breezy hill
   These stately antlers wilt thou toss:
   Here, shining with unfading gloss,
A trophy of the hunter's skill,

They hang upon the pictured wall,
   And memory paints the lofty swell
   Of the green hills of San Rafael,
That saw thy freedom and thy fall.

Fair trophy of a huntsman's skill,
   Dear token from a kindly heart,
   To which I pray Heaven may impart
The blessings which that heart can fill,

With all the choicest gifts that crown
   A life of usefulness and love,
   A life whose aim is far above
This earth's dark turmoil, care, or frown.

CHEER UP.

KEEP a stout heart, friend, though fortune may frown;
Let not life's burdens thus weigh thee down.

What are earth's pleasures but glittering dross?
Tread in His footsteps who carried the Cross.

Sink not aweary, faint not with fear;
Angels are with thee to comfort and cheer.

Life's path not always leads through joy's bower;
Griefs will assail thee and tempests will lower.

But as the morning follows the night,
After the shadow cometh the light—

The light of that morning which ever endures,
Whose beauty no storm-cloud of sorrow obscures;

The light of His presence in whose love is found
An armor unfailing to compass thee round.

Girt with that armor, what is there to fear?
Then up, friend, and onward! Be of good cheer.

Not to the coward the battle is given,
Nor to the faltering the glories of Heaven.

A MEMORY OF MAY.

THE Autumn's bright crown is with golden hues
    tinted,
  And the dead leaves like moments are drifting
    away;
But this bloom of Collinsia, as pure as the dawning,
  Recalls to my spirit a memory of May—

A memory of hours when it, with its kindred,
  Like fairy lamps lighted a lone mountain dell,
Whose tree-clothèd sides gave a musical echo
    To the strains whose glad chorus the wild song-
    sters swell.

From the hearts of the flowers sweet perfume was
    stealing,
  And the green branching ferns hid the rough rocks
    away,
The Columbine's rubies burned bright 'mid the
    thickets,
  And the wild roses, blushing, bent down to the
    spray;

While fair as the blossoms that May-day adorning,
  And pure as this bloom from the rude hill-side rent,
Were the laughing-eyed, glad-hearted girls who wan-
    dered
  Amid those wild scenes, and in ecstasy bent

Where some rare floral gem in its beauty was spring-
 ing,
 Or wonderingly gazed where some wild bird with
 skill
Had cunningly woven its nest, and had hidden it
 In safety away 'mid the grass on the hill.

Young hearts paid their tribute of homage to Nature,
 And blithe voices wakened the echoes that slept
Lulled away in the depths of the mountains, whose
 secrets
 The ages so long and so jealously kept;

'Till the noontide's warm hours of tropical beauty
 Were treasured away with the dreams of the past,
And the sweet-sighing zephyrs stole downward to
 wander
 Amid the cool shades that to westward were cast.

Then all gathered round an old oak by the fountain,
 A reft in whose moss-covered trunk formed a shrine
Which fair hands had decked with bright flowers and
 tapers,
 And there in their midst smiled the Mother Divine,

Whose praise, in sweet accents of music up-swelling,
 Flowed forth from the hearts of the children who
 came,
To quaff from the full cup of Nature's pure pleasures
 Amid these wild scenes, from their home Notre
 Dame.

Oh! never before had that sylvan dell witnessed
   A sight as entrancing as shone in it then,
When each young heart was lifted in praise to its Maker,
   And angels knelt with them that day in the glen—

Knelt with them to catch every breath of their worship,
   Sweeter far than the odorous gems of the sod,
To bear it aloft, like the fragrance of incense,
   To their home in the beautiful presence of God.

How the rugged old hills must have thrilled to their centre
   As they echoed the praise of the Mother most pure!
What a beautiful tale for the great oaks to whisper
   In tremulous murmurs while they shall endure!

And here, while the dead leaves around me are drifting,
   And the old year in beauty is passing away,
While the red tapers brighten the shrine of the Autumn,
   My heart turns with joy to this memory of May.

TO NELLIE.

WHILE the tints of early autumn
    Over hill and valley fall,
And September's gentle fingers
    Spread her azure veil o'er all,

Upon this thy bridal morning,
    Nellie dearest, do we pray
That thy future be as cloudless
    As the fairest summer day;

Bright and beauteous as the wild rose
    Blushing by the winding streams;
Joyous as the wild birds' accents
    Sounding where the sunlight beams;

Fresh as morning's draught of nectar
    Perfumed by the violet's breath,
Hallowed by a love whose fervor
    Will prove faithful unto death.

Crowned with Heaven's choicest blessings,
    Faith and Hope and changeless Love,
Whose bright angel-hands will lead thee
    To the heart's true home above.

A TRINKET.

YOU smile, pretty one, at this token,
    This token so battered and gray—
This symbol of Hope, which, though broken,
    I wear my sole trinket to-day.

But know, of all things that I treasure,
    Is this symbol most precious to me ;
For it slept on the grave of my darling
    In the Island far over the sea.

Kneeling there when my heart was nigh broken,
    When earth seemed all dark to my eyes,
I found on her low grave this token,
    Like a messenger sent from the skies.

It whispered of bright days before me,
    Of strength with my trials to cope :
Since that hour all my life's stormy battles
    Have been won 'neath the banner of Hope.

THROUGH IDLE HOURS.

THE roses blossom by the gate,
    The roses clamber up the wall;
The birds sing when the morning breaks,
    The birds sing at the evening's fall.

The breezes idle through the woods,
    The breezes loiter o'er the grass;
The clinging vines, with bloom aglow,
    Nod gaily to them as they pass.

The scene is fair the long day through,
    But fairest when the twilight thrills
With her deep sense of restful calm
    The bosoms of the mighty hills;

When day has passed, and with it borne
    The petty cares that try and wound,
And in the peaceful trance of even
    A joyous benison is found.

Then it is sweet through idle hours
    To sit and muse as daylight fades,
Till all the shining stars of heaven
    Glow in the Night Queen's ebon braids;

To sit and watch the crimson waves
    Of sunset lave the shores of gold,
While argosies of amber hue
    By giant cliffs their courses hold—

Rare argosies that drift away
  With every snowy sail unfurled,
To anchor in some quiet bay
  Shut in the wondrous cloudland world,

As kindly thoughts, when clothed in words
  Of kindred kindliness, will rest
Freighted with power to soothe and cheer
  The weary pain in sorrow's breast.

And so, with spring's rich fragrance fraught
  The golden-wingèd hours depart,
And peace, like twilight dew distilled,
  Falls softly on the dreamer's heart.

"GOLDEN SANDS."

INSCRIBED TO SISTER MARY CORNELIA, S.N.D.

GAZING back o'er the years now as swiftly receding
    As clouds float at even to far-away lands,
I take from Time's glass the bright moments passed
    with thee,
    To hold, as a treasure, my life's golden sands.

They gleam on the shrine where fond Memory has
    laid them,
    Dear moments that sped all too swiftly away—
Links forged in the chain of a friendship undying,
    Which absence nor distance can bow to its sway.

They have brightened dark days till the shadows departed,
    Left the seal of their power impressed on my heart;
And my soul thrills again, as I read, with the pleasure
    And peace which thy presence could ever impart—

A ray of the peace that abideth for ever
    Where the white dove is brooding with unruffled
        wing,
And the cares of the world may not enter to sadden
    The soul of His chosen, the bride of the King.

I turn o'er the leaves of the volume before me,
  Where precious gems gleam in the red gold of
    thought;
But less brightly they shine in the sight of the Maker
  Than the marvels thy teachings on hundreds have
    wrought.

In numberless homes by the tranquil Pacific,
  From the north to the south of this beautiful land,
In all ranks of life, unto blossom and fruitage
  Are springing the seeds that were sown by thy hand—

Seeds of Faith, Hope, and Love, seeds of knowledge
    and duty,
  That are strengthening the spirit and firing the brain
To walk 'neath the shade of the Cross without swerving,
  And carry the banner of life without strain.

In the triumphs they win o'er the world and its legions,
  In the numbers who strengthen home's duty-gemmed
    bands,
In their love, fond and grateful, for ever outpouring
  For thee, lies a wealth of the soul's "Golden Sands."

GOD CARES FOR ALL.

"BEHOLD the lilies of the field—
   They labor not, nor do they spin;
Yet Solomon's most royal robes
   Wore not the lily's beauteous sheen."
So God's eternal words declare;
And lo! he holds them in his care.

The grasses of the plain arise,
   Grow, bud and bloom, fulfil their part;
And Christ's dear words of mercy fall
   To blossom in the human heart:
For in his love he guards us all,
And stoops to lift us when we fall.

The birds that through the trackless air
   Wing their swift flight from land to land,
Find food and shelter everywhere,
   Made ready by the Master's hand;
And He who guides them in their flight
Points out to us the path of right.

For more than birds or grass or flowers,
   That gladden in his gracious sight,
Are our immortal souls, where shine
   A spark of Heaven's celestial light—
Our souls, for whose offences dread
Christ's blood on Calvary's mount was shed.

Most precious Blood! the priceless key
  That opened wide the shining gates;
Thoughts of the kingdom bought with thee
  The faithful heart with joy elates—
Thoughts of the home God's loving care
Hath given for us to seek and share.

O blessèd heritage prepared
  By Mercy's hand for one and all;
Thrice holy love whose shield extends
  Alike above the great and small;
O happiness, that all may claim
The shelter of our Father's name.

THE TRUE COMFORTER.

WHEN the sorrows of earth, when the shadows of woe,
    Fall dark o'er the path which we tread,
When the sunlight of love's rare illumining glow
    Is lost in the grave of our dead,
In that dread hour of anguish, where, where shall we turn?
What pillar of light through the darkness discern?

Vain then is the comfort that friendship can give;
    Each hope that we trusted seems fading away;
We shrink from the years we are destined to live,
    As we mourn o'er the dear one death summoned away,
And, sadly but trustfully looking from earth,
Fix our gaze upon Heaven, true land of our birth.

There is hope, there is peace, there is comfort divine,
    There love that ne'er fails us, there hope that ne'er dies;
There the sore, stricken spirit no longer shall pine,
    There joys pure and lasting await us. The skies'
Cloudless arch bending o'er us but veils from our sight
A realm of pure and unending delight.

Thus I mused as I stood by the flower-wreathed
 mound
 That hid from my gaze the dear face of a friend,
And heard through the calm, breathless azure around
 The prayers of the Church for his spirit ascend,
While parting and sorrow, and heartache and care,
Seemed floating to Heaven on the white wings of
 prayer;

There to rest in the light that for ever flows down
 From thy fountain of mercy, O merciful Lord!
Whence the dews of thy pity shall rest as a crown
 On the hearts where the vials of sorrow, outpoured,
With bitterness floodeth their fond souls who weep
For the loved one reposing in death's dreamless
 sleep.

Dear ones rendered desolate, God is your stay;
 He is mercy and love, the one only true friend;
Trust, trust in him ever, and, safe 'neath his sway,
 Press onward and upward till life's day shall end,
And in Heaven's shining courts he will give you
 again
The loved ones whose loss rends your bosom with
 pain.

SAN DIEGO'S CENTENARY.

THE waters throb along the beach,
    Chanting their summer roundelay,
Where San Diego's quaint old town
    Looks out across its quiet bay;
The hazy glamour o'er the land,
    And on the hills the azure glow,
The veil of beauty which they wore
    To-day one hundred years ago:

One hundred years ago to-day,
    When Spain's proud banner, floating free,
Proclaimed the advent of the faith
    Of Christ beside the western sea;
When Padre Serra and his band—
    Fresh from the desert rude and wild
Where savage man alone had trod,
    Where vegetation never smiled,

Where, on the tempest-scathèd rocks
    And sandy hollows parched and dry,
In deathless characters are traced
    The anger of the God on high—
Wearied with journeying many a day,
    But filled with zeal's celestial glow,
Raised here the Cross to mark the land
    As Christ's one hundred years ago.

Here rang the anthems of their praise,
  In hymns of worship sweetly poured,
While, blending with their earthly strains,
  The angels sang in sweet accord.
Banner and pennon waving free
  Lit up the summer's arid plain,
Floating above the flashing arms
  That girt the warrior sons of Spain.

For, blended in the holy cause
  Of love and faith, together came
Friar and soldier, each to work
  For Christ's dear glory and his fame—
Friar and soldier, each to work
  Together, yet not interfere
With either's task to train, to rule,
  To guard, to guide, to bless, to cheer.

And thus they wrought. Fame's pages hold
  The record high of many a deed,
Yet bards are silent in his praise
  Whose life deserves their noblest meed—
Padre Junipero, whose name
  A golden halo crowns our land,
Though time and ruin now deface
  The temples builded by his hand.

But in the fallow soil he sowed
  The flowers of Faith have blossomed fair;
The cross he loved with such a love
  From many a spire now cleaves the air.

His prayers are answered : o'er the land
  Religion daily brighter glows,
And God has bade this wilderness
  Blush with the beauty of the rose.

Still faithful in the path he traced,
  The soldiers of the Saviour tread
Through cities fair or deserts waste,
  Where'er the foot of man has sped;
Gathering the harvest from the seed
  Thy sons, Saint Francis, sowed of old,
Leading with tenderest care and love
  The strayed souls back unto the fold;

Bearing Love's balm to all who sink
  Oppressed by sorrow, sin, or care;
Making God's desecrated fanes
  Smile in glad beauty, rich and rare.
And thus, in love and faith and trust,
  Another people stand to-day
Where San Diego's quaint old town
  Looks out across its quiet bay;

The summer's glamour o'er the land,
  And on the hills the azure glow,
The veil of beauty which they wore
  To-day one hundred years ago.
Where then a few brave spirits came
  To rear the Cross, to plant the seed
Of Faith, now hundreds throng around
  Of every race and clime and creed.

But o'er them Spain's proud banner flings
  No more its folds upon the breeze ;
Her day is dark, her crown is lost,
  Her empire over by our seas.
Yet homage to her sons whose task
  Is still to loftier heights to guide
The souls of men ; their fervent zeal
  We honor with a loyal pride.

As now our holy Bishop stands
  'Mid prayer-wreaths rising to God's throne,
And consecrates with solemn rite
  And lays with praise the corner-stone—
The corner-stone on which will rise
  A temple to Our Lady's name,
Where faithful hearts with filial love
  May come her tender care to claim.

And honor to the happy thought
  Which binds to-day the links of years
With this memorial hour which breathes
  Of present joy, of vanquished fears—
This hour which bids us turn again
  To the bright morn of long ago,
Which unto California gave
  Faith's heavenly light, Truth's fadeless glow.

THANKSGIVING HYMN.

FOR all the beauty of the passing year,
    Its music, mirth, and glee,
Its song of birds and wealth of blooms, we give
    Our thanks, O Lord, to thee.

For days that rose in clear, unclouded calm,
    For peace on land and sea,
For breezes fraught with health's electric thrills,
    We give our thanks to thee.

For plenty in the harvest's bounteous yield,
    The orchard's laden tree,
And the full fruitage of the purpled vine,
    We give our thanks to thee.

For joys that crowned our lives with summer's glow,
    Fervid and deep and strong,
Till all the earth around about us seemed
    As kindling into song;

For Sorrow's hand which smote with cruel blow
    Our hearts' most tender chord,
But led us through the darkness of Grief's night
    Nearer to thee, O Lord;

For countless graces poured into our lives
    And strewed around our way,
For thoughts that lightened earth's oppressive cares,
    We thank thee, Lord, to-day.

WELCOME TO THE FIREMEN.

WELCOME! welcome! This our greeting,
    Gallant Firemen, unto you,
Soldiers of our land's best army,
    Heroes tried and proven true.
Brighter, greener are your laurels
    Than the war-scarred veterans wear;
Nobler is the ceaseless conflict
    You are called upon to share.

Let the bugle's ringing challenge
    And the loud drum's fierce tattoo
Summon them to martial glory:
    Loftier task awaiteth you.
For their fame is won by slaughter,
    Ruined home and bloody grave,
While your mission, dauntless spirits,
    Is to comfort and to save.

When across the solemn midnight
    Clangs the loud alarum-bell,
And the hearts of startled listeners
    Hear in it hope's funeral knell;
As the city wakes in horror
    At the tidings fell and dire,
As from lip to lip goes echoing
    The dread word of portent, "Fire!"

While the awe-struck eye beholdeth,
   Spreading broad and red and high,
Sheets of flame like demon banners
   Flaunted 'gainst the starry sky;
When they think what lives imprisoned
   May fall victims to its rage—
Manhood's strength and woman's glory,
   Helpless youth and feeble age—

How their hearts recoil in anguish,
   And their trembling lips are dumb,
Till they hear your cheers resounding,
   And the cry, "They come! they come!"
When the haunts but late so silent
   Echo to the rush of feet
And the clatter of the engines
   Dashing wildly down the street,

Then the gathering throngs grow eager,
   And with fervent spirits pray
Many a pure and sweet "God bless you!"
   As you pass upon your way.
Who will mount the lifted ladders
   Where the fierce flames hiss and leap?
Who will save the lives fast sinking
   Into stupor's deadly sleep?

Ah! no Fireman's heart e'er faltered
   At the sound of duty's call,
Though his pathway leads through danger
   Which the stoutest might appall.

WELCOME TO THE FIREMEN.

You have trod the smoke-filled chamber,
    You have dared the death of flame,
When, from walls that reeled and tottered,
    Down the blazing roof-tree came.

You have rescued lives most precious,
    Wife or husband, sire or son,
And a wealth of love undying
    From our people you have won.
Yet you passed not through unscathèd—
    Tenderest homage do we yield
To our brother Firemen lying
    Dead on honor's battle-field.

And again we breathe our welcome,
    Warm and heartfelt, fond and true—
Welcome from our smiling city,
    Gallant Firemen, unto you.
Welcome! welcome! ever welcome!
    Hear us still and once again:
Welcome, Firemen of our country,
    To our city of the plain!

TO A FRIEND.

THEY tell us that friendship can only
   Be perfect when blessed day by day
By the smiles of the dear ones we cherish;
   That in absence it fadeth away;
That those whom we love with most ardor
   Will bow to the rulings of change,
And time, with its varying fortunes,
   Have power true hearts to estrange.

But, dear friend, though the years in their passage
   Have given us of sorrow and joy,
We have felt that the bond of thy friendship
   Was something they could not destroy;
And often when shadows were darkest
   They have fled from the light of thy smile,
And hours that else had been dreary
   Thy gift has had power to beguile.

And then as we read we have likened
   Thy heart to those women whose lives
The author has drawn with such beauty
   As models for mothers and wives—
The "Heroic Women" whose story
   Is written on history's page,
And fills with an unfading glory
   Each kingdom and station and age.

For life in its every-day trials
  Has need of a courage as high
As that which, when bugles are pealing,
  Nerves warriors to battle and die—
A courage as high, ay, and higher:
  A courage supported by love,
A courage which looks for its guerdon
  In the realms of glory above.

Such courage is thine. May its ardor
  Continue to fire thy soul,
And the angels of Peace and of Pleasure
  Thy life and its fortunes control,
Till the hour when, the earth-shadows lifted,
  In the glow of the " Beautiful Land "
Thou shalt listen to sweet words of welcome
  From that gentle and heroic band.

A FAIR SPRING DAY.

'TIS March, but the voice of the storm is hushed;
    No more with a quivering wail
Do the leafless oaks of the woodland bend
    Their crests to the sweeping gale.

But the sun looks down from a cloudless sky,
    And the green grass seeks to hide
The gaping wounds in the valley's breast,
    Which were torn by the rushing tide

When the river, leaping its narrow banks,
    Bearing ruin in its train,
Through the solemn hours of the stormy night
    Sped over the fertile plain.

The air is filled with the wild birds' song
    In ringing notes of glee,
And the humming-bird flits from flower to flower
    With the butterfly and the bee.

Lo! charmed by the sceptre which **Flora waves**,
    The hill-tops to gold now turn,
And league after league o'er the vale we behold
    Thy fires, Calandrinia, burn!

With what tender voices earth's beauties call
    To the inmost heart to-day,
Pleading for praise for the hand that strewed
    Such blessings around our way!

And a cloud of incense is wafted up
    From the fragrant gems of the sod.
Oh! fair as a dream in this sweet spring glow
    Is this wondrous footstool of God.

TO MRS. M. E. B.

SHALL we search for lofty symbols,
    That our language may impart
A more eloquent portrayal
    To the feelings of each heart?

Nay, when love sincere gives greeting,
    Few and brief the words it says,
But what wealth of sweet emotions
    In each sentence it conveys!

So, dear friend, our heartfelt phrases
    Short and simple, are sincere,
Voicing the deep love which kindles
    The fond spirits gathered here—

Voicing all the grateful feelings,
    All the friendship warm and strong
Won, through years of gentle patience,
    By thy service true and long.

Morning's dawn or sunset's moments
    Found thee ever at thy post,
Urbane, smiling, genial, courteous
    To the questioning, troubling host.

Ever faithful unto duty—
    Oh! no loftier meed of praise
Crowns at last the victor warrior
    Or the statesman's weary days.

TO MRS. M. E. B.

Ever faithful unto duty,
  Ever thoughtful, ever kind—
Thus, dear friend, thy name for ever
  Will in memory be enshrined,

And the years before us stretching
  Find our friendship warm and true,
While bright blessings round thy pathway
  Daily added joys renew.

Oh! we fain would bring a token
  Worthy of the love we bear
And the gratitude unspoken
  It is ever ours to share—

Something that would mutely render
  Praise for duty nobly done,
Better than the gift we tender.
  Take with it the hearts thou'st won:

Take their warm appreciation,
  Take their friendship, love, and praise,
And their prayers that God will bless thee
  And make beauteous all thy days.

WAITING.

WHEN the dead leaves drifted lie,
    And the long moss streamers swing
To the passing zephyr's sigh;
    While the blackbird plumes his wing,

And the blithe lark's merry note
    Fills with music all the air—
Sounds that skyward float and float
    From the valley's bosom fair;

When the sycamores arise
    In their mantles brown and gold,
Foreheads lifted to the skies
    Like the giant kings of old—

Then the Winter's sway begins
    In this sunny land of ours,
And his mighty cohort wins
    Refuge in the Summer's bowers.

While the green grass starts to life
    O'er the valley brown and sere,
And the earth with hope is rife
    For the coming of the year,

For the joys that will elate,
    For the blessings it will bring,
Doth the land in patience wait
    For the bridal of the Spring.

GREETING TO THE PIONEERS.

"THERE'S a land beyond the mountains where
perpetual summer reigneth,
Where the soil is rich and fertile and the air is soft
and bland,
Where the wealth of field and forest lieth ready to
be garnered
As the whitening grain of autumn waits the mowers'
sturdy band."

Thus they told us of the beauties of the Queen of the
Pacific,
The secrets of whose vaults of gold the genii
guarded still;
Told us of her smiling valleys where uncounted herds
were roaming,
Of her cloudless skies o'erarching rocky peak and
sloping hill.

Why, the legends of the Orient seemed to pale before
her glories,
And with youth's enraptured fancies we would
often sit and dream
Of a life of calm contentment, dwelling 'mid her rare
luxuriance,
Like the Lotos-Eaters resting by their own belovèd
stream

Then the cry of "Westward!" sounded. "Westward ho!" we answered blithely;
   And we trod with heart undaunted dreary plain and lone defile,
Till we passed the tall Sierras, and for many a league before us
Saw this land of our adoption in her bright young beauty smile.

Here we rested, toil and danger 'mid those tranquil scenes forgotten.
   We have loved her as a mother: she has given a mother's care.
She has blessed us with all blessings, Pioneers of California;
   Who could win a richer dowry than she freely bids us share?

From her mountains' rugged fastness golden streams are yearly flowing,
   And her valleys give in harvest shining stores of golden grain;
While her vineyards, sun-empurpled, pour for us the sparkling nectar
   Which might lure the merry Bacchus here to linger with his train.

And to-day, the past and present blending fondly in our memories,
   Here we meet with heartfelt greeting, cordial smile, and clasp of hand,

GREETING TO THE PIONEERS.

Living o'er again in fancy all the changes years have witnessed
  Since we met and hailed each other first as pilgrims in this land.

Some who journeyed then amongst us have been summoned to their crowning;
  They have laid aside life's burden, all its duties nobly sped;
But their names will live for ever, haloed by our hearts' affections.
  Honor to their fadeless memory, tears and reverence for our dead!

Friends of years! the friendship plighted in the long-ago still gloweth
  Fresh and fair within our bosoms, drawing closer year by year
The brave men and noble women, wearing now Time's silvery colors
  'Neath the well-earned honors crowning every loyal Pioneer.

By the dangers met and vanquished, by the sorrows shared in common,
  When, as brother upon brother, we for sympathy relied
Upon hearts that never failed us, once again with joy we greet you,
  Once again with pleasant converse bridge Time's chasm deep and wide.

Children of such noble parents, may their bright ex-
    ample lead you
    Up the shining paths of honor to the land whose
        cloudless shore
Is the goal to which we journey; there, our labors
    past and ended,
    We shall meet in joy exultant—we shall meet to
        part no more.

May the days that wait our coming in the future's
    shadowy vistas
    Hold for us the priceless treasure of your great
        love, warm and true ;
And each glad reunion, brothers, find us still un-
    changed and faithful,
    Prompt as now on Friendship's altar early pledges
        to renew.

May the blessings of our Father—he whose guiding
    hand extended
    Led us safe o'er sea or desert, lonely plain or rocky
        shore—
Fall upon us, O my brothers! and our lives be closely
    guarded,
    Safe from every fear and danger, in His love for
        evermore !

SUNRISE IN WINTER.

THE morning herald sounds his warning trumpet,
    And lo! the clouds away
From hill and valley roll, while earth awaketh
    To greet the dawning day.

Dim shadows cluster 'neath the leafless woodlands,
    And on the mountains there
Where Santa Anna lifts her noble forehead
    High in the eastern air.

Round her behold the nimbus of the Orient,
    And o'er her lofty head,
Gleaming and glowing in rare, rosy splendor,
    A crown of rubies red—

A crown as brilliant in its gorgeous tinting
    As if the heavenward cry
Of blood for vengeance pleading had been painted
    Upon the cloudless sky.

But lo! the sun his mighty host advances,
    And in mysterious lines
Flings on the virgin snows of lofty hill-tops
    The shadows of the pines.

And at his coming Winter's jewels, scattered
    O'er grassy meads below,
Blaze in refulgent splendor ere they vanish
    Before his fervid glow;

While farm and village brighten in the glory,
    And far the noisy hum
Of life is heard where late all nature slumbered
    In silence cold and dumb.

THE LITTLE HAT AND SHOES.

THEY hang upon the chamber-wall
   The little hat and shoes
That never more in field or hall
   My darling boy will use.

For 'neath an angel's crown of light
   The fair head shines to-day,
And safe for aye the tireless feet
   That cannot go astray.

Ah! when I touch my Bonnie's hat
   My eyes with tears grow dim,
And fancy paints his smiling face
   Beneath its jaunty brim.

I see the brow so pure and white,
   The eyes of earnest brown,
And, shining in the sun's soft light,
   The fair hair floating down.

O mother-heart! O mother-love!
   What feelings burn and glow,
What memories of the cherished one
   For ever lying low!

And yet, although I mourn his loss,
  I feel that he is blessed,
And sin or care, or grief or pain,
  Can never mar his rest ;

For 'neath an angel's crown of light
  His fair head shines to-day,
And safe for aye the little feet
  That through heavenly meadows stray.

TO ANNIE.

LO! without the skies are misty,
   Cold and misty, dull and gray;
While the rain-sprites, bent on pleasure,
Move in mad and mischievous measure,
Whispering, calling from the tree-tops
   And the roofs of San José.

But within the air is vocal
   With the merry notes of glee,
And no dreamy shades are drifting,
For each cloud of care uplifting
Flies before the voice of music,
   Or of laughter ringing free.

What to us the wind's low moaning
   Or the Storm-King's boding strife,
As we twine joy's threads so golden,
Clasp the links of memories olden—
Memories of the May we journeyed
   Side by side the path of life?

Oh! those May days, bright and balmy,
   Linger with us sweetly still:
Dreams of leafy forest alleys,
Dreams of flower-gemmed mountain valleys,
And of rambles when the twilight
   Purpled many a distant hill.

Musing thus, I pray the moments
   Of thy future, Annie dear,
Ne'er may know a cloud of sorrow,
But the light of each to-morrow
Shine as jewels for the crowning
   Of each swiftly passing year.

A TOKEN.

TO SISTER MARY OF ST. GEORGE, S. N. D.

BRIGHT with no wealth of Orient pearls,
   No precious gems, no shining gold,
But loftiest type of love and faith,
   This little Cross behold—
Symbol of hope beyond compare,
Key of the treasures which we share.

'Twas for the Cross, in days of old,
   The Christian warrior died;
Nor bribe nor threat could shake his trust
   In Jesus Crucified.
Saint George! true flower of chivalry,
Sealed with his blood his loyalty—

Saint George, the valiant knight who met
   The dreaded dragon foe
In combat close, and with his sword
   The furious beast laid low,
Bidding the city's terrors cease,
And filling it with joy and peace.

And you, dear friend, his client here,
   Have battled long and well
Against the hydra-headed foe,
   Against the demon fell
Of Ignorance, whose crushing power
Would rob the earth of Truth's bright dower.

Yours is a sterner fight than his
  Who heard the trumpet's peal
And in his sinewy fingers felt
  The electric touch of steel;
Yours is the hidden martyr's crown,
His the world's homage and renown.

But in the angel's book above
  The record shineth fair—
The story of your toil for those
  Committed to your care,
The faithful love, the patient zeal,
For earthly and for heavenly weal.

Oh! dear unto Christ's Sacred Heart,
  Most precious in his sight,
Are they who guide the steps of youth
  Unto the living Light,
And with good counsel, true and wise,
Make plain the pathway to the skies.

And as I mark Time's sunset hours
  Draw closer round my way,
I feel the lessons of your life,
  Your words of strength, a stay
That lifts my spirit from the dust
To Heaven, the haven of our trust.

APRIL 23, 1885.

THE ROBIN.

AMONG the quiet peasants in Brittany they tell
    This legend of the robin, by children loved so
        well—
This legend of the robin, whose merry accents ring
Through every glade and covert sweet welcome to
    the Spring.

They say that when the Saviour, to Calvary's rugged
    crest
Bearing his cross, moved forward, sore, wounded,
    and oppressed,
When foemen thronged around him, and friends fled
    far in fear,
Above the angry multitude a robin hovered near,

And, reckless of the tumult and angry cries of scorn,
From out Christ's bleeding forehead it snatched one
    cruel thorn;
Then o'er the robin's bosom the sacred blood flowed
    down,
And with its ruby tinting dyed the plumes of russet
    brown.

And evermore the sweet bird bore upon its tender
    breast
The warm hue of the Saviour's blood, a shining seal
    impressed.
Hence dearest to the peasants' heart, 'mid birds of
    grove and plain,
They hold the robin, which essayed to soothe the
    Saviour's pain.

A CHRISTIAN HERO.

[Suggested by the perusal of the Life of Right Rev. J. N. Neumann, C.SS.R., and inscribed to Rev. H. Giesen, C.SS.R.]

THE laurels of the hero,
    The martyr's shining palm,
The sage's wreathèd oak-leaves
    For one so wise and calm,
The heart's most tender homage,
    Sweeter than words can frame,
For memories undying—
    Are twined around his name.

Great heart where love celestial
    In quenchless radiance burned,
Whose thoughts and aspirations,
    To Heaven alone were turned;
Who 'mid earth's many children
    Accounted himself least,
Yet wore its noblest title—
    God's consecrated Priest.

Hunger and cold and labor,
    Dangers by sea and land,
Hatred and stern privation
    Leagued 'gainst him hand-in-hand;
But, clad in faith's strong armor,
    With childlike patience sweet
He laid his heavy burden
    Down at the Saviour's feet,

Then rose refreshed and strengthened
    Life's duties to fulfil,
In sunshine or in shadow
    Owning his Master's will.
For him no cross too heavy,
    No toil but seemed as light,
If but one straying spirit
    Came back to truth and light.

How thrills the soul on reading
    That miracle sublime
Of the bleeding Host reproaching
    The apostate for his crime,
When He who died to save us,
    Who dwells with us for aye,
Pitying the erring wanderer,
    Revealed Himself that day!

True son of Saint Alphonsus,
    With graces richly blessed,
The first-born of the Order *
    Within the favored West—
The first-born of the Order;
    And well-won honors came
To add a Bishop's merits
    To his unclouded fame.

Though few the years God left him
    To lead his people here,
So careful was he ever
    Of souls to Christ so dear,

---

* Right Rev. Bishop Neumann was the first novice of the Redemptorist Order in America to make the religious vows.

Each thought, each deed, each moment
  Through every passing day,
Was given to prayer and labor
  For those beneath his sway.

Thus, conning his life's pages,
  With love's pure lessons rife,
I thank God for the blessings
  That crowned his servant's life,
And beg the holy Bishop,
  Who now before him stands,
To lift for us in pleading
  His consecrated hands.

Mossy Woodland, March, 1886.

SUNSHINE AND SHADOW.

DAY after day we hear, with inward shuddering,
    The death-bell's solemn toll,
Marking the exit from its earthly dwelling
    Of an immortal soul.

Day after day the brightest links are broken
    That form the chain of life,
As from our closely clinging arms are taken
    Parent or child or wife.

Day after day we feel the cold breath blowing
    From out the opened tomb,
And the Death Angel's pinions waving softly
    In sunshine or in gloom.

And yet through life's unceasing round of duties
    We smile and pass along,
Marking some saddening note of lamentation
    In every voice of song;

Hearing the organ's rolling notes of triumph
    Where late the requiem sighed,
Looking on lips, that quivered o'er the dying,
    Smile-wreathed to greet a bride.

We drink the perfume of the wildwood blossoms
    Blown by on every gale,
And think of one who in the by-gone summers
    Trod with us through the dale.

The tiniest flower that raises up its petals
    To gaze upon the sky,
The kingly laurel lifting up his forehead
    Upon the hill-tops high—

Each scene we tread recalls to us the memory
    Of loved ones passed away
From the dark shadow of this earthly valley
    To God's eternal day.

TO FANNIE R.

LOVE, wandering through the garden bowers,
  Toyed idly with each glowing bloom
And said: "For me the fairest flowers
  Pour forth their delicate perfume;
For me each tiny bud was made,
For me they bloom, for me they fade."

"Nay," Friendship cried, "the rose's blush,
  The lilac's glow to thee I yield;
The warmer tints of Flora's brush
  Wear thou upon thy gleaming shield;
But lo! she bids her fairies twine
Sweet blooms to lay upon my shrine.

"The pansies, purple, blue, and gold,
  The violets, darlings of the year,
The sweet forget-me-nots, I hold
  To Friendship consecrate and dear."
And these the offerings which I make:
Take them and wear them for my sake.

DEAR MOTHERLAND!

O MOTHERLAND! so long by tyrants stricken,
    So long by chains weighed down,
From hand and brow the cruel stranger wrested
    Thy sceptre and thy crown;

Laid waste thy children's homes by hill and valley,
    Left town and village bare;
Gave to the beasts thy broad fields, once so fertile,
    Gave to the birds of air

Grim heaps of slain—sons whom thy love had cherished,
    And who, with sword in hand,
On many a hard-fought field for thy dear honor
    Fell 'neath the foeman's brand.

Then—direst wrong to thee, O Mother Erin!—
    God's fanes they overthrew;
And at the altar, in their holy vestments,
    His ministers they slew.

For at their posts thy pastors stood undaunted—
    Bishop and monk and priest—
Gathering again the flock the wolves had scattered,
    Spreading the Mystic Feast

In hidden caves amid the mountains' fastness,
    Or by the sounding sea,
Where with warm, filial love thy sons uplifted
    The Sacred Host for thee.

They with their blood bore witness to their teaching—
    Blood which thy own green sod
Drank in red torrents when thy sainted heroes
    Died for their faith in God.

And not in vain flowed out that crimson current,
    As all thy records show :
It fed the tree of Faith with quickening nurture ;
    It fired with fervent glow

Thy children's hearts through years of bitter suffering,
    Of persecution dire,
Writhing 'neath wrong and rapine, force and treachery,
    Tortures by sword and fire ;

The weary days dragged out in dungeons dreary,
    Each woe thy history paints,
The crown of thorns which pierced in glorifying
    Thy forehead, Isle of Saints !

Not thine the crowning joy of happy mothers;
    Far from thy doors to-day,
With hearts that ache with an unconquered yearning,
    Thy hapless children stray.

Not thine to cheer them as a mother cheereth,
    Not thine their joys to know,
But thine to share their hope, strong and undying,
    For freedom here below.

Freedom for thee!—such freedom as shall quicken
    Thy pulses as of old,
When o'er thy hills, now desolate and stricken,
    Will shine the age of gold;

When from thy spires, once more to Heaven uplifted,
    The joyous bells shall ring,
And earth re-echo to the grand "Te Deum"
    Thy own true bards will sing.

1874.

IN THE DAWN.

THERE'S a voice in the air
    Where the clouds drift along
On the wings of the breeze :
    'Tis a cadence of song
That thrilleth aloft at the gates of the day,
As though kindled to life by the dawn's earliest ray,
And, down in a torrent of melody falling,
Hark ! hark to the voice of the meadow-lark calling.

    As his summons rings clear,
      Lo ! his brethren behold
    Soar up far and near
      From their nests on the wold.
And hither and thither, aloft and alow,
Now answering, now blending, their mingled notes flow,
A shower of music like benisons falling
All over the earth, as the sweet larks are calling.

BRIDAL WISHES.

MAY the Angel of Love on your pathway attend,
  Never veiling his splendor or soaring in flight,
And into your hearts his best blessings descend,
  Ever rich in their splendor and pure in their light.
Rejoicing go forth on life's pathway untried,
  Linked heart unto heart by that magical band,
Type of union unending, whose circle to-day
  Laid its fetter of love, gentle Bride, on your hand.
In the future which waiteth your coming may joy
  Imprint on the hours her seal of pure bliss,
Nerving you with new zeal, till the world above
  Enters into each pleasure God gives you in this.

Blessing all with your happiness, blessing and blessed,
  Dear Cousins, I pray that your future may be
Most rich in each gift by God's chosen possessed,
  In peace richly dowered and from sorrow set free;
Loving each with a love which no shadow can mar;
  Loving on till the end with an undying love,
Ever faithful and fond, ever gentle and true,
  Reflecting the peace of the world above.

GLORY TO GOD.

THERE is a strain of worship
    Resounding evermore
By mountain and by moorland,
    By woodland and by shore.

The stars that cross the heavens,
    A bright, harmonious throng;
The rivers rushing seaward
    In currents deep and strong;

The voices of the zephyrs,
    The thunder's solemn tone,
The deep, unceasing murmur
    Of ocean's monotone;

The seasons' march perpetual,
    The myriad wild birds' strains
That ring through forest arches,
    That echo o'er the plains—

All chant the self-same chorus,
    All hymn the song of praise
To God, whose love unceasing
    Crowns all our nights and days.

Shall man alone, ungrateful,
    Refuse to lend his voice,
And in sweet Alleluias
    With Nature's choirs rejoice?

Nay, praise unto the Maker,
   Sweet praise from morn till night,
And thanks for all the blessings
   That fill our lives with light,

With worship and thanksgiving
   Win in God's home a part;
For dearly doth he cherish
   Each fond and grateful heart.

TO RT. REV. EUGENE O'CONNELL, D.D., BISHOP OF JOPPA.

CONGRATULATION ON HIS SILVER JUBILEE.

COUNTLESS friends to-day are breathing words of sweet congratulation
  On the glad and glorious advent of thy Silver Jubilee,
Joying with thee in the blessings which have crowned thy zealous labors
  Since fond hearts first hailed thee Bishop of thy wide-extended see—

Crowned thy years of faithful labor, years whose moments drew thee closer,
  Ever closer, to the Master whose blessed trust 'twas thine to keep,
Pastor of the souls so precious to the wounded Heart of Jesus;
  Shepherd who, o'er mount and desert, sought afar thy straying sheep;

Noble pioneer, who bravely dared the dangers and the trials
  Strewn so thickly in the pathway of the missionary priest.
Thine the victory, thine the laurels, thine the crowning, faithful servant
  Who hath spread for hungering thousands love's sweet Eucharistic feast;

Who hath led to smiling pastures, watered by the
    streams of Heaven,
  Thy great flock, which else had perished famine-
    stricken by the way,
Blinded by the glare and glamour of the false, false
    world around them,
  Whelmed beneath the mighty torrent of the evils
    of the day.

And from far the heartfelt wishes of thy faithful
    friends are wafted,
  Freighted with love's tender greetings, honored
    prelate, unto thee;
Wingèd words the precious burden of their spirits'
    homage bearing,
  Earnest prayers that all thy future may one cloud-
    less summer be.

And as Joppa greets the pilgrim, greets and speeds
    him on his journey
  To Jerusalem's holy city, to its Tomb, the Shrine
    of shrines,
Pilgrim hearts to thee, its Bishop, turn for counsel
    and for guidance—
  Guidance to the Heavenly City, where God's fade-
    less splendor shines;

There to rest for aye enraptured in his love and light
    and radiance,
  There to hear his praises flowing ever in a silvery
    tide,
Where his angel-hosts are keeping honors for thee,
    well deserving,
  Where love's crown of crowns awaits thee, Bishop,
    Counsellor, and Guide.

FREEDOM.

THANK God for freedom! ye who dwell
    As brothers in our land to-day,
Who mark upon the breezes' swell
    Our Flag its shining stars display;

Who hear along the balmy air
    The echoes borne from sea to sea,
The deep tones of a nation's prayer,
    The "*Laus Deo*" of the free.

For oh! few greater boons than this
    His boundless mercy could bestow
Upon the sons of earth. What bliss
    So sweet, so perfect as to know

That here nor stripes, nor gyves, nor chains,
    Nor penal laws, nor exile long
In rocky isles or desert plains,
    May curb the feelings pure and strong

That spring within a Patriot's soul,
    That fire his heart, and nerve his hand,
And all his loftiest thoughts control
    For God and home and Fatherland?

Lo! Freedom here dominion holds
　　Unchecked alike o'er life and mind,
And on her annals are enrolled
　　The names most honored by mankind.

Not hers the tyrant's iron hand,
　　For Justice with impartial sway
Protects the throng that round her stand,
　　While Knowledge, with the steadfast ray

That burns within her lamp of gold,
　　Enkindled at immortal light,
Pierces the darkness, and behold!
　　Our country smiling at the sight.

Freedom! for thee our fathers gave
　　Their lives upon the battle-field,
And won with thee on shore and wave
　　The rights their rulers would not yield.

Through toil and sorrow, want and woe,
　　Through war's red sea they nobly pressed,
Till, crowned with Victory's deathless glow,
　　They hailed thee "Empress of the West,"

And taught their children to revere
　　The precious gifts thy hands bestow,
To hold thy cause than life more dear,
　　To guard thee closely 'gainst each foe.

To thee the warrior's heart of fire,
　　The poet's fervid strains of song,
The statesman's knowledge, strength, desire,
　　And loyalty alike belong.

And all are faithful to their trust ;
  They pledge their filial love again,
And vow, O Freedom pure and just!
  To keep thy honor without stain.

And humbly do they pray that ne'er
  May treason's clouds obscure the ray
Of joyous peace whose beauties rare
  Enrich and cheer thy perfect day.

AT DAYLIGHT'S CLOSE.

ANOTHER day is passing from our sight,
    Yet, ere its latest hour
Falls tremblingly before the scythe of Time,
    To fade like some sweet flower,
While twilight's violets linger in the west,
    And stars begin to shine,
With grateful hearts we come to breathe our thanks,
    Lord, for all gifts of thine—

For blessings countless as the wide sea-sands;
    For strength against our foes
When, fanned to flame by fierce contending thoughts,
    Our evil passions rose;
For hours of peace within whose holy calm
    The heart with rapture thrilled,
And over earthly wounds the healing balm
    Of heavenly dews distilled.

Who can tell o'er the gifts unnamed, untold,
    One passing day can bring,
The joys and graces still an hundredfold
    Given to us by our King?
For these, O Father of eternal love!
    Our heartfelt prayers ascend
In meek thanksgiving for Thy tender care
    And mercies without end.

BESIDE THE SEA.

A SOUVENIR OF SANTA CRUZ.

LAVING the feet of gold and purple mountains,
  The ocean, veiled in haze,
Chanted its strain of grand and solemn worship
  That glorious day of days.

Across the smooth beach where the waves were beating
  The gray gull winged its flight,
And the Abronia's countless blossoms painted
  The sands with rosy light.

There fled the white-maned breakers racing landward—
  Great Neptune's coursers fleet,
Hasting to quaff a draught of mountain nectar
  Where bay and river meet.

Bathed in the golden sunlight whose rare splendor
  Was flooding all the west,
Throned on her regal hills, the sea-side city,
  Seemed like a dream of rest.

No waves of traffic through her streets were flowing,
  No voice of toil arose,
But wayward zephyrs, through her gardens blowing,
  Just stirred the opening rose.

The Sabbath's calm and beauty o'er her rested ;
    The tranquil hour of prayer,
Marked by the peal of church-bells far resounding,
    Fell like a blessing there.

O gentle scenes, to which the toiler, wearied
    In the pursuit of wealth,
Hies for a while from breezy hill and billow
    To quaff the cup of health.

How many charms are thine, how many graces,
    Let bards more favored tell ;
I, but a wanderer through life's pleasant places,
    Bow to thy magic spell:

The sense of peace which, like a great libation,
    Thy mountains ever pour
From rose-wreathed vials in each shady cañon
    And by thy sounding shore ;

The crystal waters of thy river flowing
    By many a happy home ;
The favored bowers where, amid bloom and beauty,
    Joy, Love, and Friendship roam.

But not alone the gifts that Nature gave thee—
    The charms of sea and air,
Or fadeless glories of thy fragrant gardens—
    Combine to make thee fair.

The gentle hearts 'tis thine to hold in keeping,
    Dear friends so true and tried,
Whose names are linked with thine in love undying
    By memory glorified.

AMID THE PINES.

AROUND me rise the hills, their brows uplifting
    Through the clear, sunlit air,
Grand, still, and solemn, earth's great high-priests
      offering
    Their beauty as a prayer.

No noisy hum of life's unceasing tumult
    Breaks on the peaceful calm
Of this secluded spot where pine and laurel
    Are breathing forth their balm.

Far up the mountain-side, like rugged heroes
    Proud of their battle-scars,
Won by long years of stern, unyielding battle
    'Mid elemental wars,

The old Pines stand, their children round them
      clustering,
    As though they loved to hear
Told o'er again in every breeze that murmurs
    Their fathers' proud career.

Now through their boughs, with undulating motion,
    The zephyrs glide along;
Then Echo startles from her sleep to answer
    A stormy burst of song.

Anon it dies away in gentle cadence—
    A whisper, and no more—
As though the love-vows of some summer idler
    Were murmured o'er and o'er.

For oh! how oft the wooer's words of rapture
    Have thrilled the listening leaves
When Hesper's star, in peerless beauty shining,
    Illumed those glorious eves.

'Tis a fair spot of deep, unbroken quiet,
    Here on the mountain's breast,
Where hearts grown weary with earth's toil and
    trouble
    May pitch their tent of rest;

Letting life's cares drift out of reach and vision,
    Like bubbles on a stream,
And pass the hours wrapped in the trance per-
    vading
    A fair Elysian dream;

Lulled by the sound of distant water falling,
    The insects' droning hum,
The jay's incessant chatter, and the beating
    Of the woodpecker's drum;

While down with steady fall the leaves are drifting:
    Their fading beauties lie
A rare mosaic of Dame Nature's tinting,
    To please the gazer's eye.

For lo! the angel of the Autumn, passing,
    Flung down a flaming brand,
And all the funeral torches of the Summer
    Were kindled o'er the land.

There shines in living flame the poison ivy,
    And there the maples burn,
While the old oaks, their conqueror still defying,
    Slowly to amber turn.

And while her colors dance by moor and meadow,
    And float from every tree,
They own imperial Autumn's sway, whose sceptre
    Now shines from sea to sea.

RAISING THE STARS AND STRIPES AT MONTEREY, JULY 7, 1846.

A SEA of molten silver calmly lying
   Under the fervid glances of July;
A breath of balsam borne by breezes hying
   Across the olden town from mountains high;

A dreamy rest on earth, in air, on ocean,
   A voiceless calm. Yet human hearts that day
Were rent and torn by many a fierce emotion
   Of patriotic zeal in Monterey.

For war's dread voice, o'er Mexic valleys ringing,
   Found on these shores remote an answering sound,
And busy rumors to our fair land winging
   Whispered of foemen thronging closely round.

But calmly here her gallant sons awaited
   The change they feared each passing day would bring,
Dreading the foreign rule, so fiercely hated,
   'Neath England's Cross or France's Eagle's wing;

Hearing within the north the tread of strangers,
   The conquerors by prophet lips foretold,
Yet bearing still stout hearts to meet the dangers
   The future hours might in their keeping hold.

RAISING THE STARS AND STRIPES.

When lo! around Point Pinos' clear outlining,
   Marking her path with glittering diamond spray,
Her white sails set and starry banner shining,
   The swift *Savannah* sped across the bay.

And watching eyes, from town or fort outgazing,
   In that bold ship a happy omen saw,
And read upon her flag's bright crimson blazing
   The promise blest, Security and Law,

As there below the town she came to anchor,
   And soon across the glittering sands sent forth,
Fearless of foemen's frown or words of rancor,
   A gallant corps of "strangers of the North";

With martial tread the rugged streets ascending,
   Their brave hearts burning this fair land to claim,
Their loyal love for their great nation lending
   A halo to their dream of deathless fame.

And there that valiant band of soldiers planted
   The Stars and Stripes within the quiet town,
Where once in pride upon the breezes flaunted
   The silken banner of the Spanish crown.

Up in the crystal air the glad winds lifted
   The grand old Flag, and waved it broad and free,
While, peal on peal, the cannon's thunders drifted
   Far up the land and echoed out at sea;

Cheer answering cheer, in tones of heartfelt greeting
   From loyal lips—tones floating far away,
Which, clamorous voice of rock and mount repeating,
   Hailed the bright Stars and Stripes o'er Monterey.

And thus for aye from foreign rule was wrested
  Our glorious land, the fair Queen of the West,
Who shines each year with added grace invested,
  The fairest jewel on Columbia's breast.

SAN CARLOS DEL CARMELO.

(AUGUST 28, 1884.)

WHERE the waters of Carmelo, between fertile
    meadows winding,
  Bear adown the crystal tribute of the mountains to
    the bay,
And the old pines on the hillside rank and dress their
    scattered columns,
  Flinging out their greenest banners in meet honor
    of the day,

Stands the old church of San Carlos, to whose doors,
    as loving pilgrims,
  From the State's remotest borders eager hundreds
    thronging came
On that glad centennial morning when, from cloudless
    skies above it,
  Strewed the sun o'er earth and ocean rich largesse
    of golden flame.

Smiled the heavens in summer splendor, laughed the
    earth in heartfelt gladness,
  And white-crested waves came leaping lightly,
    lightly up the shore,
As though joining in the revel of the joyous breezes
    waking
  On the forest harps faint echoes of the deep's sub-
    limest roar.

And a living stream was pouring o'er the roadway to
    the Mission—
  People of all ranks and nations, by one common
    impulse led
Unto fair Carmelo hastening, in its shrine, from ruin
    rescued,
  There to render love and reverence to our land's
    illustrious dead.

Oh! how sweetly, how sublimely from the sounding
    arches echoed
  Once again the solemn music of the grand Grego-
    rian chant,
Breathing requiem for the hero who o'er countless
    dangers triumphed,
  Bearing to the last a spirit which no earthly foe
    could daunt.

Through the open doorway gazing, we could see white
    vapors rising
  Softly o'er the southern headland, and then vanish-
    ing in air,
Like the floating robes of angels from the cloudless
    ether bending,
  To bear back to Heaven the incense of love's fra-
    grant wreath of prayer.

Fancy turned to dwell enraptured on the past whose
    crowning halo
  O'er Carmelo's lovely valley fadeless rests for ever-
    more,
With its chain of memories linking years of sunshine
    and of shadow
  Since Spain's banner first was lifted by Viscayno on
    this shore;

When, storm-tossed and ocean-driven, from these
 green hills, winter-gladdened,
He beheld a mighty river leaping downward to the
 strand,
And the calm, blue deep around him, and the pleasant
 scenes before him,
Seemed a vision of far Carmel—seemed the prophet's holy land.

Then he named the place Carmelo, and he paid a
 glowing tribute
To its beauties in his letters to his monarch far
 away,
When telling of the harbor where his storm-worn galleons rested,
And the wealth of field and forest round the shores
 of Monterey.

Years passed on, till from the south-land came the
 band whose noble leader
Claims our heart's sincerest homage—came the pioneer whose hand
Wrought with tireless zeal, uplifting from the depths
 of pagan darkness
The wild dwellers of the forest, the poor children
 of the land.

Not Spain's gallant caballeros, nor her warriors
 famed in battle,
Made Carmelo's valley famous, make its memories
 bright and fair,
But because the meek Franciscan, the pure-hearted
 Padre Serra,
For the Indians whom he cherished lived and
 taught and labored there.

There he rests amid his brethren, waiting for the last
    day's dawning,
  In the old church of San Carlos, which has risen
    once again
From its crumbling mass of ruins, and in gracious
    beauty smileth
  O'er the fallen Mission round it—greeting to the
    hill and glen.

There he rests; and we who, pilgrims on that glad
    centennial morning,
  Stood beside his tomb and pondered on the great
    deeds he had done,
From his glorious example of a hope that never fal-
    tered,
  For life's daily round of duties have a loftier cour-
    age won—

Courage for life's daily duties, and a wealth of plea-
    sant memories
  Framing hill and shrine and forest in a glory all
    their own,
Happy thoughts and joyous fancies, in our hearts to
    sing for ever,
  With the soft, low murmur blending of the ocean's
    monotone.

California's Welcome

TO

His Grace Most Rev. P. W. Riordan, D.D.

RECITED BY THE PUPILS

OF THE

College of Notre Dame, San José, Cal.

CALIFORNIA'S WELCOME.

CALIFORNIA:

HERE let us rest; the hours wear on apace,
And we would fain converse of bygone days,
When o'er these wilds the Indians, in the chase,
   Pursued the flying deer through trackless ways;
Or when Cabrillo's sail a meteor shone
   Along the coast, then vanished from our sight
As vapor by the hurrying breeze is blown
   From northward, and the surging waves are white.
But on our land he set Hispania's seal;
   He raised the Cross which all our homage claims,
And gave our broad domain, with loyal zeal,
   To God, his monarch, and the great St. James,
Long ere the pirate Drake, with bloody hand,
   Unfurled the English flag in crimson sheen,
And claimed the wondrous beauties of our land
   As a new kingdom for his haughty queen;
Fresh from the scenes of rapine and of blood,
   Enriched with many a plundered galleon's freight
Which vainly had his cruel horde withstood—

ANGEL OF THE OCEAN:

   But Heaven hid from him the Golden Gate!
Robber and murderer, steeped in every sin
   That fills the heart with horror and with dread;
Despoiler of God's Altar, who, to win

Its sacred vessels, blood in torrents shed:
The mighty ocean which Balboa gave
   To God and to His holy Mother's care,
Recoiled, with horror in each trembling wave,
   When it beheld the impious monster dare
Lift to his lips, amid the wassail wild,
   The cup that held the consecrated wine—
The holy chalice by his touch defiled,
   'Mid scoffings at the Mysteries Divine!
And then no more Pacific, rose and hurled
   Its angry surges round his vessel's way,
While veiling mists, by unseen hands unfurled,
   Hid from his gaze the entrance to the bay.

ANGEL OF THE SHORE:

And he departed, knowing not that here
   An empire richer than the Indies slept,
Where in sweet solitude, year after year,
   Their simple ways the land's rude children kept;
No foreign voices waked the echoes round,
   Through winter's hours or summer's days aflame
With golden glory, till we heard the sound
   Of cheers when here Spain's ships to anchor came.

CALIFORNIA:

We still remember how our children drew
   Together, filled with wonder and affright,
When o'er the waves Spain's royal banner flew
   And her proud vessels shone upon their sight.
Sons of the wilderness, they ne'er had seen
   Nor stately ships nor men of other climes,
But deemed that some winged creature hither brought
   The deities of their forefathers' times.

"Are these," they cried, "the gods our fathers knew,
    Whose hands the mighty thunderbolts control,
Who give the winter's rain, the summer's dew,
    And bid the ocean waters landward roll?
Oh! have they sought once more our fallen race,
    And come they here amid our glades to dwell,
To share with us the pleasures of the chase
    Or bid the air with warlike anthems swell?"
We marked each savage head in awe incline
    When they beheld, with reverent, startled eyes,
The holy Priest before the Altar shrine
    Offering to God the Mystic Sacrifice,
And heard, upborne upon the morning breeze,
    The solemn chant, the sweetly-breathèd hymn—
Faint echoes of celestial melodies
    Poured out in Heaven by the Seraphim:
The very hills seemed thrilled with sudden life,
    The lofty pines caught up the clear refrain,
And ever since their sylvan haunts are rife
    With the low murmurs of the angelic strain.
But soon Viscayno's sails were homeward set;
    Spain's conquering banner vanished from our sight,
Leaving our land to silence and regret,
    Mourning the darkness, longing for the light.

ANGEL OF THE FOREST:

    The vision faded; many a weary year
        My sister Spirit of the Hills and I
    Kept eager watch along the waters near,
        And answering to the questioning rills, would sigh:
    "They come not yet, the holy men of God—
        They come not yet whom we so long to see;
    Still must our people blindly onward plod
        Till consecrated hands shall set them free."

But time moves ever; patience crowneth all :
  And when the earth was glorious with the May,
Far in the south we heard the bugle's call,
  The tramp of martial men, the charger's neigh,
And from their weary march o'er rugged heights,
  And barren wastes of cactus and of sand
Whose loneliness the pilgrim's heart affrights,
  They came to plant the Cross within our land.
Good Padre Crespi led them on their way ;
  And when June's light in golden splendor died
Came Padre Serra, 'neath whose gentle sway
  Was won for Heaven our country fair and wide.
How the hills echoed to their centres then!
  What gladsome strains of joyous greeting soared,
And wild reverberations pealed again
  When from the ships the brazen cannon roared,
As San Antonio and San Carlos gave
  To Serra and Portala welcome due,
From the drear desert to the flashing wave
  Bidding "All Hail!" to friends so tried and true!
And then beside the blue, far-reaching bay—
  The summer's light on earth and sea, the air
Athrill with their melodious psalmody—
  They gave the land to Santiago's care.

ANGEL OF THE STREAMS:

O day of joy! when from the founts I guard
  They drew the sparkling waters for the feast
And Sacrifice of Love—O sweet reward!
  Desired since first Heaven's Day-Star lit the east.
No more compelled to tread the cañons lone,
  Or cross 'neath scorching heat the valleys wide,
Unblessed, for blessings on each stream were thrown.
  The name, the presence of the Crucified

Seem lingering in each crystal drop that fell
   Since that bright hour when 'neath the sheltering
     Cross
I saw its waves exorcised from each spell
   And every stain of earth's defiling dross.
And its regenerating stream was poured
   Upon the forehead of the neophyte ;
The angels sang when their meek hearts adored,
   In faith and trust, the Lord of Love and Light.

Angel of the Vales:

And not alone to thee, O sister mine !
   From holy men came blessings on that day :
Within my vales they builded many a shrine,
   And taught the savage how to work and pray ;
Taught them to love the God, for love made man ;
   Taught them that Heaven love's recompense
     would be
When death cuts short life's frail and fleeting span,
   And sets the weary soul from bondage free ;
They bade them lay the bow and spear aside,
   And from the fruits of orchard and of field
Win the reward to labor ne'er denied—
   A generous harvest's overflowing yield ;
Taught them to till the earth and dress the vine,
   To fell the mighty monarchs of the wood,
And build their homes around God's holy shrine,
   And dwell in peace, as brothers ever should.
Sons of Saint Francis! grateful hearts should give
   To you a meed of praise in deathless song ;
Your ceaseless labors, prayers, and fastings live
   In faithful hearts, a memory pure and strong—

Serra, Portala, Crespi, and the band
 Of brave Franciscans who from day to day
Met toil and death with courage high and grand,
 To win the wandering tribes to Faith's bright
  way.

Angel of the Forest:

From dusky aisles and lonely heights I gave
 Of my domain the fairest and the best
To rear the lofty temples to His Name
 By every tribe and people loved and blessed.
I saw with joy the children of the soil
 Tread through the bosky depths from morn till
  eve,
And heard them chanting at their daily toil
 Such strains as made my heart no longer grieve.
The *Aves* soared upon the fragrant air
 That echoed once to war's wild, piercing yell;
And where I heard the meek Franciscan's prayer
 Had rung of yore the orgies born of hell.

Angel of the Hills:

No more in lonely caves, on mountain-sides,
 Like the wild beasts which they themselves pursued,
Dwelt the red warriors in their want and pride,
 No loftier aim in view than daily food.
Great was the change wrought by these holy
  men :
 I from my lofty heights looked down and smiled
To see the white-walled Missions rise in view,
 And hear the praises of the undefiled

Ring musically from the silvery bells
  Along the air at morning, noon, and night;
Like the low ripple of the wavelets' swells
  The murmurous echoes sped on pinions light.

CALIFORNIA:

Great was the change wrought by these holy men,
  And many years of happiness we knew,
While faithful pastors labored for their flocks,
  And flocks were to their noble pastors true.
But bitter sorrow came to cloud and mar
  The perfect peace of Virtue's tranquil reign,
And fell Ambition, Avarice, and War
  Disturbed our realm with their seditious train.
Then was the toil of long years overthrown,
  The laborers driven from the homes they loved,
And Freedom, falsely named, a monster grown,
  The efforts of God's ministers reproved.
Bereft as orphans of the Fathers' care,
  The Indians, childlike in their simple trust,
Clung round the Missions while blest hands could share
  With their poor neophytes their latest crust.
And when death came—as come it did to some,
  With hungry eyes, and visage grim and gaunt,
The presence and the power of famine, dumb
  With the last moanless agony of want—
The latest prayer breathed by the dying priest
  Was for his people, begging God to send,
In his great mercy and his boundless love,
  Unto their flocks a Father and a Friend

That prayer was answered. When the strangers came
  And from the spoiler wrested home and land :
True hearts aglow with apostolic flame,
  Bearing God's shining seal on brow and hand ;
Bishops and priests to tend the scattered flock
  And win them from the desert paths of wrong
Back to the Church Christ builded on the rock,
  Back to the law of love so sweet and strong—
Came with Rome's blessing to this western shore
  To kindle once again Faith's fervid glow,
Religion's balm on wounded hearts to pour,
  And bid the songs of praise rejoicing flow—
Once more the sons of Spain our altars served,
  Their voices stirred our people, and their toil
Won back the weak hearts that had failed or swerved ;
  And like the bounteous yield of virgin soil
Were the rich harvests which God's reapers found
  White for the sickle in the tireless hand.
From north and south, and east and west, the sound
  Of voices calling them to hasten fanned
The fire of holy zeal within each breast.
  Hither from every land beneath the sun
New laborers for the dear Lord's vineyard hied,
  A glorious army. Of their triumphs won
No need to tell ; behold on every side
  The monuments that of their victories speak.
No need to praise ; Heaven keeps the records fair :
  There waits the guerdon that their spirits seek,
There the eternal glory they will share !

ANGEL OF THE AIR:

  But lo! there comes into our midst to-day
    Another Shepherd, a true chief and guide,
  Whose dauntless heart no labors can dismay,
    Who sweeps opposing obstacles aside.
  Pastor of Pastors! For him let us wreathe
    Again the shamrock with the olive bough,
  And bid our land's loved children haste to breathe
    To him most cordial words of welcome now.
  For oh! believe me that no worthier choice
    Among God's faithful soldiers could be made.
  Have ye not listened to his people's voice?
    Have ye not heard the loving tributes paid
  Unto their gentle Pastor, kind and wise,
    Who wrought for them with such untiring zeal,
  And read the sorrow in their tear-dimmed eyes—
    The grief too deep for language to reveal?
  He comes to share the labors of this See
    Dear to St. Francis; consecrated too
  Upon the solemn feast when faithful hearts
    Weep o'er our Lady's sevenfold griefs anew.
  Upon the eve of that most glorious day
    When our dear Lord impressed his wounds divine
  Upon Assisi's Saint, oh! may the ray
    Of their united splendors round him shine.
  But hark! the children come, fresh from the quest
    Of floral treasures in the garden's bower,
  Their youthful spirits fired with eager zest.
    Dear Convent Angels, rich with joy's glad dower!

The whispering leaves that o'er their playground
    bend,
  The leafy alleys where they love to stray,
The sweet-toned songsters of the wild that blend
  Their carols with each laughing voice at play,
The green grass springing on the verdant lawn,
  The waters falling in the fountain near,
The soft breeze stealing like a timid fawn
  From sun to shade, and fondly lingering here,
Have given me tidings from this home of love,
  Have told the secrets of each youthful heart,
Where innocence broods like a snowy dove :
  God grant that it may never thence depart!
"They wait his coming," this the blossoms tell ;
  "They long to greet him," so the breezes say,
The merry birds the tell-tale chorus swell;
  The dancing leaves ask, "Will he come to-day?"

CALIFORNIA :

He comes to-day—yea, even now is here !

ANGEL OF THE AIR :

  Haste, children, haste! your gleeful voices lend,
And, sweet as bird-notes echoing pure and clear,
  Hail with delight your Father and your Friend.

CALIFORNIA :

Be theirs the pleasant task to welcome, then,
  Saint James' pastor to the land that first
Learned the celestial truths from holy men
  Under Saint James' shining banner nursed.

                     [The children approach.]

Dear children, angels spoke of you but now—
  You come, an answer to their loving thought,
With smiles of happiness on lip and brow ;
  And we, beholding, see that you have wrought
Into the clustered blooms you gaily bring
  The loving fancies we would see expressed,
Symbolic of the spotless buds that spring
  In the bright gardens of the youthful breast.
And knowing that you long to welcome him
  Whose loving care for children has been told,
On earth by men, by angel choirs in Heaven,
  We bid you greet him, dear lambs of the fold.

WELCOME.

THE CHILDREN:

  With the rapture that kindles the brow of the dawn
  When the rose-tinted curtains of morning are drawn,
  And the music of birds and the ripple of rills
  Wake the echoes that lurk in the nooks of the hills;
  With the joy that we feel in the sun-lighted air
  When the flowers of the spring-time are fragrant and fair ;
  With the pure pleasure born of all beautiful things,
  We have waited and watched as on glittering wings
  Hour after hour floated softly away,
  Till we revel at last in the light of this day,
  When we, loved Archbishop, with spirits aglow,
  Bid our glad strains of greeting to welcome thee flow

From the great city, Queen of the North and the
  West,
From the scenes that thy love and thy labors have
  blessed,
From the hearts that still follow with blessings and
  prayers
The dear Guide that lightened their burdens and
  cares,
Do we welcome thee here to our sweet home that
  lies
In the fairest of lands, 'neath the bluest of skies;
To the hearts of thy children, who fondly implore
The hand of our Heavenly Father to pour
On thee, beloved Prelate, his blessings divine
In uncounted measure. May angel-hosts twine
The roses of peace in thy pathway to strew,
And fair be the vistas life opes to thy view.

And we, though the least of thy little ones, dare
In thy love, dear Archbishop, to ask for a share,
A fond Father's blessing, a prayer at God's shrine,
A thought in His presence, Supreme and Divine :
That through life we may ever be valiant and strong,
Never yielding to falsehood or pandering to wrong,
But joyous and free, as we stand here to-day,
Our hearts' warmest feelings of welcome to say,
As the " Caed Mille Failthe " awakens a thrill
In the soul of the exile ; oh ! think of it still
As a symbol that even but faintly conveys
The feeling of joy that each rapt bosom sways,
As we seek—oh ! so vainly—to thee to impart
The thousand-fold welcomes that spring from each
  heart.

Sacred Subjects.

TO THE HOLY FACE.

THE PRAYER OF REPARATION.

FACE Divine! with awe and rapture
   In thy presence do I bend;
Image of my Lord and Saviour,
   Let my humble accents blend
With the thrilling psalms of millions,
   With the Seraphs' songs sublime,
In the prayer of reparation
   For the evils wrought by crime,

For the insults heaped upon thee,
   For the outrage and the scorn,
For the thorns that pierced thy forehead,
   The revilings meekly borne,
Angry words and blows commingled,
   Impious oaths that rent the air,
All the anguish of the Passion:
   Listen, listen to my prayer!

Face Divine! thy royal beauty
   Stained with blood in grief I see;
Well I know thy countless sufferings—
   All were borne for love of me.
O the angry tide of passion
   Sweeping on through heart and brain!
And my hourly faults, my Saviour,
   Wound thy Holy Face again

Face Divine! thy drooping eyelids
    Seem in pity thus to close,
Lest their splendor, Heaven-illumined,
    Would deal death among thy foes.
And the lips whose tender accents
    Speak alone of God and love,
With no word of stern reproval
    Of thy ingrate people move.

"Pity! pity! Hear, oh! hear me!
    Pity on me!" Thus I pray,
Joining in the fervent pleading
    Of earth's purest hearts to-day:
For my sins, the sins that wound thee,
    For each scorned, rejected grace,
For each insult, vile and hideous,
    Offered to thee, Holy Face;

For the sins of the blasphemers,
    Torrent-like that ceaseless flow,
With their fearful imprecations
    Filling all the air with woe;
For the sins of the profaners,
    For their sacrilege and wrong;
For the young—may they be faithful;
    For the weak—oh! make them strong.

Face Divine! may thy drooped eyelids
    Lift on me a look of love,
And thy closed lips breathe of pardon,
    Breathe of mercy, when they move.
Not in wrath, O Lord, receive me
    When I hear Death's mandate, "Come!"
And within thy awful Presence
    I shall stand abased and dumb.

THE MOST PRECIOUS BLOOD.

MOST Precious Blood of the Saviour,
    Ransom whose worth is untold,
Blood of the true Paschal Offering
    Marking the door of God's fold!

Ah! how the world-weary pilgrim,
    Fainting, and ready to sink
'Neath the burdens of trial and sorrow,
    Hastes at thy fountain to drink.

Hail! health of the sick and the suffering,
    Wisdom of scholar and sage,
Light of youth's roseate morning,
    Hope of the sad hours of age:

Life-giving wine of the martyrs
    Who fearlessly went to their doom,
The strength from thy ruby drops flowing
    Robbing each torture of gloom!

Most Precious Blood of the Saviour,
    Wash from our spirits each stain;
Grant that God's blessing may never
    Fall on our hard hearts in vain.

Strengthen our souls for the combat,
    That, after earth's toiling and strife,
They may pass, angel-borne, through the portal
    That leads to the kingdom of life.

"JESUS MEEK AND HUMBLE."

TO REV. M. W.

WEARIED with life's sorrows
    And by pain oppressed,
Turned I to thy volume
    Saying: "Here is rest."

As I turned its pages,
    Lo! a sweet surprise—
There the pictured Saviour
    Shone before my eyes.

"Jesus meek and humble,"
    So the legend read.
Golden shone the halo
    Round the Christ-Child's head;

And within its glory
    Star-like crosses three,
Emblems of the sufferings
    Borne for such as me.

Where his left hand, clasped
    His mantle to his breast,
Blue-eyed Passion Flowers
    To his Heart were pressed;

While his right hand, lifted,
  Blessings seemed to pour—
Blessings upon blessings
  On this earthly shore.

As I gazed my troubles
  Vanished from my sight;
Pain grew less in anguish
  And the earth more bright.

What were care and suffering,
  What was fever's pain,
If through all one blessing
  I might hope to gain?

So I laid life's burdens
  At my Saviour's feet,
And went forth in courage
  Daily cares to meet.

THE RESCUE OF THE KING.

OH! the earth has still her heroes,
　　Men as daring, true, and strong
As e'er wore fame's golden laurels
　　Won by deeds that live in song—
Men who lead a nobler army
　　Than the warrior-hosts that tread
To the shining goal of victory
　　Over gory heaps of dead.

Who are they? Lo! they are toiling
　　Round about us day by day,
Or are lighting distant regions
　　With Faith's Heaven-kindled ray;
Bearing with unmurmuring patience
　　Bitter hardship, toil, and loss,
That the children of the forest
　　May be gathered 'neath the Cross—

Valiant priests who walk rejoicing,
　　Happy if they may but bring
One poor soul that dwelt in darkness
　　To the bright home of our King.
Such were they whose dauntless spirits
　　Met and faced a crushing blow
At the Mission of Keshina
　　Just one little year ago,

When the holy Convent, builded
   In the wilds with care and toil,
At the silent watch of midnight
   Fell, the hungry fire-fiend's spoil.
Bravely wrought they, bravely, nobly,
   But their efforts were in vain :
The fierce strength of the destroyer
   They, alas ! might not restrain,

As it burst through door and window
   With a red and angry glare,
Flinging out its lurid banners
   From the roof-tree on the air;
While the stout walls rocked and trembled
   As the swift flames mounted higher,
And within the Chapel quivered
   A red sea of living fire.

Yet *one* strove to pass its portals,
   Sought to tread that crimson sea,
Daring death and all its horrors,
   O my Lord and God, for thee !
For within that humble temple
   Angels watched with folded wings
Where the Tabernacle sheltered
   Thee, O Lord, the King of kings !

Rose a wall of death before him ;
   Forkèd tongues of angry flame,
Like a thousand furious monsters
   Leaping forth, to meet him came.

Driven back, but all undaunted,
  Heedless of each warning call,
Though the lifted ladder trembled
  'Gainst the Chapel's smoking wall,

Yet he mounted to the rescue
  With the ardor warriors bring
When the cohorts of the foemen
  Close in battle round their king.
Courage, strength, and hero-daring—
  These were his in measure grand,
As the shattered glass and mullion
  Fell before his eager hand.

And beneath him lay the Altar,
  Fire above, below, around,
Rushing onward, upward at him
  With a sullen, roaring sound.
What though life hung in the balance?
  Still he wrought with resolute will,
And the Tabernacle lifted
  O'er the scorching window-sill.

Joy of joys! the King was rescued!
  Oh! the rapture that held sway
In that brave priest's loyal bosom
  Words are feeble to portray.
Death a thousand times were welcome,
  Could he only shield from harm
The most Precious Treasure, rescued
  By the strength of his right arm.

Saved! though, round about him sweeping,
   Through the broken casement poured
The mad flames, that in their fury
   Like to baffled demons roared.
Oh! to him that dreadful moment
   Seemed by balmy breezes fanned,
Though the furnace-blast was beating
   Fiercely upon brow and hand.

Joy and gratitude to Heaven
   Filled his heart with pure delight;
Lost was all the toil and terror
   And the dangers of the night.
Not for earthly honors wrought he,
   Yet our meed of praise we bring
To the priest so brave and loyal
   In the service of his King.

FEBRUARY, 1885.

AT BENEDICTION.

OH! 'twas like a glimpse of Eden when I passed the
    chapel portals,
  And upon its well-loved altar saw the lighted tapers
    shine,
Where the brightly-wreathèd blossoms seemed to
    smile as if in welcome
  While I waited for the blessing of our Lord and
    King Divine—

For the blessing far surpassing all that human thought
    can picture.
  Then the organ's deep-toned music thrilled and
    filled with joy the place,
And the voices of the singers, soaring up in psalms of
    worship,
  Caught my heart and bore it upward, out beyond
    the bounds of space.

Vanished dreams of earthly pleasure, fleeting hopes I
    fondly cherished,
  As I listened, all enraptured, to the grandly thrill-
    ing strains,
Till the pulsing of the organ seemed the sound of
    waving pinions,
  And the hymns the songs of angels as of yore on
    Bethlehem's plains.

Ah! I well might fancy Heaven had been opened at
    that moment,
  When the Lord of Hosts uplifted blessed his chil-
    dren kneeling there,
And as manna in the desert came the solemn bene-
    diction,
  Filling with a golden glory all the thorny paths of
    care.

Sweet hour fraught with peace, whose memory will go
    with me on life's journey,
  Shining 'mid my fairest treasures as a gem of purest
    ray !
May that blessing of my Saviour, shining ever in my
    bosom,
  Keep my straying steps from wandering from " the
    straight and narrow way "!

COLLEGE NOTRE DAME, SAN JOSÉ, CAL.

OUR LADY OF PERPETUAL HELP.

OH! 'tis a sweet, consoling thought,
   Whate'er life's lot may be,
Dear Mother of Perpetual Help!
   That we may call on thee,
And through thy fond maternal care,
   Thy all-embracing love,
Know that each fervent, pleading prayer
   Is heard by thee above.

O loveliest Maid! Heaven's crownèd Queen,
   How may we best essay
To strew the fragrant flowers of love
   Before God day by day?
How win the favor of thy Son,
   Supreme in awful power,
Save by true service unto thee
   Through every passing hour?

Blest Virgin, in whose spotless soul
   The fount of pity springs,
How sweetly thou dost plead our cause
   With the great King of kings,
And, spite of all our wandering ways,
   Our weakness and our sin,
From the unfailing source of grace
   For us such treasures win!

OUR LADY OF PERPETUAL HELP.

O Lady of Perpetual Help!
　　We hail thee once again,
True solace in each bitter grief,
　　Blest comfort in our pain.
Too oft we falter in the path
　　Or idly turn away;
Oh! in the dreadful day of wrath
　　Be thou our shield and stay.

Be with us in life's daily cares,
　　When clouds obscure the light,
And onward the sad pilgrim fares
　　Through murky clouds of night.
Be with us in joy's rosy glow;
　　Ah! most we need thee then
To bid in purer channels flow
　　The restless thoughts of men.

Be with us—oh! with fond desire
　　The priceless boon we crave—
Be with us at the hour of death;
　　Then, Mother, come and save
From the foul demon's cruel power
　　The souls thy Son redeemed—
The souls he gave thee as thy dower,
　　For which his life-blood streamed

To wash away the mark of sin,
　　The dark, defiling stain
That rested on the spirits bound
　　By Satan's fettering chain.
Receive each beating of our hearts,
　　Each slowly laboring breath;
Befriend us, Mother of our Lord,
　　In the dread hour of death.

THE ROSARY.

AUTUMNAL fires with ceaseless glow
  Have tinged the woods with brown,
And all day long, with sighing fall,
  The leaves are drifting down;
The faded foliage on the breeze
  Is borne afar and near,
And mingles with the common dust
  The glories of the year.

O month whose wondrous sunsets light
  The hills with red and gold!
Amid thy treasure-stores 'tis thine
  A jewel fair to hold;
For as the month of flowers is given
  To Mary's honored name,
So does the chaplet of her love
  Thy earliest Sunday claim—

The precious chaplet of her love,
  Which link by link doth bind
To Jesus' Heart and Mary's life
  The children of mankind;
The Rosary, which, bead by bead,
  In one unending chain,
Is joyous in our Lady's joy
  Or mournful in her pain;;

Which winneth from Heaven's fount of grace
  All solace for our needs.
What aching heart hath sought nor found
  Sweet comfort in "the beads"?
Prayer dear to prince and peer alike,
  To peasant and to saint,
Whose mysteries with such perfect art
  Joy, grief, and glory paint.

No thrilling eloquence of man
  Such knowledge can impart;
No artist with his matchless skill
  So deeply move the heart;
No volume ever yet contained
  Such wealth of precious lore;
No prayerful practice ever yet
  Such heavenly fruitage bore.

O holy feast whose blessings crown
  Our bright October days!
Illuminate our pilgrim paths
  With Faith's inspiring rays;
May every bead we humbly tell
  Win us our Mother's love
And link by link our spirits bind
  To her dear home above!

NOTRE DAME DE FRANCE.

OUR Lady, Queen of Heaven and Queen of France,
    That land which owns thy sway,
By many a shrine where holy fountains glance
    And pilgrims kneel to pray;

That land which thou hast honored with thy love,
    Which thou hast made thine own,
Where often to the meek and pure of heart
    Thy beauty thou hast shown—

Thy love, dear Mother, grew in splendor there
    Since Faith's first shining ray
Kindled the darkness of the pagan night
    And turned it into day.

Gaul's children owned the Saviour of the world,
    They followed his command,
But, childlike in their faith, they loved to yield
    Their homage through thy hand.

And thou hast pleaded for them not in vain,
    Mother most chaste and pure;
Thy voice has taught them in their days of grief
    In patience to endure.

Thou hast been joyous with them in their joy,
    Wept with them in their woe,
And spread thy mantle's triple shield of power
    Betwixt them and the foe.

When clouds of war lowered darkly o'er the land,
 And civil strife oppressed,
Lady of Pity, thou wert with them then,
 The dead Christ on thy breast.

Lady of Pity, many a lonely shrine
 Grew vocal with their grief ;
Thou hadst known sorrow, thou couldst feel for them,
 Thou only bring relief.

They clung to thee as some fond, favored child
 Clings to its mother's breast,
Certain within thy great, all-pitying love
 To find relief and rest.

Within the fair and favored clime of France
 How many names are thine,
Breathed o'er with tenderness and love supreme
 Around each holy shrine !

In shadowy groves, by Gemme's lofty tower,
 Garaison, fount of prayer,
Famed Cahuzac, and every gift that gives
 To thee Aude's valley fair.

But there is one fair province wholly thine,
 Miraculously so,
Where like twin roses in thy crown of love
 Lourdes and Beth Arram glow.

The noisy Gave on its tumultuous way
 Pauses before the shrine
Of sweet Beth Arram, as in homage meet
 Unto the Babe Divine ;

As though the shadow of the holy Cross
    Upon the Calvary there
Had power to change its loud and clamorous voice
    To one of praise and prayer—

The Cross by hands of angels consecrate,
    And to whose shadow came
Monarchs, and prelates, and the holy men
    Whom France still loves to name.

Here came the peasants of the Pyrenees,
    Here the Crusaders prayed,
Claiming the shelter of thy " beauteous branch,"
    Thy comfort and thy aid,

Long ere the Gave heard echoing o'er its waves
    The far-resounding swell
Of pilgrims chanting round the holy cliff
    And cave of Massabielle—

Of pilgrims chanting there thy praises sweet,
    Lady of Lourdes, whose love
And mercy for the suffering ones of earth
    The sternest spirits move.

Lady of Lourdes! the name that fills with joy
    The stricken and the weak;
Healer, consoler, comforter, and strength
    Of all who humbly seek.

The wide world sends her pilgrims to thy shrine,
    They claim thy powerful aid.
Thy Son's dear Cross is graven on their hearts,
    They preach a new Crusade:

NOTRE DAME DE FRANCE.

A new Crusade—an old but ever new—
    Against the demon band,
Impiety and sacrilege and wrong,
    That ravage every land.

Aid them, dear Mother, in their ceaseless toil,
    The shepherds of the fold,
Thou purest pure, thou Virgin without stain,
    Their lives in keeping hold.

Our Lady, Queen of Heaven and Queen of France,
    Queen of the Sacred Heart!
In the great treasures of whose boundless wealth
    We humbly claim a part;

Thou who didst fire with love the royal hearts
    Of Clovis and Charlemagne;
Thou whom King Louis, by a solemn vow,
    Made Queen of his domain.

Her queens have sought thy cloister's holy shade,
    Leaving the song and dance,
And there, in garb of sackcloth rude arrayed,
    Have wept and prayed for France.

Lady of Victory! whose blessings crowned
    The banners of the land
When Jeanne de Arc, Domremy's Virgin Saint,
    Expelled the English band.

Mother Immaculate, Mother most pure,
    Blessed Virgin without stain,
The sons of Gaul are crying unto thee,
    Nor do they cry in vain.

A long, illustrious line of holy men
    Bear witness to thy power—
Men who have laid earth's fleeting joys aside
    And taken Christ for their dower;

The countless saints whose lives of virtue crown
    Thy chosen land with light;
Martyrs who laid their lives down for the cross,
    Bishop and anchorite;

Martyrs whose blood e'en in these later days
    Poured out a crimson rain,
Blood which has quickened into vigorous life
    The tree of Faith again.

Hail, Queen of Saints! Who loved to honor thee,
    What lips but hath addressed
To thee the prayer thy own Saint Bernard framed,
    The "Memorare" blest?

O Queen of Saints! from thy bright home on high
    Look down with pitying glance;
Plead for us with thy Son and hear our prayers,
    O Notre Dame de France!

THE ASSUMPTION OF OUR LADY.

LO! the mighty heavens are opened, and a tide of living splendor
  Poureth forth in golden glory from the shining courts above,
Whence the white-winged angels hasten forth, elate with rapturous gladness,
  To hail their Queen, our Mother, with a pure and reverent love.

Ay, they come to bear her from us, she who for our sake has suffered
  In her heart the woes and sorrows that her Son, the Saviour, bore;
She has shared his thirst and hunger for the souls that scorned and spurned him,
  Felt the cruel nails and scourges that his sacred body tore.

Now she goes to share his triumph in the kingdom of his Father,
  Loving yet her mortal children with a love both fond and deep.
Yea, in Heaven we still may claim her: were we not bequeathèd to her,
  In Christ's hour of awful anguish, as a precious trust to keep?

O ye angel-hosts attendant on our Lady's blest Assumption !
  Ye whose happy lot was near her in that hour of joy supreme,
Ye whose lips were never sullied by the taint of earth's corruption,
  Ye alone may chant the numbers worthy such a glorious theme.

But the words of pious authors and the visions of the artist
  Have portrayed its royal pageant, till, with Faith's inspired eyes,
We behold the Queen of Angels, by her subject throng attended,
  Upward borne 'mid sounding anthems to her crowning in the skies.

O, the sense of rapture thrilling through her bosom at that moment,
  Love and rapture thrilling, filling every fibre of her breast,
As, clothed in awful splendor, the Trinity appeareth
  Where seraphic hosts are chanting in the mansions of the blest.

Well may the angels turn to her with looks of rapt devotion,
  Seeing in her face reflected the bright scene that she beholds
When the glory, far surpassing all that human thought can fathom,
  As she nears the throne of Deity, upon her gaze unfolds.

Ah! we feel they glance with pity on the earth thus sadly orphaned,
  And we bid them bear our pleading to our gracious Mother's throne,
Ask for us the gifts and graces she can give in generous measure,
  And the strength and courage needed for our errors to atone.

"Queen of Angels," lowly bending in thy presence, do we offer
  Heart and hand and life to serve thee, happy if we may but claim
From thy Son's o'erflowing mercy this great boon, that we be worthy
  To be ranked with those who humbly seek to glorify his name.

In the joy of thy Assumption, oh! we would not be forgotten:
  Share with us its light and beauty, purify each faithful soul;
Make us worthy of the ransom Jesus paid for us on Calvary;
  Lead us on life's rugged pathway, safe beneath thy chaste control.

By thy glorious coronation on this day of days, dear Mother,
  Do we hail thee Queen of Heaven, Queen of Angels and of Saints,
Queen of that celestial kingdom where the praise of God for ever
  Echoes amid scenes transcending all that fairest fancy paints.

There, we pray, our exile over in this world of toil
 and sorrow,
 When the immortal soul upspringing leaves its
  prison-house of pain,
Where seraphic choirs are chanting on this feast of
 joy exceeding,
 We may hear with hearts rejoicing the great beauty
  of their strain.

"NOTRE DAME DE BON SECOURS."

AN INCIDENT OF THE FEVER-PLAGUE IN CANADA.

TURNING from the pictured pages
   Lying open in my hand,
Fancy leads me forth a pilgrim
   To my distant native land—
Leads me to her shrine who yieldeth
   Ready succor when we call,
She who with a Mother's fondness
   Guards the homes of Montreal;
To her shrine, Hope's only beacon
   In that hour of bitterest woe
When the Plague-King slew his thousands
   Of our people long ago.

O those days of gloom and horror!
   Lips will tremble, tears will fall,
As the mothers to their children
   All its bitterness recall—
How, as leaves in autumn falling
   When the stormy winds rush by,
Stricken by Death's mortal anguish,
   Sank the sufferers to die;

When that bold, unfaltering legion
   Of Christ's chosen servants trod
Daily 'mid the sick and dying,
   Leading countless souls to God.

Lovingly above the sufferers
 Did these mercy-angels bend,
Watching, caring, soothing, tending
 To the dark and bitter end.
But they passed not through unscathèd:
 Fell the Pastor at his post,
And the patient Sister-nurses
 Joined the shining martyr-host.

Then the holy Bishop Bourget
 Sought Our Lady of Prompt Aid,
Saying: "For my suffering people
 Let thy power be displayed.
Oh! to stay the fever's fury,
 And to save my orphan band,
And to send my flock new pastors,
 Holy Mother, stretch thy hand.
Lo! with humble, contrite spirit
 Do I seek thy holy shrine.
Save us, Mother, or we perish!
 Made us wholly, truly thine.
Mark my vow: to toil unwearying
 Here thy homage to restore,
And to bring my people pilgrims
 To thee as in days of yore."

And they came; the air re-echoed
 To the hymns the people sang.
Ne'er before such heart-appealing
 Through thy streets, fair city, rang.
Who can plead like those who suffer?
 Who so well portray their woe
As the hearts that bleed and quiver,
 Freshly wounded by grief's blow?

And Our Lady heard and answered :
   Swiftly as the north wind's breath
Stays with frost the dread malaria,
   Stayed his cruel work King Death.
From its haunts the fever vanished,
   Health came back with smiling face,
And the people sang thanksgiving
   To Our Lady full of grace.

TELLING THE BEADS.

OVER the hands that are shining
    With the brightest of jewels aglow—
Hands where toil's stain never rested
    To sully their tinting of snow—
Bead after bead dropping downward
    Bear pearls for the casket of Heaven,
Prayers breathed for joys in the future,
    Thanks murmured for favors God-given:
              "Ave Maria!"

Over the hands that are hardened
    And rough with the toiling of years—
Hands that have done a stout battle
    With hunger and heartache and fears—
Bead after bead dropping downward
    Waft prayers full of hope and of trust
From hearts that, through bitter temptation,
    Strove to tread in the paths of the just:
              "Ave Maria!"

Over the hands of the statesman,
    Grown weary with guiding the pen
In the framing of laws and commandments
    For the guidance and bettering of men,

Bead after bead dropping downward
  Fall freighted with pleadings for light,
That the whole world may revel in beauty
  Which is born of the rulings of right:
          "Ave Maria!"

Over the hands of the beggar,
  As he crouches alone by the way,
Drawing his rags closer round him,
  Teaching his sad heart to pray,
Bead after bead dropping downward,
  His weary voice broken with sighs,
He claims the sweet aid of his Mother,
  The merciful Queen of the skies:
          "Ave Maria!"

Over the hands of the hermit
  Shut away from earth's turmoil and jar,
When the light of the day has departed
  And brightly shines eve's silvery star,
Bead after bead dropping downward
  Tell each a sweet prayer for the world,
In the hour of its sorest temptation
  'Neath the banner of darkness unfurled:
          "Ave Maria!"

With love in her heart for the Saviour,
  With peace in each line of her face,
The nun in her humble attire
  Bends low to "Our Lady of Grace";
And the beads from her white fingers dropping
  Seem to me brightest jewels of worth,
As the pure bride of Heaven kneels pleading
  For the fallen and outcast of earth:
          "Ave Maria!"

O Mother of God, who hast given
    Thy children this chaplet so fair,
Take thou each and all of the pleaders
    Close under thy sheltering care;
May each bead that is told in thy honor
    Shine fair in the records of love,
And win for thy servants sweet guerdon—
    A home in the mansions above:
                  "Ave Maria!"

OUR LADY'S DOLORS.

THE CHILDREN'S TRIBUTE AT HER SHRINE

The Prophecy of Simeon.

MOTHER of Sorrows, at thy feet
   Sweet blossoms from the wilds we lay,
In memory of the cruel swords
   Through thy pure heart that forced their way.

The fairest buds that crown the spring
   We offer for that hour of care,
That hour of anguish sharp and keen,
   When, borne upon the throbbing air,

Prophetic Simeon's words of awe
   Filled thy meek breast with dread alarms,
Forebodings of the future ills
   Waiting the Infant in thy arms;

That hour whose sorrows comprehend
   The sorrows of thy spotless life,
Whelming thy spirit as when waves
   Sweep shoreward in the tempest's strife.

Oh! let the perfume of our flowers
   Plead with thee for the hearts that stray
Far from the shadow of the Cross,
   Lost in the world's tumultuous way.

The Flight into Egypt.

We offer now these callas fair,
    Children of Egypt's sunny land,
Where thou, belovèd Queen, didst dwell
    An exile from thy native strand;

In memory of thy anguish keen
    Through the long hours of dreary flight
When the world's Monarch stooped to flee
    An earthly ruler's cruel might.

With thee we trace the rocky path;
    With thee we tread the desert's sand;
With thee we bear the heat and thirst,
    And face the armèd robber band.

With thee we fondly watch and ward,
    Through all thy fears and deep alarms,
The smiling Babe that calmly rests
    In peace within thy sheltering arms.

The Three Days' Loss.

Lily of Israel, by the pain
    Endured through all the three days' loss,
Foreshadowing thy greater grief
    Beneath the cruel Cross,

Bearing sweet wreathèd blooms to thee
    We crave to tread the pathway trod
Through Sion's city in thy search
    For thy dear Son and God.

Oh! teach us with unwavering faith
    To seek him ever day by day;
Oh! fire our hearts with love's pure flame,
    Whose glow will never more decay.

And guide us till with thee we find
    The Saviour in his Temple fair,
Where through thy sorrows we may hope
    With thee his heavenly joys to share.

Meeting Jesus with the Cross.

Blending our tears of grief with thine,
    Belovèd Mother, let us stand
Beside thee in this hour of woe,
    A youthful but devoted band,

While onward in an angry tide
    The maddened crowd is borne along,
And fair Jerusalem echoes back
    The cries of the infuriate throng.

And in its midst—O woe untold!
    O sight to pierce thy tender soul!—
He walks beneath the heavy Cross
    Whose word the heavens and earth control.

Striped by the keen and cruel scourge,
    Scorned by his foes, who jeer and cry,
Heaping their insults base on him,
    They hurry forth to crucify.

Our spirits long to bear with thee
    The bitter sorrow of that hour
Which saw thy Son, the Lord most high,
    A victim to his people's power;

And strew beneath his bleeding feet
  These blossoms of the glen and grove,
And our young hearts, which burn and glow
  With flames of pure and fervid love.

The Crucifixion.

The hour foretold by Prophets,
  The hour of dread, is here.
O children! gather closer,
  Draw nearer and more near.

Draw nearer to Our Lady
  In this surpassing pain;
Weep, weep with her, dear children:
  Such tears fall not in vain.

See on the cross the Saviour,
  By impious hands laid low;
The nails through flesh and muscle
  Driven downward blow by blow.

And as they tear and wound him,
  Our Lady's virgin heart
Is, by the pain he suffers,
  Stricken and rent apart.

Lo! now the Cross is lifted;
  Behold the Precious Blood
Rains down on Calvary's summit,
  A great and priceless flood.

Hark to the words he speaketh:
  He claims us for his own;
Oh! let us strive to merit
  A place beside his throne.

He gives us to his Mother,
   A legacy of love!
O pitying Mother! guide us
   Unto thy home above.

And as our humble offerings
   Before thy shrine we lay,
Of flowers and tears, we beg thee
   To plead for us alway.

The Taking Down from the Cross.

Our dear and holy Mother
   Once more shall fondly hold
Upon her breast the Saviour,
   As in the days of old—

The Blessed Babe of Bethlehem,
   But rigid, cold, and dead,
With pure flesh striped and wounded
   And thorn-transpiercèd head.

Come, let us aid Saint Joseph,
   As now, with reverent care,
He holds our dear Lord's Body—
   Blest load for man to bear!—

Or bring the fragrant spices,
   Or spread the snowy shroud,
Treading with noiseless footsteps
   And young heads lowly bowed;

In silent awe and reverence
   Our humble homage yield,
Asking His care who fashioned
   These blossoms of the field.

The Burial of Jesus.

Within the tomb they lay him;
  Earth's opened heart doth take
To its embrace the Saviour,
  Who suffered for our sake.

Around his grave, dear children,
  Our solemn guard we'll keep,
With countless angels watching
  Above his wondrous sleep;

Our hearts subdued with sorrow,
  Our bitter tear-drops shed
In wild, heartrending anguish
  Above our Mother's Dead!

O mystery far surpassing
  The reach of human thought!
O death by which the freedom
  Of man from sin was bought!

Blest Queen of Heaven, hear us:
  Accept our humble prayer,
And let thy little children
  Thy last great Dolor share.

Oh! take our hearts' best offerings,
  Their homage true and deep,
And in thy care for ever
  Our wayward spirits keep.

Accept the fragile blossoms
  We lay before thee here,
And win for us, thy children,
  A home in Heaven's bright sphere.

OUR LADY OF MOUNT CARMEL.

BY this blest badge we wear, O holy Mother!
    This token of thy love,
Look down on us with eyes of tenderest pity
    From thy bright home above—

Thou who didst tread the Via Dolorosa
    Through sorrow's bitterest gloom,
Thou who didst stand beside the Cross in anguish,
    Didst mourn beside the tomb;

Thou whose pure heart wast torn with grief whose tortures
    No mortal tongue may tell,
When died thy Son, our merciful Redeemer,
    For those he loved so well.

Then, when our sins thy loving heart were breaking,
    He gave us unto thee,
That thou our Mother and our Mediatrix
    For evermore should be.

And thou hast proved a loving Mother to us,
    Blessed Queen of love and light,
Who hast bestowed upon us this most glorious
    Badge of the Carmelite—

Gift of thy love unto that chosen servant
    Whose heart, with love aflame,
Sought daily with undying zeal to honor
    Thy pure and holy name.

A boon he craved, a gift from thee, dear Mother
    A token from thy hand,
Whose power would fan the flame of praise and worship
    To splendor clear and grand.

And thou didst hear his prayer—this badge thy answer.
    What rapturous surprise
Flooded his soul when from the opened heavens,
    To glad his loving eyes.

Thou camest to earth, the Infant Saviour bearing
    Upon thy spotless breast,
And to thy sainted servant gave this armor
    And shield for souls oppressed.

Mount Carmel's caves, within whose shadows lonely
    God's priests and prophets prayed,
Thrilled to the music which uncounted angels
    Singing around thee made.

And thence for evermore sweet strains of comfort,
    Thy words of promise, flow—
Words which have fallen with a balm of healing
    On many a wound of woe.

O dear, dear Mother! through each passing moment
    Look from thy home above,
And shield from tempting wiles the thousands wearing
    This livery of thy love.

Pray for thy children found in every station,
    Peasant or prince or peer,
Merchant or soldier, or the rugged sailor
    Whose stout heart knows no fear.

But oh! all blessings choicest still and rarest
    Flow round their hearts to-day
Who for Christ's sake leave home and friends and kindred,
    To tread the " narrow way ";

Whose every aim in life is consecrated
    To God, and God alone ;
Whose prayers, a grand, perpetual adoration,
    Like incense seek his throne.

Win them, sweet Mother, faith's celestial guerdon,
    To each give strengthening grace,
And let the influence of their lives heroic
    Be felt in every place.

MY LADY'S JEWELS.

(The month of October being dedicated to the Rosary of Our Lady and to the Holy Angels, and the month of November to the Holy Souls, may our good angels bear many a chaplet of Aves up to the Throne of Grace as suffrages for our loved ones who have passed before us through the mystic gateway of the tomb!)

THEY are my Lady's Jewels,
   And that is why I prize
As a treasure what seems so common
   And worthless to other eyes.

They are my Lady's Jewels,
   And all through life's sad years
They have been to my heart a comfort
   That soothed its darkest fears.

Holding them close in sorrow,
   In sickness and bitter woe,
I have felt the cross grow lighter
   And my heart with courage glow.

They are my Lady's Jewels,
   And no monarch's caskets hold
Gems of such wondrous splendor
   As these in my hands unfold.

True, they are brown and homely,
   And fashioned of common wood;
But I see in them shining diamonds,
   And rubies as red as blood,

With milk-white pearls that emblem
    The purity of soul
We all must keep while striving
    To win the heavenly goal.

And lo! as upon them gazing,
    Clasping them bead by bead,
See how they open unto me
    A volume of light to read.

Chapter and page and column
    Are shining before me here:
The life of our blessed Mother,
    And the Saviour we love and fear;

Mary's joys and her sorrows,
    Mary's glory and pain,
And the graces we win through Mary,
    Falling like precious rain—

Graces that bless and brighten,
    Graces won by her prayers,
As down at the throne of Jesus
    She layeth her children's cares.

Dear are my Lady's Jewels,
    Most precious and dear to me,
For the sake of the poor souls waiting
    Our Aves to set them free—

The poor souls watching and waiting,
    In purgatorial pains,
Till the prayers of their earthly kindred
    Move Our Lady to break their chains.

O lovers of Mary's Jewels!
  Think as you bend to-day,
That some one you loved most dearly,
  Some one who has passed away,

May now unto you be calling,
  Asking an alms of you,
Prayers that our holy Mother
  May pour on their souls, the dew

That quenches the flames and loosens
  Each closely prisoning band,
And free and lead them rejoicing
  To their home in the heavenly land.

They are my Lady's Jewels,
  And earthly cares and needs
Vanish away as vapor
  At the touch of my Rosary beads.

What were the wealth of Ophir,
  What were the Indies' store,
If this chaplet of Mary's roses
  I could claim as mine no more?

Ah! I would guard them closely,
  With their graces to heal and save,
And still would my hands enfold them
  When I rest in the silent grave.

OCTOBER, 1881.

OUR LADY OF KNOCK.

THROUGH years of persecution, of bitter woe and wrong,
The glorious Faith of Erin has shone with radiance strong;
It lit the lowly hovels, the mountain glens so lone,
And caverns where the ocean's voice rang out in thunder-tone.
For, banished from their churches and abbeys' holy shade,
'Mid Nature's rugged fastness the priests their dwelling made.
Then, holy hills of Mayo, your rocky heights became
Temples unto God's honor dear and Mary's spotless fame,
When all your glens were peopled by that heroic band
Driven exiles into Connaught by Cromwell's fierce command;
The angels bent in pity above them day by day,
And thoughts of Mary's sorrows were still their strength and stay.
Then by the sobbing ocean or on the sterile sod
How many a nameless martyr gave up his soul to God!
And as the years rolled onward their children still have borne
The tyrant's vengeful anger, the tyrant's cruel scorn

Upon their quivering vitals has the vulture Famine fed,
Till Heaven alone could number the dying and the dead.

But still their Faith they cherished, nor threat nor promised power
Could win from Erin's children Saint Patrick's treasured dower.
And now, amid their sorrows, Our Lady from above
Comes down to bless and cheer them with tender, pitying love;
And, holy hills of Mayo! ye thrill with glad acclaim
As hour by hour recordeth new marvels to her name,
Where to Knock's lowly chapel the eager pilgrims haste,
Of Christ's dear mercy, given through Mary's hands, to taste.
For there our heavenly Mother, Saint Joseph, and Saint John
Upon the startled vision of Erin's children shone;
There on a glittering altar rapt eyes beheld again
The Lamb, type of the Saviour on Calvary's mountain slain—
The Saviour on whose shoulders the whole world's sins were laid,
Whose Blood, a priceless ransom, our reparation made;
The Saviour whose loved Mother comes in these days of fear,
Of hunger, and of heartache, our mourning land to cheer,

With her two chosen guardians 'mid earthly joy and
    loss :
One watched beside Christ's cradle, one stood beneath his Cross;
One guarded his fair childhood, its labor and its rest,
One at our Lord's Last Supper reposed upon his
    breast.

And while the thronging pilgrims—the sick, the worn,
    the weak—
Hear in each healing marvel our Mother's mercy
    speak,
We, dwellers o'er the ocean, lift up our hearts to-day,
Begging of thee, sweet Virgin, for Erin's sons to pray;
Win for them strength and courage their heavy cross
    to bear,
And bid the smile of plenty dispel want's cloud of
    care ;
Grant freedom to thy children, but, dearer blessing
    still,
Teach them, with faith unswerving, to do God's holy
    will.

True to their pledge now given
To thee, O Queen of Heaven!
The promise their young voices
   Breathe forth for one and all.
Guard them, guard us, till Heaven
Opes on life's closing even,
And we will stand forgiven
   Where shadows never fall.

OCTOBER ROSES.

NOW is the time when garden haunts
    Are gay with bright October roses,
And morning's dawn or sunset's glow
    In turn their varying tints discloses;
With their white blooms we deck thy shrine,
    O Virgin ever pure and glorious!
And with their red and gold adorn
    His throne who rose o'er death victorious,
Thanking his generous love that crowns
    The waning year with radiant splendor,
As humbly at his feet we lay
    The blossoms with our homage tender.

But wealth more precious than these blooms
    October guards as lord and warden,
For through his golden hours we cull
    The roses in our Lady's garden.
How beautiful, how bright, how sweet,
    With fragrance from Heaven's realm of beauty,
These flowers that lift our souls above
    The wearing cares of earthly duty!
They speak to us of Jesus' life,
    Of Mary's sorrow, joy, and glory,
And soft as dew their petals fall
    Upon the fires of Purgatory.

O precious flowers! O holy beads!
    Of our dear Mother's love the token;
How often unto listening hearts
    Your messages of joy are spoken!

More fragrant than the rose's breath
  Your Aves rise to Heaven appealing,
And visions of your mysteries stir
  The hidden founts of holiest feeling;
While all the universal Church
  The praises of our Queen is singing,
And joyous echoes far and wide
  With strains of filial love are ringing.

We, too, ere yet thy chosen month
  Within Time's silent vault reposes,
Lay at thy feet, belovèd Queen,
  Wreaths of thy own October roses;
And beg thee that each lovely bloom
  Before thee now in beauty lying,
Each Ave sweet, may win from thee
  Release for souls in prison sighing.
They plead with us; for them we plead.
  Queen of the Rosary! win them pardon,
And dower their spirits with the light
  And graces of thy own rose-garden.

And for the living, too, we pray,
  But most for Christ's dear standard-bearers—
His noble priests who toil to make
  All hearts in heavenly joys true sharers.
And as Saint Dominic taught of yore
  The Rosary's untold power and beauty,
May its blest fruits ne'er cease to cheer
  His children's arduous path of duty;
Its shining Aves light their way
  Till Death Heaven's golden gate uncloses,
And at thy feet they haste to lay
  Pure wreaths of thy October roses.

"HAIL, FULL OF GRACE!"

"HAIL, full of grace!" 'Twas thus the angel spoke
When from high Heaven he came to thee to bring
The message and the mandate of his King.
Thou who ne'er bent 'neath sin's defiling yoke,
Who ne'er God's laws by word or action broke,
To thee we turn, O Maiden pure and mild!
Thou fair, thou spotless one, thou undefiled,
Thine aid the children of the earth invoke;
Oh! by thy sevenfold joys, thy sevenfold pains,
Win us the strength that fainting hope sustains!
Turn upon us those mercy-beaming eyes;
Hark to our prayers, and plead for us once more,
That when life's dreary pilgrimage is o'er
We may salute thee, Mother, in the skies!

CAUSE OF OUR JOY.

HOLY Mother, to thy care
    Do I yield this life of mine;
Listen to my pleading prayer,
    Suing by thy joys divine.

Highest of Heaven's subject throng,
    Than the angel choirs more high,
Throned within the awful light
    Of our God's all-seeing eye.

Brightest where all earthly thought
    Of celestial beauty dies,
Fairest where the lustrous light
    Dazzles e'en angelic eyes.

Honored with an honor meet
    By the blessèd and the pure,
With an homage that shall last
    While the heavenly courts endure.

All are clients at thy feet;
    Thou canst win where others fail:
Stretch thy helping hand to me
    When the tempter's wiles assail.

At the right hand of thy Son
    Thou art placed that thou mayst win
For thy children one and all
    Freedom from the thrall of sin.

By the favors God bestows
 Upon all who honor thee,
By thy sevenfold joys in Heaven,
 Holy Mother, succor me!

AVE MARIA.

As the angel hailed thee first
 With the Spirit's words of power,
Do thy praises still ascend
 From the cloister, from the bower;
From the busy scenes of toil,
 From the homes of ease and rest,
From the soul of childhood pure,
 From the prisoner's guilty breast,
From the hearts by sorrow bowed,
 By the voice that melts in tears,
Faltered slow, or sung aloud,
 Ring thy praises through the years.
O'er the wide domain of earth
 There is not a single place
Where thy children are not found
 Bidding thee "Hail, full of grace."

Blessèd art thou amongst all
 Daughters of the human race,
Thou whose royal lineage high
 Priests and prophets loved to trace.
Star of hope to fallen man
 Wert thou since earth's earliest dawn,
Since at Eden's closing gates
 First the flaming sword was drawn.
Light of Israel's darkest day,
 Princess of King David's line,
Never daughter of thy race
 Bore such noble Son as thine.

He was Lord of that domain
    Which nor air nor oceans bound;
In his praise through earth and Heaven
    Strains of sweetest worship sound—
Lord of that dominion fair
    Which his presence doth illume,
At the Father's right hand throned
    Shines the blest fruit of thy womb.

Holy Mary, Mother pure,·
    Holy Mary, Maiden sweet,
Hear thy pleading children call,
    See them kneeling at thy feet;
Listen to their anxious cry,
    Hold them closely in thy care;
Guide them to thy home on high,
    Shield them from the tempter's snare;
Bless them in their days of toil,
    Soothe them in their hours of woe,
Lend them comfort and support
    On their journey here below;
Lift their hearts above the earth,
    Aid them, Mother, in that hour
When they tremble in the clasp
    Of the dread death-angel's power.

THROUGH MARY'S HEART.

I KNOW a way by which to reach
  The Sacred Heart on high,
A path round which ring echoes sweet
  To each appealing cry;

A pathway odorous with flowers
  Most fragrant and most fair,
Such blossoms as ne'er brightened yet
  Spring's glittering parterre.

The caves of ocean never hid
  Such pearls as strew the way;
Ear never heard before such songs
  As thrill there all the day.

It leadeth through the garden where
  The Bridegroom loves to tread,
The chosen spot on which his smile's
  Most radiant light is shed;

It leadeth through her holy Heart,
  The Virgin meek and mild,
The stainless Heart that shade or spot
  Of sin has ne'er defiled.

It follows where the cruel sword
  Of sorrow oped the way,
Whence light and grace and boundless love
  Flow on us day by day.

O Mary, Mother, chaste and pure!
　　Look from thy home above,
And lead me safely unto God
　　Through this bright path of love.

By every precious gift he gave
　　To make thy Heart so fair,
By all his love for thee, beloved,
　　I claim thy sheltering care.

Through thee, my hope, I seek to gain
　　Grace from his Heart divine;
For evermore I hear his words,
　　"Come through her Heart to mine."

"Come through my Mother's Heart to me;
　　Whate'er she asks I give."
Then, holy Mother, hear my prayer,
　　And teach me how to live—

To live and work for God alone,
　　To win his strengthening grace,
Till, dying on thy loving Heart,
　　I may behold his Face.

TO SAINT JOSEPH.

[Suggested by the opening of St. Joseph's Free Schools in San Francisco by the Rev. Hugh P. Gallagher.]

SAINT JOSEPH, stainless, meek, and mild,
Meet foster-father of the Child
Who, leaving Heaven's celestial bowers,
Dwelt in this sinful world of ours,
And by his meek example showed
To youthful hearts the shining road
Which leadeth to the promised prize,
The golden gates of Paradise.

How blest, dear saint, thy lot to share
From day to day the Infant's care;
And, after toil, what precious rest
When by the Saviour's love caressed—
Sweet foretaste of the world of bliss
Given to thy holy heart in this!

Dear saint, by all the joys then given
When thy home held the Lord of Heaven
Look from his cloudless home above,
And by thy pity and thy love
Pray that this school beneath thy care
Good fruit a thousandfold may bear;
That choicest blessings flowing down
Its noble founder's life may crown.

For bravely has he wrought to win
Youth from the luring path of sin,
From dangers ever lurking near—
The unbeliever's scoff and sneer,
The constant taunts, the scorning eyes,
The words that wound in friendly guise,
The thousand bright, deceptive arts
That weaken faith in youthful hearts
And early teach their steps to stray
Far, far from where Religion's sway,
Undimmed 'mid persecution's wrath,
Beacons for us the upward path.
Patron of all, to thee he brings
These tender souls as offerings,
That thou mayest lead with guiding hand
The little children of our land.
For lo! upon their future waits
The country's peace, the law of States;
And as to good or ill they grow,
Follows a nation's weal or woe.
But thou canst mould each heart aright
Until, as lilies in God's sight,
Fragrant and fair their good deeds show,
Brightening earth's darkness with their glow,
Till he who for them toiled and planned
Shall be called "blessèd" in the land.

SAINT PATRICK'S DAY.

O MORN of grace and beauty!
   We fondly bid thee hail,
With the welcome true and hearty
   Of a love which ne'er can fail.

For shrined within our spirits,
   Close twined around each heart,
Lives the love for Erin's Patron
   Which can never thence depart.

Dear Apostle of our country,
   Who through weary years of toil
Spent his boyhood a meek captive
   To a proud lord of the soil!

How Heaven's love and pity blending
   Grew within him day by day!
How he grieved to see the people
   Amid pagan darkness stray!

Ah! he wept the thousands dying
   With no future hope to cheer,
Ever praying God to send them
   Faith unclouded, pure, and clear.

He was heard. The lowly captive,
   From his servile bonds set free,
Sought once more his native country
   O'er the blue waves of the sea.

But the memory of green Erin
  On his heart its burden laid,
And in dreams he heard the wailing
  As her babes for baptism prayed,

Till he knelt in humble pleading
  At the Sovereign Pontiff's throne,
Begging that to Ireland's children
  He might make the Gospel known.

With the blessing of Christ's Vicar
  To the Irish isle he, came,
And no conqueror earth has honored
  Won such pure and lasting fame.

Kings and princes, peers and peasants,
  Answered his impassioned call,
And with meek and contrite spirits
  Owned the Saviour, Lord of all.

And he left to us, the children
  Of that land where'er we stray,
Faith's pure light to guide and cheer us
  With its strong and steadfast ray.

Grateful for the gift he gave us,
  Fondly, earnestly we claim
Graces for our sorrowing country
  Through Saint Patrick's glorious name;

Joining in the world-wide chorus
  Which to-day thrills every clime:
"May Hibernia's Saint be honored,
  Loved, and reverenced through all time!"

SAINT BENEDICT'S DAY.

I HEARD the linnets 'mid the vines
    Sing at the dawn of day,
And from the budding trees o'erhead
    There came an answering lay;
And larks' and linnets' thrilling tones
    Rose blending gladly then,
Till all the woodland songsters gave
    Sweet echoes o'er again.

It is the morning of his feast,
    The saint by angels led
To Subiaco's desert lone,
    Monte Casino's head—
Monte Casino, where he reared
    His home of toil and prayer,
And framed the rule that guideth still
    His children everywhere.

Saint Benedict, the blessèd saint,
    Belovèd from his youth,
Who sought in solitude and peace
    The shining path of truth;
Who fled the city's luring snares,
    And, in the desert wild,
Within his lonely cavern dwelt,
    Our Lady's favored child.

Saint Benedict, the humble saint:
  Devoid of earthly pride,
He sought, but sought in vain, his love
  From all but Heaven to hide—
The love that from his spotless soul
  A fragrant incense soared
Up to the awful Presence where
  The angel-hosts adored.

Saint Benedict, the patient saint:
  In vain around his way
Envy and hatred raging strive
  His holy work to stay;
Meekly he followed in the path
  The Saviour glorified,
Without a murmur or complaint
  Toiled bravely till he died.

Saint Benedict, the favored saint,
  Who signed the sacred sign,
And lo! the goblet shattered fell
  From round the poisoned wine;
The saint whose vision pierced beyond
  The shadows of the grave,
Whose voice had power to make the steel
  Float on the river's wave.

Saint Benedict, saint of the Cross:
  None ever loved as he
Faith's holy rood, Love's mystic sign,
  Mount Calvary's fruitful tree.
Beneath the shelter of its arms
  His holy laws he gave;
It was his armor during life,
  Companion in the grave.

Saint Benedict, thrice blessèd saint,
    Father of Monks, we hail!
Before this title of our love
    All other titles pale;
All other titles merge in this,
    For first beneath his sway,
In Occidental lands, men learned
    To labor and obey.

Saint Benedict, whose holy rule
    Such wondrous lessons taught,
With knowledge of God's love divine
    And saving maxims fraught;
Who with such heavenly wisdom filled
    The hours of praise and prayer,
Of prayer and praise, till either seemed
    The joys of Heaven to share.

Saint Benedict, teacher of saints:
    A long, illustrious line
Of priests and bishops, martyrs, popes,
    Sprang from that rule of thine—
Apostles of the Faith, who bore
    Its light to pagan lands,
And watered with their hearts' best blood
    Its seed on desert sands.

Saint Benedict, thy spotless fame
    Knows not the touch of years;
Thy virtues and thy holy name
    Ring through both hemispheres:
Though Old World tyrants slay and spoil,
    Still there thy Order clings,
And 'mid the New World's fertile fields
    In fullest vigor springs.

Saint Benedict, whose gentle heart
  Loved birds and streams and flowers,
Because they showed the Maker's love,
  Pray for this land of ours—
Pray for the land whose lifted voice
  Calls on thy name to-day;
For blessings on its every home
  Plead with the Lord, we pray.

Saint Benedict, by all thy love,
  By all thy toils and prayers,
By all the graces thou didst win,
  And which the wide earth shares,
The children of the Faith who dwell
  Within the golden West
Beg thee to guide them on the way
  To Heaven's eternal rest.

And while the birds' sweet matin songs
  Go echoing far away,
And while the bells for *Ave* ring,
  And while thy children pray,
Let this poor wreath of wild-wood flowers
  I lay before thy shrine
Whisper the love which fain would fire
  This simple lay of mine.

MARCH 21, 1877.

SAINT DOMINIC.

WHEN the dreams of bygone ages rise before me in their glory,
   Painting in undying colors names of honor and renown,
And the shifting vision shows me rulers of long-buried empires,
   Kings whose royal race no longer bears the sceptre and the crown ;

Warriors once the shield of nations ; statesmen brave and bold and earnest ;
   Orators whose words so golden thrilled and held the hearts of men ;
Artists who will live for ever in the pictures they have left us ;
   Poets, authors who have moulded all the future with the pen ;

Valiant knights who lived devoted to their ladies' love and honor,
   Wearing upon wrist and helmet favors given by snowy hands,
Daring for their sake the dangers of the battle and the tourney,
   Journeying at the loved ones' bidding into wild and distant lands—

Then, amid the many figures passing upon fancy's canvas,
  Lo! one robed in white outshineth 'mid the loftiest of our race—
Leader of a noble army, fearless in earth's fiercest battles,
  Dauntless champion of a Lady hailed by angels "full of grace!"

Bravely went he forth to conquer in the armor of her choosing,
  With the shield of spotless innocence, the shining sword of prayer;
And he bore his Lady's colors all unsullied in their beauty,
  Till, the long, fierce conflict over, he resigned them to her care.

Dear Saint Dominic! One fair legend of his life is e'er before me,
  And I see his wondrous writing by the red flames unconsumed,
Firm and lasting as the Order that his love called into being,
  And whose labors have the darkness of so many souls illumed.

Saint whose miracles are countless as the graces which Heaven gave him,
  And whose name is linked for ever with Our Lady's love and fame,
When we tell our humble *Aves* on the beads she gave unto him,
  Then we feel the sweet charm dwelling in Saint Dominic's honored name.

Saint who toiled, from dawn till twilight, for the hearts
by error darkened,
Never pausing, never faltering at the dangers in the
way;
Saint whose rest was ever sweetest when, his daily
labors over,
He might kneel before the altar all the long night
hours and pray.

Saint whose actions shine as brightly on the pages
Time has written
As the stars that burn and glitter in the deep blue
arch above;
Model of all noble virtues, pure in hand and heart
and spirit,
His great genius ever glowing with the fervent fires
of love.

Dear Saint Dominic! 'mid the glory of thy home in
realms celestial,
Basking in the light and beauty of our tender Mother's smile,
With the happy souls around thee whom thy earthly
labors ransomed,
Oh! we beg thee to remember us who dwell 'mid
sin and guile.

Lo! the dark and gloomy shadows cast from evil
hours surround us,
And toil's bitterness and heartache, press upon us
day by day,
While a countless troop of tempters, who would wean
us from allegiance
To our Maker and our Saviour, seek to bend us to
their sway.

As children turn with confidence and pleading to their father
    When night's sable robe is hiding the fair world from their sight,
So we call to thee, imploring thy guidance and assistance
    That our course may still be upward to the Lamb's unclouded light;

That our course may still be upward, and the luring smiles of pleasure
    And the hopes and aims earth-centred may no more have power to hold
Our spirits in their bondage, but, all baser thoughts repelling,
    We may long with ceaseless longing 'mid the saints to be enrolled.

Champion of Our Lady's honor! Preacher of her fame and graces!
    Dauntless knight, whose crest was never veiled to foeman in the field!
Win for us the grace of courage, fervor, strength, and perseverance;
    Stand beside us ever, ever, lest we weakly fall and yield.

Pray for us!—thy prayers were ever heard with favor by our Mother,
    And her Son will ne'er refuse her when she offers him thy prayer.
Pray for us, for us thy children; hear us calling, calling humbly;
    Shelter us beneath the mantle of thy tender love and care.

SAINT THOMAS OF AQUINAS.

THINE a name to live for ever in the world thy life illumined
  With the sweet, seraphic lustre burning in thy spotless soul,
Where each lofty aspiration tended only to God's honor,
  And no wild, contending passions ever swept with fierce control.

"Angel of the Schools," thy wisdom like a stream of living waters
  Gladdens all the arid desert of the earth, and vivifies
With a never-failing vigor minds that humbly and sincerely
  Draw their knowledge from Truth's fountain where all purest science lies.

Lover of the Saviour lifted for his people upon Calvary,
  For their sake upon the rude cross in such agony enthroned,
How the wounds that rent his body filled thy gentle heart with anguish,
  Drawing thee still closer, closer unto him whom men disowned!

From sweet Jesus' wounds descended light to guide thee in thy labors,
  Thence flowed forth all grace and learning to enrich thee with their dower,
Thence the deeply hidden meaning of each theme sublime and mystic
  Was revealed to thy rapt vision by his love's celestial power.

To thy heart a precious volume was the Crucifix, unfolding
  Unto thee the wondrous secrets thou so well couldst understand:
That the measure of man's loving was to love God without measure,
  And to yield him praise unceasing, earnest, fervid, deep, and grand.

By thy songs which seem as echoes of the glorious strains that seraphs
  In the golden courts of Heaven chant in joy before his face,
By the all-consuming fervor of the holy zeal that fired thee,
  And which made thy humble spirit as a very fount of grace,

It was given thee that the Saviour of thy work should speak approval,
  Saying from his cross: "O Thomas! thou hast written well of me;
What wouldst ask of me as guerdon?" Winning thy enraptured answer
  Which surrounding angels echoed: "I desire naught but thee!"

O great Saint in Heaven rejoicing, in the glory of
    God's presence,
  May the sweet desire that filled thee all our hearts
    with love inflame,
Till life's only aim and object, every thought and
    word and action,
  Be an offering to the honor of his dear and holy
    Name.

SAINT BENEDICT JOSEPH LABRE.

"OUR Lady's Pilgrim Saint," "Saint of the poor,"
"The Client of Dei Monte's Virgin Queen,"
"Loretto's Pilgrim," and the faithful "Guard"
Who watched with tireless love and fervent prayer
Our Eucharistic Lord—
      O blessed Saint Benedict,
These were the titles love bestowed on thee
Ere, answer to the prayer of myriad hearts,
The Sovereign Pontiff Pius—who, like thee,
Was Mary's chosen servant—to the world .
Proclaimed thy name, long hallowed, crowned at last
With the great honors which the Church decrees
To those who of her faithful children bear
The glorious name of Saint.
      In this age of ours,
When Infidelity holds regal sway,
'Mid wealth and luxury with all their train
Of crying evils which o'errun the land,
Meet was it that to oppose these ravening foes
Such perfect model should be given to us
Of poverty, of penance, and of prayer.

How shall we praise thee, grand, heroic heart,
Tried in the fiery crucible of pain
Till all of earth and self are burned away,
And naught remained but the consuming love

Whose deathless flame its daily fuel found
In contemplation of Love's mystery,
Where on the altar, veiled in humble guise,
God deigns to dwell with mortals?

What were thy arms in life's great conflict? These :
The Crucifix at once thy sword and shield,
The wounded image eloquent to thee
Of all the Saviour's attributes divine
And his great mercies to the human race ;
And Mary's Rosary beads, which seldom left,
Even for a moment's space, thy holy hands—
The beads which link by link, a shining chain,
Bound all thy heart and heart's pure love to her,
The Queen Immaculate of earth and heaven,
Who laid thy pleadings at her dear Son's feet
And won prompt answer to thy fervent prayer.
Nor were thy victories won by prayer alone :
Thine was a soul that shrank not from the pain
Of self-inflicted penitential stripes,
So often blended with thy sorrowing tears,
Till 'neath the blows the crimson blood flowed forth
An offering for the sins that weighed thee down ;
Not thine own sins—virgin in life wert thou,
And stainless as a child that knows no guile—
But for the countless crimes which day by day
Cried out unceasing to the Throne of God
For vengeance, not for mercy, on mankind ;
For all who scoffed, derided, wounded him,
Renewing Calvary with all its woes,
Were given thy prayers, thy penances, thy fasts,
Which made each day throughout the livelong year
A rigorous Lenten vigil unto thee.

Wedded to holy Poverty from youth,
Still from thy scanty means a generous alms
Thou gavest to the hungry ones around.

Saint of the poor, to thee a needy throng
Of pleading clients cry aloud for aid ;
They ask of thee, with confidence and love,
Prayers that their lives may be as God desires,
Humble and earnest, faithful and sincere,
True to the teachings of our guide the Church,
And filled with charity and holy zeal
To do his will unmurmuringly below ;
Prayers for His Church, for Rome so well beloved,
Prayers for thy hapless native land, fair France,
Who hails with joy a noble son in thee.
List to their pleading, O beloved Saint!
Make their petition thine, and 'twill be heard.

SAINT AGNES.

VIRGIN Spouse of Christ the Saviour! dear Saint Agnes, we salute thee
  With the tender love and reverence thy angelic virtues claim,
Yielding to thee, holy maiden, homage high and pure affection,
  Echoing the praises sounding through long ages to thy name.

Child in years, in heart a hero, earth has never honored braver,
  For thy spirit passed unscathèd through temptation's ordeal dread.
Fear within thy gentle bosom found no trembling chord responsive,
  For thy firm, undaunted courage was by founts celestial fed.

Wealth and power in vain allured thee with the shining gifts they offered,
  Pleading words or threatening mandates could not make thee break thy vows;
Thou couldst triumph 'mid the tortures which the cruel tyrant fashioned,
  Welcoming death, whose coming gave thee sooner to thy Heavenly Spouse.

Glorious saint! pure virgin martyr! in God's presence
    now rejoicing,
  By the Bridegroom's hand rewarded with the price-
    less palm and crown,
Thou who art so near and precious to the Sacred
    Heart of Jesus,
  Plead with him that we may never feel his anger's
    dreadful frown.

Win for us thy dauntless courage to resist the powers
    of evil,
  Thy God-given strength in trial, and thy purity of
    heart;
Ask, dear Saint of love and innocence, and, answer-
    ing thy pleadings,
  Thy chosen Spouse his blessings to thy clients will
    impart.

SAINT VIVIANA.

HID in the catacombs of Rome while centuries
    rolled away,
Saint Viviana's form reposed until that happy day
When Science led her searching bands their silence to
    invade,
And found where, 'neath the marble cold, the martyr-
    child was laid,
And brought the sacred relics forth. What changes
    earth had known
Since, welcoming the martyr's doom, she won the
    martyr's throne!

The Roman Empire's pomp and pride for ever passed
    away,
The tyrant and his subject hordes long mouldered
    into clay,
The memory of their lives a name, their palaces laid
    low,
Naught left unchanged but the true Faith she died for
    long ago—
The Faith the Saviour planted first, which his apostles
    spread,
That lives of saints have glorified and blood of mar-
    tyrs fed;

The holy Faith whose fadeless light illumines every clime,
The rock-built Church whose cross-crowned walls have triumphed over time—
The Church whose children fondly own, where'er their land or home,
Allegiance to God's Vicar here, the holy Pope of Rome,
Our noble Pontiff-King, who gave unto this Western fold
The relics of the martyr-saint, a treasure fair to hold.

When pleading for his scattered flock our reverend Bishop stood
And gave the promise years of toil and holy zeal made good :
A proud cathedral he has raised in Viviana's name,
And the fair land beside the sea an added grace doth claim.
The " City of the Angels " holds the precious treasure now,
More precious than the royal gems that wreathe a monarch's brow—

The relics of the holy saint, the virgin pure and mild,
Who witnessed for the faith of Christ while yet she was a child ;
The saint whose pleading prayers for us a bounteous wealth will bring
Of graces from the treasure-house of Heaven's most gracious King :
The stainless life, the holy death, the virtues manifold
Of our dear Patroness shall win joys for the land of gold.

Her courage as a shield of power will guard the young from sin,
And cheer them on the upward way, the heavenly crown to win ;
But closest round our Bishop's life her tender care will twine
With blessings still a thousandfold on him who reared her shrine,
Whose zealous heart and tireless hands have toiled for God alone,
Till whitening harvests brighten now the desert he hath sown.

EVENING PRAYER TO MY GUARDIAN ANGEL.

MY angel-guide, with thee I kneel
    Before God's throne to-night;
Oh! beg of him to be my shield,
My strength upon life's battle-field,
    And with his fadeless light
Illume for me the upward way,
Where in his beauty's cloudless ray
My ransomed soul at last will feel
    The joys that ne'er decay.

Sheltered beneath thy loving care
    Since childhood's earliest hour,
My heart has felt from day to day
Thy watchful love, thy tender sway,
    Thy chaste enlightening power.
Oh! blend thy earnest prayer with mine,
Win for me from his grace divine
    Patience, the heavenly dower,
Which makes my cross less hard to bear,
    Till peace and rest are mine.

I do not beg of him to take
    All suffering from my life,
Only for grace and strength to bear
The cross his mercy bids me share,
    The cross with blessings rife;
To hail with joy the cross he blessed,
The cross his holy hands caressed,
The cross he carried for my sake
    And all earth's wrong redressed.

FOR THE SOULS IN PURGATORY.*

IN thy mild and sweet compassion we beg of thee, O Mary!
   To hasten with assistance to the souls that writhe in pain
Amid purgatorial fire, languishing 'neath keenest tortures,
   While the cleansing flame effaces every sin's defiling stain.

To the souls of the departed, O Mary! be propitious,
   Thou whose voice of pure entreating is all-powerful with thy Son;
Daughter of the world's Creator, Mother of its King and Saviour,
   Ask him that the bonds which hold them by his mercy be undone.

The dead, O pious Mary! send up their sighs and longings,
   Desiring, oh! so fervently, that they may be set free
From the torments laid upon them, and within thy glorious presence
   Dwell 'mid joys that are eternal for evermore with thee.

* A free rendering of an old Latin hymn.

Oh! haste, dear Mother Mary; show the depths of thy compassion
 Unto those who are lamenting in the bitterness of woe;
Obtain for them that Jesus by his Sacred Wounds would heal them—
 Wounds from which flowed forth the Precious Blood that gladdens all below.

True hope of those who cry to thee, O Mary! hear the pleading
 Of the multitude of faithful who for their brethren pray,
Beseeching thee in mercy to appease thy Son's just anger,
 And win for them the blest reward of Heaven's unfading day.

O good and gracious Mary! grant that the tears of sorrow
 We shed before the Judge's feet may quench the avenging fires,
And the souls set free from prison soar up on wings exultant
 To chant their Maker's praises amid angelic choirs.

And when in God's awful judgment the Son shall come in splendor,
 Searching all hearts with a rigor language but too poorly paints,
Judging all with strictest justice, pray for us, for us, O Mary!
 That we then may be found worthy to be numbered with the saints.

THE CALLA.

O FRAGRANT flower, pure and sweet,
   Whose parent blossoms sprang to birth
Where Egypt's mystic river laves
   The ruined wonders of the earth.

All-spotless as the gleaming snow
   When drifted on the trackless height
Of mountain-tops, I see thee glow,
   Emblem of purity so bright,

The fairest of fair Nature's gems
   Love offers at Our Lady's shrine,
As though her pitying glance had lent
   An added beauty unto thine.

And looking on thy chalice white,
   A thought came o'er my spirit there,
Where incense burned, and music throbbed,
   And sweet psalms filled the house of prayer.

'Twas thus: that when the Virgin dwelt
   An exile by the slumbrous Nile,
The fragrant lilies on its banks
   Basked in the glory of her smile.

And there the Infant Saviour touched
   Some opening blossom as He passed,
And to its gleaming petals gave
   A beauty evermore to last—

A beauty meet, as now, to glow
  Peerlessly lovely at the shrine
Where our dear Mother fondly clasps
  Within her arms the Babe Divine.

REMEMBER THE DEAD.

[The church bells throughout the diocese of Monterey and Los Angeles are tolled every evening at eight o'clock to remind the faithful to pray for the souls of the faithful departed.]

THE trembling stars look down
   From their far azure throne,
As though with dewy tears
   Answering the bell's sad tone,
As through the tranquil eve
   With solemn sound it tolls,
Calling on all to pray
   For earth's departed souls.

    "Remember those who sleep
      Cold in each narrow bed;
    Remember them and pray,
      Pray for the loved and dead."

And waked by this appeal,
   Fond memory points again
To dear graves scattered far
   By mountain and by glen;
To fields where banners flew,
   Where battle's thunders rolled,
Where many a mother's joy
   Sleeps 'neath the cold, damp mould.

And ocean's deep voice names
  Its silent guests once more—
Brave hearts who sank to rest
  Amid the tempest's roar.
From scenes where plenty ruled,
  Or famine held her sway,
From many a nameless grave,
  Friends plead with us to pray.

    "Remember those who sleep
      Cold in each narrow bed;
    Remember them and pray,
      Pray for the loved and dead."

O holy thought, to keep
  Our lost ones still in view,
With sweet largesse of prayer
  To prove that we are true.
Then while across the vale
  The solemn summons rings,
Let prayers for their repose
  Mount to the King of Kings.

A MESSAGE.

"Let us strive to love our dear Lord and his and our Blessed Mother every day a little more, so that we may meet in Heaven."—F. G.

Oh! sweet that daily task should be;
   For love, love in return would gain
In measure boundless as the sea,
   And unalloyed by care or pain.

So on the unwritten page of Time
   Given by the New Year do I trace
Thy message, with its power sublime
   To make each day a day of grace;

To make each day a link of light
   In love's great chain, that more and more
Our souls may feel the radiance bright
   Reflected from Heaven's golden shore;

Taking as motto for the year,
   And lesson for the hours of life,
That sentence, ringing like a cheer
   Across earth's sounding sea of strife—

The thought that thrills me as I read,
   That fills my mind with sweet desire,
And bids me humbly bend to plead
   For one spark of celestial fire;

One little ray of zeal divine
  To set my darkened soul ablaze,
And make this faltering heart of mine
  A holocaust of joyous praise;

That it may know no earthly love,
  No music save my Jesus' name,
And, yearning for his home above,
  His Mother's sweet protection claim;

Drawn nearer to her day by day,
  Nearer to her, nearer her Son:
Held safe beneath their gentle sway
  Till life's sad pilgrimage is done.

IN MISSION TIME.

WE had waited, watched and waited, for the golden
    hours of spring-time,
  For the glad mid-April moments and the blessing
    they would bring,
For the grand and glorious message, royal edict of
    the Master,
  Borne to us in love and mercy by the envoys of
    the King;

Till the first morn of the Mission, dawning over hill
    and valley
  Where in darkly ominous masses hung the rain-
    clouds brooding low,
Shot one long, broad ray of splendor over all the land
    around us,
  For a few brief moments lighting up the scene with
    vivid glow.

Happy omen of the beauty and the joy of heavenly
    rapture
  Which would pierce so many bosoms, waking them
    from dangerous sleep!
Then the storm arose in fury, shook abroad its misty
    banners,
  And the hail beat fiercely round us from the frozen
    upper deep.

But before the lighted altar all was calm and holy quiet,
  As, by cross and priest preceded, up the sounding aisle they came ;
The brave soldiers of Christ's legion, messengers of earth's Redeemer,
  Conquering hearts the hardest, sternest, by the power of Jesus' name.

Ah! our spirits gave them greeting as we gazed on them with reverence,
  Gathering from the lessons taught us messages of truth divine,
As, with tones where love vibrated—love of God and of his creatures—
  They poured forth on wounded spirits Faith's blest chrism of oil and wine.

Oh! with eloquence impassioned they portrayed the priceless value
  Of the soul, which Christ our Saviour became man to save from loss ;
Pointing out to us the dangers that surround life's flowery pathway,
  Showing how they may be vanquished by the all-protecting Cross

And the powerful intercession of the glorious Virgin Mary,
  Whose voice is ever pleading for the erring sons of men,
Who wins for sinners mercy, who averts from us God's anger,
  Who when we fall would lift us to love's lofty heights again—

The Virgin Mother Mary, the beautiful, the spotless,
   The Lily bloom of Israel, the angels' crownèd Queen,
Hailed by a thousand titles her attributes proclaiming,
   Mary given us as a Mother amid Calvary's tortures keen :

God's Mother, pure and clement, made ours by that adoption,
   Earth and Heaven alike are thrilling to her songs of praise sublime.
Oh! we felt her blessed influence by the ceaseless tide of graces,
   By the peace and joy and comfort, of the holy Mission time ;

By the reverent throng of worshippers the angel's "Hail" repeating,
   Their blended voices rising, from the greatest to the least ;
By the penitential spirits pardon in confession seeking ;
   By the hearts regenerate hastening to Love's Eucharistic Feast ;

By the glad, pure-hearted children round the shrine where, fair and fragrant,
   Shone a wealth of wreathèd blossoms, while the waxen tapers' light
Shed a soft, illumining radiance o'er the youthful votaries bending,
   Tendering to their holy Mother all life's morning fair and bright.

Shall we trace the daily lessons? Nay, for they are
    deeply graven
  On each faithful heart, imparting courage for the
    years to be,
Lessons linked and interwoven with rare gems of light
    celestial—
  Gems of Faith and Hope encircled by the gold of
    Charity.

Lessons ne'er to be forgotten. Lo! the Mission Cross
    bears witness
  Unto each and all, recalling what these grand Re-
    demptorists taught;
Glorious symbol of salvation, with such solemn rites
    erected,
  It will be to us for ever with the brightest memories
    fraught.

It will speak to us in pleading, or in voice of solemn
    warning,
  Breathe of sin and death and judgment, tell of
    pardon, joy restored
Through the prayers of our fond Mother, hope and
    solace of earth's pilgrims,
  Or, in eloquence undying, speak the mercies of the
    Lord.

As we gaze on it the picture of the solemn cere-
    monial
  Will arise upon our vision : we will see the reverent
    throng
Standing where the locust blossoms showered to earth
    their snowy petals,
  And the lofty pines seemed listening to the choirs'
    sweet strains of song;

See the earnest faces lifted as the Cross was borne
   amongst them,
  And the priest, white-robed and stately, following
   Faith's symbol came ;
Then, as 'neath the starry heavens in its place the
   Cross was planted,
  Mark the blazing tapers round it shining like a
   ring of flame—

Emblem of the Faith that quickened with its deep
   and strong pulsations
  Hearts whose parent blood was nurtured under
   many a foreign sun ;
Europe's varied nations blending here their children
   with the people
  Whose brave sires the Cross had planted when
   Spain first these wild shores won ;

Men of many lands united in one faith and hope and
   purpose,
  That where'er their steps might wander, and whatever might betide,
The true Cross would be their Labarum, be the sign
   by which to conquer
  All the legions of the foemen, all the demon hordes
   of pride.

"Holy Cross whose blessèd shadow falls with vivify-
   ing power,
  Wooing dews of grace to brighten the parched desert of the soul,
Which sin's simoom sweeping over had left seared and
   dry and arid,
  And the passions, chained no longer, rule with stern
   and fierce control,

"May thy shadow rest for ever with its great and
    countless blessings
  Upon all who stood around thee, upon every home
      and heart
Where salvation's sign is honored with meet homage
    due and reverent,
  And the peace thy presence bringeth from amidst
      us ne'er depart.

"Be to us, through gloom or sunlight, voice of warn-
    ing or of pleading ;
  Woo us to the joys of Heaven, warn us of the woes
      of crime ;
Be to us a sweet reminder of those precious days of
    graces,
  Of the heavenly joy and comfort of the holy Mission
      time ! "

ALL SOULS' DAY.

"We have loved them in life, let us love them even after death."—St. Ambrose.

WE keep as days of solemn prayer
   The anniversaries of our dead,
   Counting the moments that have fled
Since last we held them in our care,

Striving with tenderest love to ease
   Each fevered form, each pain-racked brow,
   Each heart so cold and pulseless now
When death has bade its sufferings cease.

And we are lonely in our grief,
   And murmur, "Never woe like ours
   O'ershadowed earth's love-haunted bowers;
No joy, alas! was e'er so brief."

But lo! on this November day
   One universal grief controls
   The great, wide world, which weeps all souls
Passed from their tenements of clay.

From pole to pole, from sea to sea,
   The cold, calm, crystal air is stirred,
   The same imploring prayer is heard
Of "Miserere Domine."

"Eternal Rest" all voices plead:
"For those whose labors past and o'er,
  Await us on the other shore,
Be thou, O Lord! their glorious meed."

All nations, howsoe'er remote,
  In the communion of the Saints
  Pour forth the solemn, dirge-like plaints
In mournful strains that heavenward float.

And, bound together by this tie
  Of Faith's fond prayer for those we love,
  While here we linger let us prove
Not deaf to their appealing cry; *

But, bending humbly at the shrine,
  With contrite hearts uplifted plead
  God's mercy for the souls in need,
And by the Sacrifice Divine

Offered by consecrated hands
  Upon the altar day by day,
  Beg of Love's Victim sweet to stay
The purging fires, and bid his bands

Of angels bear to him on high
  The spirits longing for their rest
  Within his presence, pure and blest,
Who rules alike the earth and sky.

Not fruitless for ourselves each prayer
  We offer for the souls in pain:
  For us will rise their grateful strain
When called the joys of Heaven to share.

---

* "Have pity on me, have pity on me, at least you my friends, for the hand of the Lord hath touched me."

Then through the sad November days
  Give, give your spiritual alms,
  Join in the universal psalms
Of pleading love will turn to praise,

And win for those whose loss we mourn
  The right to pass the shining gate
  With spotless robes, and stand elate
With joy at their celestial bourne.

NOVEMBER 2, 1884.

LEGENDS AND BALLADS.

THE CROSS.

A GASPESIAN LEGEND.

[The following curious incident is related in the *Annals of the Propagation of the Faith*, by Father Le Clercq, a Recollet monk.]

BENEATH the tall Canadian pines
   The council-fire burned bright,
And the old Cross, with moss o'ergrown,
   Shone crimson in its light.
Around it in deep silence sate
   Stern chiefs and warriors brave,
And 'mid them one, a priest of God
   From o'er the ocean's wave—
A Teacher of the Word of God,
   Who dared the deep's wild storm,
With Christ's undying love and faith
   The chill north winds to warm;
A teacher of the Word of God,
   Whose youth's impassioned glance
Had kindled 'mid the storied scenes
   Of glory-loving France.
But, at the summons from on high,
   Home, friends, and land left he,
To win new kingdoms for his Lord
   Beyond the rolling sea.
His banner was the Cross of Christ,
   Zeal for the Faith his sword,
His armor all invincible
   The Gospel of the Word.

His chapel was the spreading woods
  In grandeur dense and dim,
The river sang his Matins sweet,
  The birds his Vesper hymn.
No need of organ-notes had he
  'Mid nature's ringing choir,
When the weird zephyr's fingers smote
  The pine's impassioned lyre.
He sought the savage of the wild
  By forest, mount, and stream,
And lit the gloom of pagan night
  With Faith's celestial beam.
Chief 'mid the many tribes that ruled
  That rugged northern strand
Dwelt one which bore the honored name,
  Cross-bearers of the land.
He travelled through their wide domain,
  And found by town and fell
The emblem of God's peace with man:
  The Indians loved it well.
And on that evening, as they sat
  Around the mystic sign,
He questioned whence amid them came
  That symbol so divine.

Then spoke the wise man of the tribe:
  "It chanced, long years ago,
The pestilence with breath of fire
  Our mighty tribe laid low.
Day after day men sank to die
  By forest, hut, or cave,
And those who loved them could not stretch
  A pitying hand to save;

Day after day our teachers made
  Oblations at the shrine
Of deities tradition taught
  Our sires to deem divine.
But still the sun no mercy gave,
  The stars no healing shed,
The spirits of the hill and grove
  Looked calmly on our dead.
Till one called out in agony
  On Him whom all men fear—
The Manitou whose fingers guide
  The chariot of the year.
That night, when o'er the sleeping camp
  The pall of silence lay,
Around the wise men's slumbering forms
  Shone a celestial ray,
And in its golden light revealed
  A grand, majestic form:
No voice was needed to proclaim
  Him Ruler of the Storm.
In waves of beauty to his feet
  A seamless robe flowed down;
The glory of the opened heavens
  His kingly brow did crown;
Within his hand he bore a Cross,
  And bade our sleeping sires
Raise such a sign within their homes
  And near their council-fires,
And that the honor which they paid
  Unto the sign he gave
An offering of peace should be
  The dying tribe to save.

"The vision fled, the morning broke,
  The wise men gathered round,
And called in haste their followers
  Unto the council-ground.
Then in its centre there they raised
  Yon Cross, now mossed and old,
More precious to Gaspesian hearts
  Than wealth of gems or gold.
Yon honored symbol, gray with age,
  Looked on our nation's growth,
Won by its power from awful death
  To health and vigor both.
For this impressed upon our robes
  The sacred sign we bear,
And, safe from harm, 'mid dangers walk
  Beneath its sheltering care.
For this, when from our midst we send
  A messenger afar
To bear to other chiefs our words
  Of good-will or of war,
Our chieftain from his bosom takes
  The fairest Cross we own,
And to the bravest of his band
  The message maketh known;
Then round his neck he hangs the Cross,
  To guard, with holy spell,
His body from the foemen's snares,
  His soul from charms of hell.
We bear it when our light canoe
  Speeds down the summer tide;
In forest dense, or lone morass,
  'Tis ever at our side.

The treasure in whose healing balm
  Was found a power to save,
The object of our nation's love;
  Rests with us in the grave;
Else, when our footsteps free shall press
  That bright and golden strand,
Our kindred would not know their own
  Who join the spirit band."

PHILIP'S MOTHER.

WHERE the Connemara mountains rise in rude
    and rugged grandeur,
  Towering o'er the "Old Land's" beauty, stretching
    many a mile away,
In an humble, low-roofed cabin lay an aged widow
    dying
  When the evening shades trod westward in the foot-
    steps of the day.

By her bedside sat the pastor, speaking words of
    heavenly comfort—
  Words whose knowledge is the treasure of the sim-
    ple Irish poor,
When God's priest, who knows and loves them, in their
    sorrow stands amid them,
  Sharing with them all the trials they are called on
    to endure.

Long he spoke to her of Heaven, and the love the
    holy Saviour
  Bears to those for whom he suffered upon Calvary
    long ago;
How to him the poor are precious—then the good
    man's accents faltered,
  For he knew the widow's life had seen but poverty
    and woe.

In the days of want and anguish, when the famine
    swept the country,
  Husband, children—all had perished, dying, starving one by one.
Save the youngest, all were taken ; but our dear Lord,
    in his mercy,
  Left the poor, heart-broken mother Philip, now
    her only son.

She had borne her cross in patience, never murmuring against Heaven,
  In her tearless anguish saying, o'er and o'er: "It
    is God's will" ;
Struggling on through that black period, through that
    night of gloom and horror,
  Till the help came which brought succor and food
    to little Phil.

"Never," would the fond, proud mother say, "was son
    like to my Philip—
  So honest and so truthful, so loving and so kind ;
And though he has crossed the ocean, it is but to win
    me comforts,
  And soon he'll send to bring me to the home that
    he will find."

Now, while she strove to listen, her eager thoughts
    would wander
  Over the wide waste of waters to the far Pacific's
    strand,
Longing for a glance from blue eyes that would never
    more behold her,
  For one fond, close farewell pressure of her absent
    darling's hand;

Till at last she said: "O father! you will write and
    tell my Philip,
    Though the news will grieve him sorely, that his
        mother is no more;
And give him my farewell blessing—God and the
    Blessed Virgin
    Be his guardians till his journey on this earth is
        passed and o'er!

And tell him to be faithful to the promise that he
    made me
    When we parted by the hillside, this spring a year
        ago:
In his trials and in his crosses to think upon Christ's
    Passion,
    And make our holy Mother his advocate in woe.

Then I gave into his keeping the Rosary, once his
    father's,
    And he promised me that daily he would seek Our
        Lady's aid;
And he tells me in his letters he has never yet for-
    gotten
    To say it over daily when at evening's hour he
        prayed.

It was all I had to give him, but no linked and shin-
    ing jewels
    Ever could have been so precious as that Rosary
        to me;
'Tis a talisman to guard him, and bind him still more
    closely
    To his Faith and all its teachings in that country
        o'er the sea."

She paused in sudden weakness, as a footstep crossed
   the threshold,
  And a passing neighbor entered with a kind "God
   save all here!
I bring you news of Philip; here's a package for his
   mother—"
  Then he ceased, awe-struck and silent, when he saw
   death was so near.

But the worn, white face turned on him, and the fad-
   ing eyes grew brighter:
  "Kind neighbor, give it to me. Ah! 'tis not in
   Philip's hand!
Read the letter for me, father; my sight is dimming
   strangely.
  Is my poor boy ill and lonely in that far-off foreign
   land?"

Kind hands undid the package, when lo! from out
   its foldings
  The old brown Rosary slipping dropped down upon
   the bed,
Where the dying woman clasped it, and to her wan
   lips pressed it,
  Saying softly: "By this token I know my boy is
   dead.

"For never, were he living, would it have left his
   keeping."
  Then the pastor read the letter which a stranger's
   hand had penned,
Full of pitying expressions for the mother whose last
   darling
  In dying left the message it was his sad lot to send.

"We all loved Philip dearly, poor boy, he was so gentle,
  Counting each day's toil a pleasure, because he seemed to see
In the hard-won gains it brought him the home of ease and comfort
  To which his love would bring you from the island o'er the sea.

But one day the camp was startled by a sudden wail of terror,
  And the news spread far and swiftly that a bank had given way;
And men were stricken lifeless, or else were lying helpless,
  Closely prisoned by the timbers and the fallen mass of clay.

Soon ready hands were toiling to clear away the barrier,
  And the slain, disfigured miners were brought forward, one by one;
Then the last—the only living one of five who on that morning
  Went forth so glad and hopefully—was lifted out, your son.

All crushed and bleeding sorely, but his right arm was unbroken,
  And his hand held close the Rosary that was ever near his heart;
With painful gasps he murmured o'er the Aves as we bore him
  To the cabin whence so joyously we had seen the youth depart.

All the aid that man could render, or the comfort that
  religion
  Could give to soothe the sufferer, were freely
    brought him here;
And he gave his hoarded savings, and the beads that
    he so cherished,
  To send to his dear mother as his latest hour drew
    near.

Saying, as he gave the guerdon of his hours of weary
    toiling—
  'To those who served me you will pay their just
    and honest due,
And send the rest to mother, with the Rosary she gave
    me,
  And tell her that her Philip to his latest hour was
    true.'

Not one of those who watched him would touch the
    poor boy's money,
  But freely from their earnings an added mite they
    gave,
That your fading years might never want raiment,
    food, or shelter,
  But the love with which he loved you still reach
    you from the grave."

When he ceased the widow softly said: "God bless
    them for their kindness!
  Their pity for the stranger will meet reward above;
Take the gold they send me, father, for the hungry
    and the needy,
  And bid them pray for Philip, as they share his
    meed of love.

I will not grieve for Philip, I go so soon to meet him
  In the home of love and mercy I pray that he has won ";
Then in sweet Irish accents she murmured o'er the Aves
  On the beads that lay so lately on the heart of her dead son.

And when bells for Vespers sounded in far-off city steeples
  The passing Angel summoned the sad soul to its rest,
And friends laid her down to slumber where her kindred waited for her,
  With the Rosary she treasured clasped close upon her breast.

THE ROSE.

A LEGEND OF HILDESHEIM.

IN Hildesheim's old forest
  When morn was dawning gray,
With nodding plumes and pennons fair,
  There met a proud array.

With waving plumes and pennons fair,
  And bugle notes so free,
Knights thronged around their emperor,
  'Mid martial minstrelsy.

For Ludwig, the great monarch,
  While summer hours were fair,
Had summoned all his noble lords
  The forest's sports to share.

Each hill and valley sent its chief,
  And every tower and town,
Within those wild and lonely haunts
  To hunt the swift deer down.

But first, before the grand train swept
  From out the trysting-place,
Each hunter knelt to beg of God
  His blessing on the chase:

The spot was reached; the morning sun
   Shone bright o'er hill and wold,
But poured its fullest glory round
   The jewelled cup of gold—

The jewelled cup wherein reposed
   The Body of our Lord,
Standing where pearly dewdrops gemmed
   The velvet emerald sward,

While o'er it with protecting arms
   A lovely rose-tree spread;
Though born within the summer night,
   Its fragrant blossoms shed

Their wealth of incense on the air.
   Men marvelled as they gazed
Upon the arch of floral light
   O'er the ciborium raised.

For yester-morn nor branch nor flower
   Upon the spot was seen,
Where now its brilliant blossoms hung
   On boughs of tenderest green.

All knelt in humblest reverence
   Around their treasure there,
'Mid silence in itself as sweet
   And thrilling as a prayer;

Till, swelling upward glad and high,
   A hymn of thanks arose;
From hearts o'erflowed with joy it rang
   Across the morn's repose.

While yet its accents heavenward soared,
    Ludwig the Pious came
And knelt with those who humbly sang
    Thanksgiving to God's name.

They told the emperor the tale,
    They showed the rose-tree fair,
Whose wondrous blossoms poured their wealth
    Of fragrance on the air.

Then Ludwig gave his order high :
    "Here shall a chapel stand,
In memory of this marvel wrought
    By the Almighty's hand."

  .   .   .   .   .   .

Years passed ; the forest arches old .
    Before the axe went down ;
The wilderness, in time, became
    A proud cathedral town.

Where Ludwig's chapel first was reared
    A mighty fane arose,
But, trained upon its carven side,
    Still bloomed the wondrous rose.

And still it blooms in beauty rare,
    Though centuries have shed
Their winter frosts and summer smiles
    Around its fragrant head.

Still 'neath the Altar doth its root
    Strike deep into the earth ;
The sanctuary has been its home
    Since its glad hour of birth.

O blessed boon! for aye to dwell
In peace anear God's Throne,
To hear the songs by angels sung
When midnight's hours are lone.

Then round the Tabernacle's walls
Their heavenly accents ring,
Commingling with their golden harps
Hosannas to the King.

("The oldest known rose-tree in the world is one at present growing against the wall of the cathedral of this town [Hildesheim], remarkable alike for its extreme age and the scanty nourishment with which it has supported itself for so many centuries. Tradition states that in the year of grace 814 the Emperor Ludwig the Pious, son of Charlemagne, was staying with his court at Elze. Being desirous of hunting in the great forest where now stands Hildesheim, Mass was said by the imperial chaplain at the place of rendezvous. By some mishap, when the service was concluded, the vessel containing the Sacred Elements was left behind. On returning to the spot the next day great was the surprise of the chaplain to find the sacred vessel overshadowed by the tender branches of a lovely rose which had sprung up during the night, and now filled the air with the perfume of its flowers. The emperor shortly after arrived, and by his command a chapel was built, with the altar standing on the spot occupied by the roots of the rose—that very rose which is now blooming as freshly as though a single decade and not a thousand years had passed over its head. So far tradition. Certain it is that the roots of the rose-tree are buried under the altar of the cathedral, and consequently are inside the building, the stem being carried through the wall to the outer air by a perforation made expressly for that purpose. The plant is held in the highest veneration by the inhabitants, and no one is permitted to gather its flowers or break its branches."—*Herr Lennis.*)

LEGEND OF SAN GABRIEL.

("San Gabriel, in the year 1776, witnessed an extraordinary event. To avenge an outrage committed by a soldier the Indians rose and came in great numbers to destroy the Mission. The Fathers alone, but in their sacred vestments, met the throng of enraged warriors, and at an opportune moment held up before them a shining image of the Blessed Virgin. As if by a miracle the fierce hearts were subdued at once; they knelt and cried, and embraced the Fathers, with whom they ever after dwelt on terms of the closest friendship."
—*B. H.*)

WHERE the south in fadeless beauty
    Smiles unceasing praise to God,
Fair as when its billowy verdure
    First by mortal feet was trod;
Amid scenes our Father fashioned
    Into beauty's perfect mould,
Gemming them with tropic splendor,
    Stands the Mission gray and old.

Many years of change have written
    Records in the book of age
Since its walls gave back an echo
    To the Indians' yells of rage
When the chiefs of hill and valley
    Their rude warriors hither brought
To avenge a guilty outrage
    By a Spanish soldier wrought.

On the dwellers in the Mission
    Fell a chilling pall of fear
As the angry foe closed round them:
    Mortal aid nor help was near.

For the few but brave defenders
  Of that outpost dared not hope
With success against the myriads
  Of their enemy to cope.

To the mighty God of battle
  Rose their pleading in that hour,
On his aid alone relying
  To escape the savage power
Of the Indians who were nearing,
  Shouting loud their demon cry,
Gloating in their hearts already
  O'er the victims doomed to die;

Challenging their foes to conflict—
  When a vision met their sight:
Not of armèd men whose weapons
  Glittered in the sun's clear light,
But in albs of snowy whiteness,
  Gleaming chasuble and stole—
Robes which well befit God's altar
  When the organ's anthems roll—

Came the Fathers of the Mission,
  Calm as though they trod the while
'Mid their people kneeling round them
  In the chapel's crowded aisle;
In their hands no warlike weapons,
  Drum nor bugle cheered their way,
O'er their heads no flaunting banners
  With the breezes danced at play.

But they bore a shining image
  Of the Virgin pure and fair;
She it was who gave their spirits
  Courage thus the foe to dare.

Loudly rang the scornful laughter
  Of the Indians as they gazed
On the soldiers of the Saviour;
  Then their weapons all were raised,

And, as nearer drew the Fathers,
  Every trusty bow was bent;
But before the barbèd arrow
  Speeding to its goal was sent,
Fell the hands so late uplifted,
  Weapons all to earth were flung,
And one cry of awe and wonder
  From the savage concourse rung.

For the glory of the sunshine,
  Cent'ring in a column bright,
O'er the image of the Virgin
  Poured a flood of living light,
Till it seemed to glow and quicken
  With the throbbing pulse of life,
While from out the foemen's spirits
  Fled each thought of blood and strife.

And they gazed, and gazed in wonder,
  As with hastening steps they trod,
Offering their hearts' glad homage
  To the ministers of God.
And the friendship which they plighted,
  At Our Lady's feet that day
They have kept with faith unswerving
  As the long years rolled away.

THE HAPPIEST CHRISTMAS.

WE dwelt in the forest, wild and free,
    Where the great Columbia rushing pours
    Its waters down betwixt wooded shores,
To blend with the waves of the moaning sea.

Of rough-hewn logs was our cabin rude,
    But, oh! it was warm and bright within,
    And sheltered us safe from the tempest's din
When it rang through that dismal solitude.

And we were happy, Lucile and I,
    And our merry children, one and all—
    Jean and Marie, Antoine and Paul—
As the busy moments went flitting by.

But the heart of each was centred and tied
    In the smiles of the baby, the loved *petite*,
    The blue-eyed, golden-haired Marguerite,
The child we cherished with tender pride.

For the others were rosy and strong and tall;
    With dusky tresses and eyes of night;
    While Marguerite was a ray of light,
Winsome and gentle, frail and small.

But there was one shadow that would intrude;
    A bitter grief bore my wife and I:
    There no cross-crowned spire, lifted high,
Blessings to earth and its people wooed.

No priest of God in that lonely wild
   Lifted his consecrated hand ;
   And we mourned, for two of our little band
Were still by original sin defiled.

On their baby brows was no seal impressed,
   Marking them heirs of God's home above,
   And the waters of Baptism's fount of love
Had not quickened the faith in each infant breast.

But we taught them their prayers, and how to sing
   The beautiful hymns to the sweet Christ-Child,
   And the *Aves* sweet of the Mother mild
Blent, too, with the praise of the Saviour-King.

And as oft as the Christmastide drew near,
   In the fair home-chamber of the house
   We fashioned a Crib of the cedar-boughs—
The Crib to the pure heart of childhood dear.

And they gathered around it to hear again
   The story so often told to them
   Of the birth of the Babe of Bethlehem,
And join in his praises loud and clear.

How I loved to kneel with my children there!
   For the blessed picture called me home
   To where the Saint Lawrence' waters foam,
To my father's house and my father's prayer.

Oh! you who have dwelt your whole life long
   Under the sheltering arms of the Cross
   Know naught of the wearying sense of loss
Filling the heart where Faith is strong ;

The longing, when sickness and death draw near,
    And the limbs are bound with pain's cruel band,
    For the touch of the priest's anointed hand,
And the sound of his voice to banish fear.

It was Christmas eve, and the tapers shone
    Round the humble Crib and the faces there;
    Outside of our dwelling the icy air
Wailed and cried with a pitiful moan.

But we clustered beside the blazing hearth,
    Where the dogs who served me nobly and well
    In the dangerous chase by flood and fell,
Slept on in spite of the children's mirth,

Who sang together the carols sweet—
    The dear French carols of long ago—
    While Jean played the violin gently, low,
Smiling into the blue eyes of Marguerite.

Then came a pause, for warily slow
    The hounds arose and gazed to the north;
    I opened the door, and they bounded forth,
Silent but eager, into the snow.

I followed with Jean, who's a hunter born;
    He, pointing away o'er the solitude,
    Said: "It is some one lost in the wood.
List! That is the voyageur André's horn."

Then, seizing my bugle, I blew a blast;
    Loud and shrill through the night it rang,
    And soon the voyageur's answer sang
A joyous peal over dangers past.

We lifted a blazing torch on high,
  And out of the forest, lo! there came,
  Straight to that glittering point of flame,
My old friend André with cheery cry,

Marshalling a weary and wayworn band,
  Whose furry garments, frosted white,
  Made them seem like phantoms of the night
Marching down through the shadowy land.

Within on the hearth the fire blazed clear,
  And already, with eager haste, Lucile
  Was making ready a welcoming meal,
As she heard of the wanderers drawing near.

A clasp of the hand, a murmured word,
  And I turned from André to greet the rest,
  When, behold! in their midst stood an honored guest,
The sound of whose voice all my being stirred.

The voice was the voice of a priest of God,
  Saying: "Peace and joy to your home to-night!
  God's blessing, my son, on your heart alight!"
My soul bloomed with pleasure, like Aaron's rod.

And I knelt at his feet and sobbed aloud,
  Crying: "Welcome, most welcome!" o'er and o'er,
  "Man of God, to this desolate shore."
And one and all for his blessing bowed.

Then André spoke: "To the fort in the west
  We were journeying down when I thought of you here,
  And hastened to bring you the comforting cheer
Of seeing your children made Christians blest."

And, lifting my golden-haired babe to his knee,
   "I thought of thee most, my pet, my sweet—
   I thought of thee most, my Marguerite,
For the dear Child-Jesus is waiting for thee."

The good priest smiled as he heard him speak,
   And questioned the children, one and all—
   Jean and Marie, Antoine and Paul—
And patted the baby's dimpled cheek.

When Christmas morning rose in the east
   The candles were lighted, the white cloth spread,
   And o'er heart and home were the blessings shed
That flow from the Eucharistic feast!

And then o'er my children's brows were poured
   The saving waters that wash away
   The stain of original sin's foul sway,
And they were made heirs of Christ our Lord.

O Christmas Day, so bright, so blest!
   Yours was the only, the perfect joy,
   That knew no trace of the earth's alloy,
For you brought to our spirits peace and rest;

And glancing back o'er the years that have flown,
   With sun or shadow, smiles or regret,
   We count your morning the happiest yet
Of all the Christmas days we have known.

"And what of Marguerite?" Child of grace,
   Her voice is heard 'mid the angels now;
   The light of heaven illumes her brow:
Ah! she sleeps in the graveyard at Saint Ignace.

THE HAUNTED DELL.

A CALIFORNIAN LEGEND.

YOU marvel at the beauty rare
　　By Nature lavished everywhere
　　　Within this quiet dell.
But marvel not, for it is true
That, hidden here from mortal view,
　　　The mountain fairies dwell,
Guarding from sacrilegious hand
This pathway of enchanted land
　　　With magic's wondrous dower;
And here, from eve till dawning gray,
On all who pass this lonely way
　　　They fling their spell of power.
For them athwart the leafy glooms
The Æsculus uplifts its plumes
　　　Tinted like Alpine snow;
For them along the rough hill-side
The branching ferns spread rank and wide
　　　To hide their caves below.
Many have felt a spell of fear
Fall on their hearts while wandering here
　　　While twilight's shadows lay
In purple lines of light and shade,
Through which the first faint starlight played
　　　Down on the haunted way;

Have felt their life-blood quivering dart
In icy terror to their heart,
　　Yet saw no cause of dread,
And heard no sound, save when the breeze
Waked the weird music of the trees
　　That crown the mountain's head;
Or 'mid the fern-leaves clustering dark
Have seen the glow-worm's trembling spark,
　　But never dreamt that there
The fairies of the haunted way
Held them as victims to their sway,
　　Close bound in gyves of air.

'Tis many a year since first I trod
The flowery beauty of this sod,
　　And then a youth I came,
With life's first ardor in my breast,
To dwell within the glorious West,
　　The savage foe to tame.
My childhood, passed beyond the main
Amid the sunny scenes of Spain,
　　Gleams bright in memory still;
Where conquest crowned her arms of yore,
At springs of legendary lore
　　My spirit quaffed its fill.
I wandered 'mid Granada's towers,
Trod through the lone Alhambra's bowers,
　　And listened to the fall
Of fountains plashing sweet and clear
In waves of music on the ear
　　Within its haunted hall;
Or from its latticed windows high
Looked forth upon the midnight sky,
　　Yet never felt the spell

Of such wild terror in my soul
As held me in its weird control
  One night within this dell—
The midnight of a glorious day,
When I had wandered far away
  In quest of sylvan game,
Unnoting still how far I strayed,
By hill and stream and flowery glade,
  Till evening's shadows came;
And then yon mountain's rugged dome
Uprose betwixt me and my home,
  While far to westward lay
The fertile plain, whose bounding streams
Glanced in the sun's expiring beams
  Upon their seaward way.
Then slowly back my course I drew
This wild and wondrous pathway through;
  And, loosening in its sheath
My trusty weapon, lest the shade
Might hide some Indian ambuscade,
  Rode on with bated breath,
While through the azure arch o'erhead,
With presence calm, and stately tread,
  Night passed upon her way;
Her raven tresses braided fair
With clustered stars of lustre rare,
  Whose brightly glowing ray
Half-lit the mantling robes of gloom
That veiled the beauty and the bloom
  Which lay on either side.
And then in robes of silver light,
Twin-sister of the lovely Night,
  Came Luna like a bride;

Her smile of rapturous radiance fell,
Illuminating all the dell,
  Till every tiny flower
Nestled amid the fern-leaves green
Flashed, jewelled by the dewdrops' sheen,
  Beneath its wondrous power.

Onward I rode. My heart kept time
To a strange, mystic Spanish rhyme,
  A tale of days of old
When Moorish chief and Christian knight,
For God, for country, and for right,
  Wrought deeds of daring bold.
It was a tale of love and fear,
Of Moorish hate and vengeance drear—
  A tale of wizard charms
That checked in mid-career the steed
When gallant knights were most in need,
  And palsied valiant arms.
So rode I, till by yonder oak,
Now blighted as by tempest stroke,
  My faithful steed stood still!
In vain I strove with whip and spur
To urge him on: he would not stir,
  Held by an iron will.
Moveless he stood; each nerve was strained;
His proud neck arched like charger reined
  By some carved marble knight,
Where then, in summer green, yon tree
Flung its bold shadow fair and free
  Against the moon's soft light.
My hot blood, kindling into rage,
Made every moment seem an age;
  And then I dared to say

THE HAUNTED DELL.

Words of such fierce, impotent ire
As burn upon my brain in fire
  E'en to this very day.
These angry words re-echoed round;
Each rock and tree caught up the sound
  With wild, discordant clang,
Reverberating wide and high,
Went up into the midnight sky,
  While bursts of laughter rang.
You dare not say I was not brave,
You dare not call me coward, slave,
  Nor mock me that my blood
Rushed back in one swift, surging start
Of icy terror to my heart,
  As lonely there I stood
And heard, in such a spot of earth,
The clearly ringing strains of mirth,
  Or held with firmer grasp
My ready weapon hard and close,
And gazed around to seek the foes
  Who held me in their grasp.

But while I gazed the hill apart
Seemed rent, and in its opened heart
  I saw a flashing throne,
On which a woman, fair and bright
As ever gladdened mortal sight,
  In peerless beauty shone.
Above her lofty brow was set
A glittering, golden coronet,
  Where gems of brilliant dyes
Gleamed forth in many a sparkling ray;
But oh! their splendor paled away
  In presence of her eyes:

And from beneath her regal crown
Her jetty tresses floated down,
   While jewels beyond price
Clasped her rich mantle's crimson fold,
Which broidered shone with threads of gold
   In fair and quaint device.
White neck and arms were gleaming bare,
Half-shaded by her flowing hair,
   And in her hand she held
A sceptre; but upon it shone
Nor glittering gold nor precious stone:
   It seemed a rod of eld—
Such rods are wizards wont to wave
At midnight in some haunted cave,
   Whene'er they seek to wrest,
By magic's supernatural art,
The secrets of the human heart
   From some foul demon's breast.
On either side their sovereign's throne
Stood maidens seven, whose broidered zone
   Bright-gleaming emblems bore;
There shone the zodiac's mystic signs,
Blending with purple-clustered vines
   And birds of sea and shore.
Fair flowed their robes of snowy white,
Bright shone their eyes in lustrous light,
   And oh! they sweetly sang,
As mingling with their flowing rhyme,
In music's most exquisite time,
   Their silvery harp-strings rang;
Re-echoed through the long arcades
Of pillared halls whose colonnades
   Sent back an answer clear,

And softly came the laughing fall
Of fountains whose low babbling call
   Rose in the gardens near.
And, save the sound of harp and song,
Which 'wildering echoes did prolong,
   All, all was silence there;
The myriad courtiers thronging round
Seemed held in silent awe profound
   Before their Empress fair.
It was a scene so bright, so strange,
So far surpassing fancy's range,
   It seemed to mock at death;
Around the hall fair faces shone,
And on each passing breeze was blown
   The rarest perfume's breath.
And I stood there as mute and still
As the grey rocks on yonder hill,
   Till in my bosom sprang
A longing wish to fling me down
Before the wearer of the crown,
   Charmed by the songs they sang.
But mingling with that longing came
A shuddering terror through my frame;
   Ah! now I know, indeed,
'Twas my good angel then who strove
To win me back to life and love,
   And save me in my need.
My better nature sought control
Of the mad feelings of my soul,
   And stilled my throbbing heart;
Then, as in agony I pressed
My right hand close against my breast,
   I felt with sudden start

A tiny Cross my mother gave
(She sleepeth now within her grave
  Beyond the rolling sea);
She bade me wear it near my heart,
And, as I loved her, ne'er to part
  With it while life should be.
And she had bade me daily pray
That God would guard and guide my way,
  And keep my soul from stain;
But reckless I of heavenly care,
Had seldom thought of daily prayer
  Since I had left old Spain.
But now within this lonely dell,
When struggling 'gainst the tempter's spell
  That held me in its thrall,
Crying: "Haste, haste! allegiance own
Before our radiant Sovereign's throne:
  O hearken to our call!"
How writ in words of burning flame,
Back on my clouded vision came
  The prayers I said in youth,
When kneeling at my mother's knee,
In the old home beyond the sea,
  I loved the Lord of Truth.
Now in what agony I cried
To him to pardon me my pride,
  And save my soul from loss;
The while with eager haste I drew
This precious treasure forth to view,
  Man's sign of hope, the Cross.
But scarcely had the words of prayer
Died quivering on the midnight air,
  When lo! the vision fled.

The glowing scene of love and light,
The fairy halls in splendor bright,
  Back into darkness sped ;
And starting with a sudden bound
My good steed left the enchanted ground.
  Forward! away! away!
O'er rock and brake his hoof-beats rang,
As down the mountain path he sprang
  To meet the coming day ;
While from my spirit's every chord
Rose mute thanksgiving to the Lord,
  Who led my straying soul
Back from temptation's luring snare,
Back to the kind and loving care
  Of Truth's supreme control.

THE POOR MAN'S TREASURES.

MY life, I know, is one of toil
   And hardship day by day,
But when the evening shadows fall
   My cares flee far away;

For as the first, faint silvery star
   Shines in the azure dome,
I clasp the little ones who throng
   To bid me "Welcome Home."

Far down within the shadowy glen
   My humble cottage stands,
Its rough-hewn sides and lowly roof
   The labor of my hands.

But vines that loving fingers train
   Around its casements cling,
And swallows build beneath its eaves
   And round it linnets sing—

And round it linnets sing at morn
   Their sweetest matin song,
But sweeter far the ringing tones
   That to my babes belong.

They are the bugle-notes that urge
   My heart to daily toil;
For them I rend the stubborn oak
   Or glean the river's spoil.

For them in winter's chilly hours
   My narrow fields I sow,
For them I reap the harvests sent
   In summer's sultry glow.

How often when with aching arms
   The gleaming axe I wield,
When hopes are few, and, coward-like,
   I fear that I must yield,

With laughter rippling from their lips,
   Light-hearted girls and boys,
Down through the waving woods they come
   My band of household joys.

They sing to me some simple strain
   Their mother loves to sing;
They share with me their berries wild,
   Bring water from the spring;

And while I list their eager talk
   Of birds and trees and flowers,
I feel a brightness o'er me steal,
   As sunlight follows showers.

And when at night we gather round
   The cheerful household hearth,
In well-earned rest my spirit tastes
   The sweetest peace of earth;

When, with our little ones around,
   My gentle wife and I
Join in the strains of praise we learned
   Beneath a foreign sky.

For we have reared a little shrine,
    And there our Lady stands,
Clasping unto her spotless breast
    The Ruler of all lands.

And, clustered round it, my dear babes
    Carol in accents clear
The hymns of Faith, and Hope, and Love
    To Christian hearts so dear.

I almost fancy our sweet Lord
    Looks down with tenderer glance,
Where lighting up each childish face
    The flickering tapers dance;

As though He smiled approvingly
    Upon their simple prayer,
And our dear Mother seems to claim
    Each as her special care.

And oh! I pray her tender hand
    Will lead them evermore,
And guard my treasures till they rest
    Upon the heavenly shore.

DOLORES.

THE beauty of the valley seemed to broaden and to brighten,
  As the morning sun came smiling o'er the hill-tops in the east,
And the breezes whispered softly to the blossoms nectar-laden
  Where the humming-bird was sipping his epicurean feast.

At her window, weak and weary, sat the pale Dolores waiting;
  She had watched the distant mountains since the coming of the dawn,
And her fevered frame drank deeply of the ambrosial wine the goddess
  Offered as her train went sweeping o'er the dusky woodland lawn.

Dolores—never surely was name so fitly given,
  For the little maiden seldom knew an hour of perfect rest
From the moment when her father to his aching bosom raised her,
  Newly born and newly orphaned, from her mother's pulseless breast.

In vain had Tia Juana tried the simples of her people,
  Each draught of power, each lotion, alike in turn essayed;
But the bent form never straightened, and the limbs, as years rolled onward,
  To the pain-distorted body refused to lend their aid.

She was waiting now the summons to make life's final journey,
  For her hours on earth were numbered, and the sands were running fast.
Ah! she felt the balmy beauty of that tranquil Sunday morning,
  And that glorious summer sunrise on earth would be her last.

Never had the vale seemed fairer, or the mountains, in their grandeur,
  More like old and trusted kinsmen, than when gazing on them now;
While each heart-throb came pain-laden, and the hand of Death was tracing
  In dewdrops cold and clammy his signet on her brow.

'Neath the giant oak-trees yonder her nurse had often borne her
  When the drowsy air was heavy with the fragrance of the spring,
Where, pillowed 'mid the grasses, she could hear the bees low humming,
  And the music of the wild birds soaring up on joyous wing.

There, beside the babbling streamlet, she had listened to the legends
  Of Our Lady's life in Israel; but the tale she loved the best
Was the story of the sorrows of the Mater Dolorosa,
  Whose dolors all her being's tender sympathy possessed.

From it she learned the lesson to bear her lot in patience,
  Remembering that the sorrows of Our Lady far surpassed,
In their awful depth of anguish, all the trials, all the sufferings
  Which upon the sons of mortals by the Maker's hand are cast.

'Twas the day the Church has given to the holy Queen of Sorrows,
  The feast-day of her Patroness, and eager hope and fear
Were blended with the longing to behold her Blessèd Mother,
  Growing stronger still and stronger as the last sad hour drew near.

Then along the valley, glowing in September's dreamy beauty,
  Pealed the Mission bells' sweet greeting, the Ave hour of morn.
For fifteen years Dolores had heard their chimes glad sounding,
  Across the sunlit plaza and o'er the red roofs borne;

Now they heralded the coming of a Guest with untold
    blessings—
  The Lord of Hosts, his splendor in humble symbols
    veiled,
Borne to the silent chamber where the dying maiden
    waited
  The coming of the King whose love for sinful man
    prevailed.

He came, and in his presence all terror of death vanished,
  And, as an infant sinks to sleep upon its mother's
    breast,
From ceaseless pain and sorrow, and nights of sleepless watching,
  Dolores, sad no longer, went forth to endless rest.

ASHES OF ROSES.

I GAVE her a rose to keep,
  And bade her remember well
Our parting upon the steep
  In sight of the ocean's swell.

I saw its red petals shine
  'Gainst the snow of her dainty hand,
And tears fall fast on that gift of mine
  As my vessel left the land.

I sailed o'er the sounding seas
  Till a twelvemonth had passed away,
And summer was on the breeze
  When once more in that quiet bay,

In shade of the rocky steep,
  My good ship to anchor came,
And up to my loved one's door
  I hastened with heart aflame.

The earth seemed devoid of pain,
  The skies were of cloudless blue,
And I murmured: "Again, again
  I will look on my love so true."

I looked on my loved one's face:
  White blossoms were in her hair,
White robes on her form of grace—
  Oh! she was a bride most fair.

But veiled were her glorious eyes,
   And hushed was her pulsing breath:
Her spirit had sought the skies
   From the arms of her bridegroom, Death.

They told me through hope deferred,
   Through watching and waiting long,
Her faith in my truth ne'er swerved,
   Her trust in my love was strong.

And when the dread summons came
   She left me the rose to keep—
The rose o'er whose heart of flame
   I had seen her bend and weep.

The red rose is ashes now,
   And close on my breast they lie—
Love's farewell pledge till we meet
   In the beautiful land on high.

LAS LAGRIMAS.

(A low group of hills situated a short distance south of San José, from the summit of which a band of the earliest Mexican settlers of the country, after having endured many dangers and privations, beheld for the first time the infant colony of San José. Overcome with gratitude for deliverance from so many perils, and joy at beholding so near their future home, the emigrant exiles gave vent to their feelings in tears. Hence the name " Lagrimas.")

WORN pilgrims from the tropic land
    That smiles beside the Mexic sea,
Allured by Hope's extended hand,
    They sought this country wild and free;

Came here to dwell amid these vales
    Where smiling Plenty reigned supreme,
Where wild flowers' perfumes filled the gales
    That dallied by each mountain stream.

They left the scenes of childhood fair,
    Severing the tenderest ties of home,
And nerved their gallant hearts to dare
    The toilsome pathway they must roam.

They crossed the deserts drear and wide,
    The rivers rolling dark and deep,
The Indians' savage power defied
    In forest lone, on rocky steep;

Till, after marches wild and drear,
    Through many a peril by the way,
Standing upon the hill-top here
    They saw thee first, O San José!

But bade no stirring shout resound
  In notes of triumph wild and high;
The silent echoes slumbering round
  Sent back no answer to the sky

The joy that thrilled each gazer's heart,
  And pulsed along each throbbing vein,
But caused the burning tears to start
  From every eye in gladsome rain.

And kneeling humbly on this sod,
  Their joy triumphing over fear,
They gave thanksgiving unto God,
  Who safely led their footsteps here.

A century has almost passed
  Since hither came that pilgrim band,
And from this spot their glances cast
  Upon their glowing promised land.

They dwelt in yonder city fair,
  They trod the scenes that now we tread,
They worshipped in yon house of prayer,
  And slumber calmly with our dead.

The swiftly passing hours have wrought
  Full many a great and wondrous change;
The seeds of enterprise they brought
  Have flowered in beauty bright and strange.

The city spreads its mighty arms,
  And far, by woodland and by hill,
Gleams out the wealth of fruitful farms
  Where Labor reaps her garner's fill.

Homesteads engirt by orchards fair
  Are clustered o'er the valley wide,
And gleaming through the crystal air
  Rise spire and dome in stately pride.

Another people rule the land,
  Another language fills the air;
The children of that daring band
  Are widely scattered everywhere.

But, grateful to God's saving power
  When pleasure triumphed over fears,
Still, still in memory of that hour
  They call this spot the "Hill of Tears."

THE BATTLE OF CLAVIJO.

A LEGEND OF SAINT JAMES OF COMPOSTELLA.

THE proud King of Cordova, the Arab Abderrahman,
   Gloating o'er the hapless people whom his power had overthrown,
Drunk with the wine of victory, sent his envoys with this message
   To Ramira, Christian monarch of the kingdom of Leon :

"I demand, O king ! a tribute, not of shining gold nor silver,
   Nor of gems whose wondrous radiance lights the hidden vaults of earth,
But a hundred beauteous maidens thou shalt yearly send unto me—
   Maidens peerless in their beauty, maidens noble in their birth."

The [hot blood of Ramira burnèd red in cheek and forehead
   As, rising from his royal throne, he cried : "Begone, and bear
To the tyrant Abderrahman our hatred and defiance,
   Our scorn and hate undying ; and tell him that we dare,

"By the aid of Santiago, to keep our realm so guarded
  That, in spite of all his armies, no foul, polluting hand
May bear Cordova's ruler one of the lovely maidens
  Whose purity and beauty are the treasures of our land.

"Ho, warders! drive these envoys beyond our palace portals,
  Beyond our kingdom's outposts, and be our mandate known
To our subjects true and loyal that they hasten, armed and ready,
  To defend the stainless honor of the daughters of Leon."

Sullen and dark and angry the envoys left his presence,
  Bearing to their haughty monarch the defiance of the king.
And soon the Arab legions, rank on rank, by thousands moving,
  Like the wind from off the desert bearing ruin on its wing.

Across Leon's fair border brought death and desolation,
  And the Spanish host, defeated, fled from Alaveda's field.
O day of woe and anguish! for, by countless foes surrounded,
  It seemed that with the morrow the Christian chief must yield.

From the height on which he rested he could see the mighty army
  Of the Moors rejoicing proudly o'er the victory of the day.
Mortal power was none to aid him; all his hopes in Heaven were centred,
  And to Saint James, his patron, he humbly knelt to pray.

Night fell; Ramira, wearied with the toils of battle, slumbered
  As calmly as an infant pillowed on its mother's breast,
When lo! Spain's great apostle, in majesty and grandeur,
  Came in the dream whose glory crowned his noble client's rest.

"Fear not," he said, "true-hearted—fear not: renew the battle,
  For help from Heaven to-morrow will aid thy little band.
God hears thy prayers and answers; his strong right hand will rescue
  From captivity and ruin the daughters of thy land."

Ramira rose rejoicing, and summoned to his presence
  The prelates and the captains of his army, one and all,
Then told his blessèd vision, and the promise of his patron
  That no stain of fell dishonor on his chosen land should fall.

Swiftly, swiftly sped the tidings, and the men, but late
   disheartened
  By defeat and threatened ruin, with one voice of
   glad acclaim,
In thanksgiving and appealing, bade the startled
   echoes round them
  Ring and thrill as heavenward soaring floated Santiago's name.

Santiago! Santiago! With a sound of dread and
   warning
  To the foemen came the war-cry of the valiant
   Spanish band,
As, with weapons flashing brightly in the rosy glow of
   morning,
  Down they swept for God and country, love of king
   and fatherland.

All in vain the Arab leaders massed their forces to
   resist them ;
On they came, but one in spirit, one in thought and
   deed and aim,
While from lip to lip went echoing the word that
   nerved and fired them,
  With their latest breath repeating Santiago's honored name.

And where'er the fight was thickest and the danger
   grew most pressing,
  There Saint James was seen in grandeur far surpassing mortal knight,
Mounted on a snowy charger, and the Spanish army
   leading·
  With a banner where the red cross shone upon a
   field of white.

With the golden light and glory of the heavens shining round him,
  With a glance like lightning dealing death upon the Arab foe,
Rode Spain's patron and apostle o'er Clavijo's field of battle,
  While the gallant Spaniards followed, fired by valor's deathless glow.

Before that glorious vision the Moslems fled in terror,
  Leaving on the field of carnage sixty thousand of their slain;
While a voice of rapt thanksgiving, of thanksgiving and rejoicing,
  Rose and swelled from joyous spirits o'er the sunny hills of Spain.

Then the king and army, kneeling, made a solemn vow to Heaven,
  Yielding as an annual tribute unto Compostella's shrine
In the golden time of harvest, from each acre of the kingdom,
  One full measure each of corn and the red blood of the vine.

Thus, a grateful offering rendering from the land the saint had rescued
  From the stern rule of the Moslem, from the captive's awful doom,
Every heart in Spain united in fond, filial devotion
  To enrich their dearest temple, blessèd Santiago's tomb.

LITTLE ELSIE.

RUDDILY the firelight glowed
In the cottage by the road;
Round the hearth the children sat,
Speeding time with song and chat—
Merry children, girls and boys.
Long they spoke of Christmas joys,
Wondering what gift would be
Hung for each upon the tree
When good Santa Claus would come
With his bugle, fife, and drum:
Wondrous dolls and fairy-tales,
Pictures of the sunlit dales
Where they loved to roam in spring
When the birds were on the wing,
And the fragrant blossoms sung
Ballads in a flowery tongue—
All the bright and varied toys
Which he gives to girls and boys.

One by one their wish they made
While the firelight danced and played:
Speaking all so loud and fast,
Little Elsie's turn came last—
Little Elsie, slight and fair,
With blue eyes and golden hair—
And she said: "I long to see
Hung upon the Christmas tree

A new robe, all fair and white,
Decked with blossoms sweet and bright:
Such a robe as should be worn
On the lovely Christmas morn,
When the angelic choirs sing
Welcome to the new-born King,
And the hearts of all should glow
Pure as the untrodden snow;
Thus to welcome from the skies
Him who came in infant guise,
Him who in his Sacred Heart
Gives to youth the larger part."

Elsie's mother sat and smiled
At the prattle of her child;
No foreboding shadow fell
With its drear and darkening spell,
Bidding waves of sorrow roll
To o'erwhelm her tranquil soul.

But when Christmas morning glowed
On the cottage by the road,
Not a merry accent stirred,
Not a sound of joy was heard.
O'er the silent, firelit room
Lay a heavy pall of gloom:
Little Elsie, robed in white,
Decked with blossoms sweet and bright,
Lay upon the flower-crowned bier;
And the children wondering near,
Grieving, weeping girls and boys,
Thought no more of Christmas joys,

For their Elsie, bright and fair—
Elsie of the golden hair,
Of the voice of rippling song,
Life of all the household throng—
In the midnight's solemn hour
Left her home's love-guarded bower,
Borne aloft by angel hands
Where the Throne of Glory stands,
Where the joyous anthems ring
In the presence of the King,
Who beheld her pure heart glow
Spotless as the untrodden snow,
And, beholding, bade her haste
Of Heaven's endless joys to taste.

LITTLE GASPARD'S DREAM.

LITTLE Gaspard, weak and weary,
   Watched the morning hours advance,
With their gold and crimson touches
   Firing all the hills of France,
Pouring in a flood of beauty
   Through his window's latticed bars,
Whence all night his sleepless glances
   Sought the glory of the stars.
And, as broader still their splendor
   Deepened over tower and fell,
From the gray old chapel belfry
   Loudly pealed the Matin bell;
Then he raised his blue eyes softly
   To Our Lady's picture fair,
While his meek young soul was lifted
   On the snowy wings of prayer.
Day by day he heard the sounding
   Of the chapel's silvery chimes,
Whispering to his prisoned spirit
   Of Heaven's fadeless summer climes.
He had learned to know and love them,
   Joining in with each refrain—
With their ringing bursts of gladness,
   With their tolling throbs of pain.
They had voices full of meaning
   For the lonely orphan child;
But he loved them best when speaking
   Of her praise, the Mother mild.

Poor and crippled, born to sorrow,
  Gaspard's life knew little joy;
But the Mother of the Saviour
  Had been mother to the boy.
Through the dreary years he numbered,
  Living on his kinsman's dole,
'Twas her love that filled and brightened
  With its summer all his soul.
And to-day was the Assumption;
  Far along the village street
He could see the children passing,
  Bearing blossoms fair and sweet—
Bearing blossoms for the altar,
  Emblems meet of trust and love,
Eloquent of Him who giveth
  Bounteous graces from above.
And the tears flowed fast unbidden,
  With a longing deep and vain
For the hours of strength and gladness
  He would never know again—
Longings to behold the altar
  On his Mother's festal day;
See her shrine all decked and wreathèd
  With the summer flow'rets gay;
Hear the organ's sweet voice filling
  All the place with music sweet,
Till the soul seemed lifted upward,
  Upward to the Saviour's feet.
And at length, in broken murmurs,
  Did he say: "O Mother mine!
I alone have naught to offer,
  Naught to lay upon thy shrine.

My poor limbs refuse to bear me
   To the fields or forest bowers,
And I cannot crown thy image
   E'en with simple wild-wood flowers."
And he wept till o'er his spirit
   Came a sense of calmness deep,
And his wearied soul was drifted
   To the tranquil realms of sleep.

Then in dreams our holy Mother
   Sought and comforted her child,
Leading him through pleasant valleys
   Where Spring's sweetest blossoms smiled.
In their midst a patient pilgrim
   Bore his cross, enwreathed with flowers
Such as never sprang to being
   In earth's fairest garden bowers—
Stainless, snowy-petalled lilies
   By no earthly sunbeams spun,
Roses flushed with glowing beauty,
   Born not of the rain or sun.

Little Gaspard questioned softly:
   "Whither doth the pilgrim go?
And whence are the wreathèd blossoms,
   Bathèd in such heavenly glow?"

"Child, that pilgrim is thy spirit,
   And thy sufferings are the cross;
And the flowers entwined around it
   Show thy patience in thy loss.

They have bloomed amidst thy silence,
  'Neath the taunting words of scorn;
They have caught their glow and fragrance
  From thy pains for Jesus borne."
"And who walks beside the pilgrim,
  Speaking words of hope and cheer?"
"'Tis thy guardian angel, Gaspard,
  Who for ever hovereth near.
He it is who culls the blossoms
  Of thy patience, love, and prayer,
Aids thee that thy spirit faint not
  In the darkness of despair."
"And whence flow those shining rivers,
  Glowing like a golden crown?"
"Child, they are the steady currents
  Of God's graces flowing down.
Strengthened by their fresh'ning waters,
  Many a weary soul shall rise,
Clasp its cross, and journey onward
  In the pathway to the skies.
Courage, child! God's love and patience
  With his children knows no bound,
And 'his sacred presence' maketh
  All the wide earth holy ground.
Courage! In life's ceaseless battle
  Prove thyself a soldier tried;
Clothe thee with the proven armor,
  Love for Jesus Crucified;
Pray to him in simple trusting:
  He will strengthen and befriend,
And will give thee—priceless jewel—
  Perseverance till the end."

Gaspard waked; the noontide's glory
  Held the wide earth in its trance,
And the Angelus was pealing
  From the thousand towers of France.
Waked to days of helpless suffering,
  Waked to nights devoid of rest;
But his dream made endless summer
  In the chambers of his breast.
Still he heard that voice so thrilling,
  In its beauty sweet and grand;
Still he saw the shining rivers
  Flowing downward through the land;
Still he bore his cross unmurmuring,
  Though with bitterest pain oppressed,
Till his guardian angel called him
  Home to everlasting rest.

THE HAUNTED HOMESTEAD.

WHERE the tree-crowned mountains tower
    Grandly o'er the fertile plain
Stands the homestead orchard-girt
    'Mid its leagues of waving grain.

Fair before the forest lies,
    Bounding its broad meadows' sweep;
In its streams the fish disport
    Where the shades lie cool and deep.

But its garden-walks are sad,
    All its roses dead and sere,
And a gloom o'erhangs the place
    Through all seasons of the year.

There the zephyr's murmuring voice
    Has a tone of one that grieves,
And men say that spirits there
    Wander through the summer eves.

Up and down the olden stair,
    When night's shadows darkly fall,
Rustling robes are heard to glide,
    Footsteps tread along the hall.

In the chambers fair and high
    Voices whisper on the air;
As the midnight hour draws near
    Ghostly eyes are seen to stare;

And the wakened slumberer starts,
    Trembling with a chill of dread,
As he feels an ice-cold hand
    Rest a moment on his head;

And his straining vision marks,
    Dim as vapor on a glass,
Through the darkness moving slow,
    Shadowy, white-robed figures pass.

Deep the mystic gloom doth lie,
    Veiling all the ancient place,
But unto its hidden source
    None the mystery can trace.

Vainly do men question why
    Hapless spirits wander here
Nightly till the old clock's chimes
    Warn them of the dawning near.

And the dwellers in that home,
    As they wander to and fro,
Pause to breathe a pitying prayer
    For the restless spirits' woe.

CONVERSION OF FATHER HERMANN.

(From *Legends of the Blessed Sacrament*, by Mrs. E. M. Shapcote.)

'TWAS the glad Month of Our Lady ; from bright-
wreathed shrine and column
  Were breathing forth their fragrance the sweetest
      flowers of May,'
And our Mother's praises echoed, chanted by the
    sweetest singers
  Of that city, crowned by fashion as the gayest of
      the gay.

On the altar tapers glittered ; evening's dusky shades
    were banished
  By the myriad lights reflected from the kneeling
      throng below;
And as clouds of incense drifted, you might deem the
    angels bending
  To glean the sheaves of worship and the breathèd
      tales of woe.

Never had such glorious anthems waked the echoes
    of that temple
  As those which, rising, falling, seemed like voices
      from on high ;
For a prince's wealth assembled there the talent of
    the city,
  To sing her praise who ruleth, Queen of the earth
      and sky.

But the leader of the choir sat all unmoved, unheeding,
  'Mid the thrilling roll of music and eloquence and song ;
No ray of Faith illumined the darkness of his spirit,
  Or made him one in feeling with the rapt, adoring throng.

The lights, the flowers, the music, the worshippers around him,
  In the world's spoiled darling wakened no thoughts of God on high,
Till the solemn "Tantum Ergo," in its grand and glorious beauty,
  Making every heart beat faster as its accents drifted by ;

Then the Sacred Host was lifted, and as o'er the kneeling concourse
  The Saviour veiled his splendor, to bless each faithful heart,
A power unseen moved Hermann to bend his knee in homage,
  And in the son of Israel waked his nature's better part.

He knelt before the Saviour, and, as dew falls, fell the blessing :
  Oh ! the Queen of Heaven was pleading for a cherished soul that day,
One of those to her bequeathèd as she stood of old on Calvary,
  And she claimed him for her crowning in that precious month of May

Then, as hyacinthine blossoms stir within the earth's
    cold bosom
  When o'er smiling, sunny uplands comes the warm
    breath of the spring,
So Faith's flowers, pure and starlike, felt the first
    thrill of existence
  As the proud musician's forehead bent low before
    our King—

Flowers of Faith, whose wondrous beauty was to
    gladden earth's remoteness
  When that heart, by love so humbled, taught God's
    mercy far and near.
The lover of the Eucharist, its Apostle, as men nam-
    ed him,
  With eloquence Heaven-given showed to all, in
    beauty clear,

The wondrous love that prompted the Saviour thus
    to give us,
  In Sacramental symbols, himself to be our food,
Dwelling ever on our altars, and the mystery of his
    Passion
  Daily in the solemn service of the holy Church re-
    newed.

So by precept and example did he lead the eager
    masses
  To a nearer, clearer knowledge of our Eucharistic
    Lord,
And formed a Guard of Honor that from midnight
    until midnight,
  In the temples once deserted, now their sovereign
    King adored.

As the Sacred Host had called him to the light of
    Truth Eternal,
  In its honor did he offer all his life's exalted
    powers,
And as an humble servant of our Lady of Mount Carmel
  He shone a bright example in this worldly age of
    ours

"BREAD UPON THE WATERS."

I.

IRELAND.

ONE Christmas Eve the soldiers
   Came hurrying through the town
With glittering sword and halberd,
   With angry threat and frown.
From street to street they hastened,
   From house to house they passed,
Searching with swift impatience;
   And when they turned at last,
Clear rang the martial bugle,
   And then, with loud acclaim,
His monarch's will a herald
   To the people did proclaim:

"Thus speaks our gracious monarch:
   A thousand crowns reward,
And lands and courtly honors,
   To peasant hind or lord
Who will to her surrender
   The accursed priest of Rome
Who, late from Madrid city,
   Came here to seek a home.
Son of a rebel chieftain,
   Harbored by traitorous men,
Haste ye to track this foreign spy
   And drag him from his den!

Then will our monarch's favor
  Unto your town be shown,
And you your true allegiance
  Prove to her power and throne."

He ceased. The crowd pressed onward,
  The troopers passed along;
But one alone moved silent
  Amid the hurrying throng:
A man with age-bowed figure,
  Whose mantle, worn and brown,
Scarce hid his tattered garments—
  A beggar of the town.
Scant seemed the heed he yielded
  Unto the herald's call,
But right and left he wandered,
  As seeking aid from all.
Sometimes his eyes were lifted
  In swift, inquiring gaze,
As though to scan the features
  Of friends of other days.
Sometimes a kindly accent,
  Sometimes a word of cheer,
A dole of tender pity,
  Fell on the wanderer's ear.
At times he heard a murmur
  Of wild, heartrending pain
That forced him, in sweet sympathy,
  To pause and turn again
With the sweet balm of comfort
  Which will through all endure—
The spirit's wealth, the only gift
  The poor can give the poor.

Before a stately mansion
　At last he paused to rest;
But loitering squire and lackey vain
　Spurned him with taunt and jest,
Till one came forth who sternly
　Forbade their cruel play,
And bade his trusty henchman
　Lead the old man away:
"Go, give him food and shelter—
　He shall want neither here:
Upon the glorious morrow
　He'll share our Christmas cheer.
'Tis said the Irish baron
　Who built this hall of yore
Vowed that no hungry beggar
　Should ever leave his door;
And I, who 'neath his roof-tree
　Now break my daily bread,
Will that a wish so noble
　Should be as nobly sped."

Midnight within the castle
　Deep calm with silence blends
Mysteriously, as slumber's veil
　Upon the earth descends.
Sleep came not to the castle's lord;
　Thought bade its spell depart,
For heavily some burden lay
　Upon his warrior-heart.
At length he rose and traversed
　The hallway's murky gloom
In stern and musing silence
　Until he reached the room

Where, by his special mandate,
   The beggar had found rest
Since Christmas Eve—three days and nights
   The castle's honored guest.
He passed the threshold, closing
   With care the ponderous door,
Drew bolt and bar securely,
   And, when that task was o'er,
Turned where his guest, to greet him,
   Surprised and silent stood,
His wan face almost hidden
   Beneath his mantle's hood.
Slowly he crossed the chamber,
   Then, sight most strange to see,
Before the seeming beggar
   Sir Francis bent his knee,
Saying: "My heart reads rightly
   What no disguise can hide:
Humbly I crave the blessing
   To mortals ne'er denied.
Lo! at thy feet, my father,
   With contrite heart I lay
The burdening cares and sorrows
   And woes of many a day."

Oh! not for pen of poet
   That blissful hour to paint,
Which saw a world-worn spirit
   Bow to love's sweet restraint,
As the poor, hunted friar
   Upon his generous foe,
From Heaven's boundless wealth of mercy,
   Bade healing blessings flow.

The moments fled unnoticed;
  At length Sir Francis said:
"No longer mayst thou tarry here:
  A price is on thy head;
A thousand snares surround thee.
  Fear not, but come with me;
Beyond the city's outposts
  A friend awaiteth thee."

II.

ENGLAND.

Years passed; the royal favor
  Smiled on the knight no more,
But prison, chains, and torture
  The brave Sir Francis bore.
His broad estates sequestered,
  His friends in exile drear,
In London's gloomy prison,
  His death-hour drawing near,
He waited, hoping, praying,
  Ere life's last hour, a priest
Would bear unto his prison
  Love's Eucharistic Feast,
To nerve him for the anguish
  Of question, rack, and screw,
And to proclaim with courage
  His Faith and Hope anew.
Only the all-sustaining
  And all-embracing power
Of God could hold unfaltering
  His spirit in that hour.

So day by day dragged onward,
  Night after night told o'er
Its moments sorrow-freighted :
  No hope the dawnings bore
Until the last fair sunset
  That e'er would glad his eyes
On earth shot golden arrows
  Athwart the western skies;
Piercing his grated windows,
  Their glory seemed to bear
A ray of hope and comfort
  Through the close, fetid air.
And, watching it, Sir Francis
  Thought of the light untold
That shineth clear and radiant
  Within God's courts of gold.
While thus he mused the jailer
  Bearing the evening meal,
Entered, and, with a sternness
  He feigned but did not feel,
Ordered a strange attendant
  To place the food aright;
Then said: "I go; but, mark thee,
  Guard well the rebel knight.
For one brief hour I leave him
  Alone unto thy care,
Awhile his last night's vigil
  In prison-cell to share."

Oh! hour too brief and fleeting;
  Fast fled its golden sands,
Moments with blessings freighted,
  Borne down by angel hands;

For in his guard Sir Francis
  Saw the priest of his desire,
His guest that long-past Christmas—
  The grateful Irish friar.

"Through toils and myriad dangers,
  By service, pleading, prayer,
I won at last this favor—
  For one brief hour to share
With thee thy gloomy vigil,
  Thus seeking to repay
With Christian aid and counsel—
  The true soul's strength and stay—
The generous love and pity
  That in thy heart I found
When in my native city,
  Fierce enemies around,
Beneath my father's roof-tree,
  E'en by a foeman's hand,
Was given sweet rest and safety
  From the pursuer's band.
I go, but will be with thee
  Through all the night in prayer,
Pleading for thee God's mercy
  And all-embracing care.
And our poor, suffering brethren—
  They, too, will watch and pray,
And will upon the morrow
  Be near thee on thy way.
Where cross-road crowds press closest,
  In their demoniac glee,
Upon the way to Tyburn,
  Thy Lord will wait for thee."

Morn dawned: the mighty city,
  Half-veiled in vapory air,
Growled like a wild beast rousing
  From slumber in its lair;
And never wild beast waking
  In hunger for its prey
Was fiercer than the rabble
  In London streets that day.
Like streams from many sources
  Joined in one current strong,
Along the road to Tyburn
  Swept the excited throng.
Denser the crowd grew, denser,
  As the last hour drew nigh,
Thirsting for blood and eager
  To see a noble die.
Beside the cross-roads waiting,
  In garments worn and brown,
His meek head bowed in silence,
  Stood a beggar of the town.
Shuddering he heard the voices
  Of those around him rise
In blasphemy and anger,
  In fierce, exultant cries.
As nearer still and nearer
  The sad procession came,
The fury of the populace
  Burst forth in sudden flame.
Closer they pressed, and closer,
  To view the pallid face
Where prison, pain, and torture
  Had left their cruel trace;

Uttering their fierce reviling,
　Laughing in mocking glee,
In suffering and in dire distress
　A noble knight to see.
The sheriff and his armèd band
　Dealt blows like falling rain
To force the angry people back, .
　An open way to gain.
Vainly. They halt. The beggar then
　Unto Sir Francis sped;
Unnoticed 'mid the surging mass,
　He raised his bruisèd head:
With reverent lips and holy
　The final words were said.
Men only saw a beggar
　Clasping in fond embrace
The gallant knight and soldier
　Sprung from a lordly race;
But angels in that moment
　Beheld with reverence dread
A contrite heart receiving
　The Eucharistic Bread.
With threat and blow the soldiers
　Drove back the crowd at last,
And 'twixt the living wall once more
　The sad procession passed,
Until the final goal was reached—
　Dread Tyburn! sanctified
So often by the martyr's blood,
　Poured out in crimson tide.
There by the headsman's dripping blade
　Was the pure soul set free,
To join its kindred hosts aloft
　'Mid heavenly harmony.

Brave Christian knight! another soul
  Was waiting for him there;
Another valiant heart had ceased
  Life's heavy cross to bear;
For, stricken by a soldier's blade,
  The faithful friar fell,
The murmurs of the maddened throng
  Sounding his funeral knell.
Thence sorrowing friends with tender love
  Bore the still form away;
With Christian prayer and Christian hope
  They mourned him many a day,
But felt that on a brighter shore
  His sweet voice swelled the strain
Of endless love, of worship grand,
  Of joy that knows no pain.
United there behold the friends
  Who, by God's wondrous grace,
Passed through the martyr's sea of blood
  To dwell before his face;
Where all the greatest woes of earth
  Seem mean and trifling things
When weighed against the great reward
  Given by the King of kings.

MAUD'S HERO.

HE never said he loved me; never told
   That tale we women like so well to hold
A precious treasure folded evermore
In our hearts' keeping, something to dream o'er
When duty calls the dear one from our side,
Or in the holy calm of eventide.
And yet I knew it: plainly I could trace
The story in the brightening of his face,
The kindling glances of his azure eye,
And tenderer accents when I lingered nigh;
For we were much together in those days
Of summer's glow and autumn's golden haze—
He a young poet, skilled in learnèd lore
And the quaint legends of the days of yore,
From wearying labor for a while set free,
And resting there beside the sounding sea.

The days sped by with pleasure's cheery zest,
Till one wild eve, when cloud-veils draped the west,
And the Atlantic, summoning its host,
Charged in mad fury on the rocky coast.
I feel its thunders thrill my spirit yet
With a strange terror I can ne'er forget.
Then, as the night closed down without a star,
Arose the cry: " A vessel on the bar!"
High o'er the storm we heard a cannon boom:
Its flash revealed the brave ship through the gloom,

With broad decks crowded with a mortal freight,
Waiting 'mid surging seas a dreadful fate,
Waiting and praying 'mid the tempest's roar
For aid and safety from the friendly shore.

And the help came, for swift the tidings flew,
And from their huts the hardy fishers drew;
In that dread moment not a hand delayed,
But all were prompt and earnest in their aid:
The dainty loiterer from the distant town
Wrought with the sturdy toiler bold and brown.
I watched them man the life-boat, saw it start,
And with it went the joy of my young heart;
For he was foremost of the brave men there—
The few brave men with strength the waves to dare.

Tossed on the breakers, 'whelmed by rushing spray,
Steadfast and true it kept upon its way,
And all were rescued, all, all reached the shore,
Save him—I looked upon his face no more.
He died as heroes die: his strong young life
Went out amid the water's angry strife.
He died for others; may the God above
Accept his sacrifice of human love.
And Amy, dear, though years may intervene,
My faithful heart will keep his memory green.

GERTRUDE.

A LEGEND OF BRUSSELS.

THEY tell this tale in Brussels, city old :
   How, years ago, a gentle maiden won
By her rare beauty and her worth untold
   The true love of a rich old burgher's son—
A rich old burgher who with bitter scorn
   Looked down on those who toiled to earn their bread,
And vowed the fair embroideress lowly born
   Should never to a son of his be wed ;
For she was dowerless, and no dowerless wife
   With his consent his hoarded wealth would share.
Then darkly o'er the lover's sky of life
   His father's anger cast its clouding care.

But youth is hopeful; and while trusting hearts
   Are kindled by love's pure and fervent glow,
The darkest shadow from their path departs,
   And Hope's sweet smile makes summer here below.
Fair Gertrude, bending o'er her 'broidery-frame,
   Watched bird and flower beneath her hand unfold,
And, calling oft on Mary's holy name,
   Her sorrow to the pitying Mother told.

And once, when bells swung in the airy tower
    Flooded the listening air with golden rain,
The chime that told the Ave's holy hour
    Chanting Our Lady's praises once again,
The maiden, kneeling in her lonely room
    With bended head, her soul absorbed in prayer,
Gave all her life, its sunshine and its gloom,
    With childlike trust into Our Lady's care;
Then rose in gladness to her daily toil,
    Singing sweet hymns as her deft fingers wrought—
Strains that the tempter's luring efforts foil,
    And unto Gertrude's soul strange gladness brought.

Lo! as she sang and worked, beside her there
    Her startled gaze beheld a woman stand
With face of beauty more than angel's fair,
    Of presence gracious, calm, serene, and grand.
She placed a cushion upon Gertrude's knee,
    And with swift motion taught her hands to trace
And weave in filmy texture, fair to see,
    Blossom and bud in dainty folds of lace.
The maiden, e'en as one mute with surprise,
    Beheld the wondrous web, that grew and grew
Until the Lady turned her heavenly eyes
    Upon her with a sweet smile of adieu.
Passing forth from the chamber as she came,
    The vision vanished in the sunlit air,
While Gertrude, all her heart with love aflame,
    Sank to the earth in meek thanksgiving prayer.
"Ave Maria," tearfully she said,
    "O gentle Mother! thou hast heard my prayer;
I thank thee, thank thee for thy loving aid;
    I thank thee, Mother, for thy guarding care."

Time passed ; wealth came, for Gertrude's wondrous
    lace
  Grew famous in the city ; soon her dower
Flowed in from many coffers ; rank and place
  Were hers. The bells rang out her bridal hour,
And she dwelt happy in her husband's love.
  Children's blithe voices filled her home with
    glee ;
Within her heart nestled the snowy dove
  Of Peace, and there abode blest Charity.

But a dark season fell upon the land
  When Labor's arm was stayed, and Want came
    forth
With gaunt-faced Famine and her mournful band,
  Sweeping the country through from south to
    north.
Amid the city's poor they reigned supreme,
  Banishing plenty, happiness, and health,
But, vanquished, fled before the magic gleam
  Of gold within the palaces of wealth.
But lo ! to happy Gertrude came one day
  The wondrous Lady whom she once had seen ;
Around her shone the heaven's illumining ray,
  But stern and awful was her regal mien.
She spoke—what thrilling power in every word !
  What love and what reproof in every tone !—
"Gertrude, hast thou forgotten me ? I heard,
  When thou wert weeping in thy anguish lone—
I heard and helped thee. All ungrateful, thou
  Hast kept a secret what I did impart.
See, all around thee wail my children now,
  Who had been happy had they known thy art.

Go forth and teach the daughters of the land,
    The balm of knowledge on their sufferings pour,
And, won back by the cunning of each hand,
    The days of plenty will return once more.
Go forth and teach them; thus shalt thou atone
    For thy forgetfulness, thus shalt thou win
Pardon from Him whose power all nations own,
    Who on the Cross paid ransom for man's sin."

And then the Lady vanished. Gertrude sped
    With eager haste her mandate to fulfil,
On many hearts the light of hope to shed,
    And teach to all the secret of her skill.
And Heaven smiled on her labors: far around
    Among the poor the art she taught them spread,
And Industry her blessed guerdon found,
    And Plenty smiled as dreaded Famine fled.

DIMAS.

WITHIN a rude and lonely cave
    Fronting upon the desert wild,
As evening shadows veiled the earth
    An Arab mother nursed her child,
Singing in soft and soothing strains
    A sweet, melodious lullaby;
But ever in its low refrain
    There lurked the echo of a sigh,
And in her loving gaze was seen
    A shadow flung from sorrow's night.
For the dear child o'er which she bent
    With the foul leprosy was white.
Ah! well might that poor mother grieve—
    The child was all her joy in life.
Her husband was a robber-chief,
    Famed for his daring deeds of strife;
O'er all the desert's wide domain
    Men fled the terrors of his glance.
No Arab like to him could ride,
    Or hurl at speed the flying lance.

Now as the weeping mother nursed
    Her child within the lonely cave,
Lo! travellers from the desert came
    A shelter for the night to crave.
One was a man with flowing beard,
    And gentle but commanding grace—
A mien befitting him who sprang
    From royal David's kingly race.

And with him came the Mother-Maid,
   The Virgin spotless, meek, and mild,
Bearing within her sheltering arms
   God's well-beloved, the sweet Christ-Child.
Commanded by the angel's voice,
   From Nazareth's humble home they fled,
To seek in Egypt's pagan land
   A shelter for the Saviour's head.
Out through the desert vast and drear
   Where Israel's children once had trod,
And owned in trembling and in fear
   The presence of the Almighty God,
All day the sun with burning ray
   Shone down upon the Infant's form,
Or cold and cutting breezes blew
   When there was naught to keep him warm.
They felt the desert's burning thirst—
   For the sweet springs were scattered wide—
And many an hour of danger knew
   Before they reached the cavern's side.
There sought they shelter for the night;
   And the kind Arab woman spoke
Sweet welcome to the stranger-guests,
   For pity in her heart awoke:
And so she bade them enter in,
   Her cave's rude comforts freely share,
And served the Mother and the Child
   With tenderest reverence and care.

The presence of the Infant God,
   The glory of his smiling face,
Within her inmost spirit wrought
   A wondrous miracle of grace.

And in the water where the limbs
  Of Nazareth's blessèd Babe were laved
She washed her leprous child, and lo!
  The darling infant's life was saved.
The snowy tint presaging death
  By the dread scourge of leprosy
Vanished, and the young Dimas smiled,
  Rosy and fair, and blithe with glee.

Years passed, and Dimas' boyhood knew
  Full many a wild and daring deed;
Years passed, and, when to manhood grown,
  His father's band he joyed to lead.
But still within his outlawed life
  Some gentler feelings held a part—
Faint traces of the kindly glow
  That warmed his gentle mother's heart.
Yet oft his deeds of ruth and wrong
  To startled listeners were told,
Till outraged Justice sprang to arms
  And seized and bound the robber bold.
The judges doomed him to the death
  Upon that wondrous day of days
When, shrinking from the world's disgrace,
  The glorious sun withdrew his rays—
The day when Israel's teachers sage,
  High-priests, and rulers all combined
Condemned to outrage and to scorn
  The heavenly Saviour of mankind;
The day that saw the pitying Lord
  Forgiving each mad Deicide,
Looking with pity on the forms
  Hanging in pain on either side,

While round him rang the jest and jeer,
  The wild, derisive scoff and 'shout,
As the fierce passions of the hour
  Swayed all the city's rabble rout.
Then Dimas, torn with bitter pain
  And agony, joined in the cry;
But, meek and silent, Jesus gave
  A loving glance as sole reply.
Then Dimas, rapt in wonder, gazed
  Upon the patient Saviour long,
Till mingling tides of love and fear
  Within his wakening soul grew strong;
And Faith, in rays divinely bright,
  Shone o'er his spirit in that hour,
And with a contrite heart he owned
  In pleading tones the Saviour's power.
"Remember me when thou wilt come
  Into thy kingdom, Lord!" he cried.
"And thou shalt be with me to-day
  In Paradise," the Lord replied.

And the forgiven one was bathed
  With blood and water from the side
Of Christ when with a spear they oped
  Unto his heart a passage wide.
O blest baptismal rain which washed
  Away the leprosy of sin!
O passage opened to God's heart
  For weary ones to enter in!

HOMEWARD BOUND.

HOMEWARD bound, we heard the billows
   Murmur ever round our way,
As the mighty waste of waters
   Widened round us day by day,
From the hour when, backward glancing
   O'er the broad horizon's rim,
We beheld the Southern Islands
   Sinking in the distance dim ;
Then we bade the ocean's vastness
   To our joyous notes resound,
As each heart gave back an echo
   To the glad song, " Homeward Bound."

Song.

Homeward bound from the land of the stranger,
   Home, home o'er the deep-sounding sea ;
Home, home to the hearts that are watching,
   And waiting, and praying for me.

Oh! red lips have grieved o'er my absence,
   And bright eyes grown heavy and sad,
But homeward I haste, and my coming
   Will render them blithesome and glad.

Oh! the voice of their welcome will cheer me,
   And my long days of travel and toil
Be forgotten when dear ones are near me,
   At home on my own native soil.

For love with her crowning awaits me
  In that spot which my soul yearns to see,
Where daily and nightly my fond ones
  Are watching and praying for me.

. . . . . .

There was one who journeyed with us,
  Gray and wrinkled, bent and old,
One who sat in musing silence
  While his comrades sang, or told
Tales fraught with adventurous daring—
  Perils upon sea or strand;
Dangers of the golden regions
  In the wild Australian land;
Stories of the lone black forest
  Where the wily bushmen lay,
Leagued with cunning convict robbers
  Bolder, bloodier far than they;
Till the youngest of our party
  Courage for the question found,
Asking: "Whither art thou journeying?'
  And he answered, "Homeward bound.

"Homeward bound—God only knoweth
  What those two words mean to me.
Many, many years of sorrow
  I have dwelt beyond the sea—
Years of bitter pain and heartache,
  Years of weary, hopeless toil,
Serving out my term of labor,
  Convict on a foreign soil;

Hearing never word or token
   From the dear ones left behind,
From my young wife fair and loving,
   From my father old and blind.
When my penal term was over,
   I, grown prematurely old,
Scorned, despised, and half-despairing,
   Toiled to win a little gold,
Just enough to bear me homeward ;
   But no smile of fortune came,
Want and sickness adding horror
   To the convict's hated name.
I have written—written often—
   But no answer came to me
Through those dreary, dreary seasons
   Since I crossed the sounding sea.
You have hopes and dreams ; your future
   Beckons brightly to you yet ;
All your crosses are but shadows,
   You have nothing to regret,
While I weary with this struggle
   Of my spirit evermore.
Will one friend be left to greet me
   When I reach my native shore ? "

Then he told his life's sad story
   To the eager, listening ring :
He had loved his fallen country
   Better than he loved his king ;
For the rest, no boy among us
   But knew well the patriot's gain,
In those days of want and bloodshed,
   Were the gibbet and the chain ;

When the country-side was swarming
  With the "Redcoats," and, in fear,
From their homes to fields and ditches
  Fled the people far and near.
And we listened to his story,
  While the waves no bond can hold,
Chanted on the song unending,
  Through the ages they have told.

Days passed on; the weary voyage
  Drew at last unto its close,
But the old man faded daily
  'Neath the burden of his woes;
And when only three days' sailing
  Lay betwixt us and our home,
From the deck no more the exile
  Watched the seething waters foam.
So we sought him; he was lying
  Calm and voiceless in his pain,
But the hand of death had sealed him
  With its signet bold and plain.
Pitying eyes were watching o'er him,
  Rude but kindly hearts were there,
Soothing him with words of comfort,
  Joining with him in his prayer
For one glimpse of dear old Ireland,
  One breath of her fragrant breeze,
Life to save him from the burial
  In the bosom of the seas.
And his prayer was heard: he lingered
  Growing weaker day by day,
Till we, watching by his bedside
  In the morning cold and gray,

Heard the sound of "Land!"
  And turning at the old man's eager cry,
"Let me look upon my country,
  Let me see her ere I die!"

Then we bore him up ; his glances
  Lingered lovingly and long
On the nearing land, whose story
  Has been told so oft in song.
And at noontide, when our vessel
  In the crowded harbor lay,
Came a priest of God to bless him
  Ere his spirit passed away.
And we laid him with his kindred
  In the churchyard's sacred ground :
Rest eternal was the ending
  Of his voyage homeward bound.

Better than to learn the story
  Of his father's helpless years,
Of his young wife's tragic ending,
  Maddened by appalling fears.

Years have passed ; the blithesome travellers
  Who sailed homeward long ago
Now are scattered ; some are sleeping
  In the grave so dark and low.
But when ocean's voice is calling
  With a sad and solemn sound,
In my heart awakes the echo
  Of the old song, "Homeward bound" ;

Though to me a deeper meaning
  In its every accent lies,
For my loved ones now await me
  In my home beyond the skies,
Where the present's toil and trouble
  And the shadows of the past,
Fade into the joys celestial
  That for evermore will last.

A CHRISTMAS LEGEND.

HOW the wild winds shouted, how they laughed in glee,
Holding their mad revels upon land and sea!
Over hill and valley pealed the thunder's tone,
But the storm seemed fiercest in the forest lone.
Through its tangled fastness, at the close of day,
Homeward bound, Sir Walter held his lonely way.
Round his path the tempest's clarion summons rang,
O'er him ice-bound branches struck with sullen clang;
Shadow upon shadow, night and winter's gloom,
Made the great Black Forest seem a very tomb.
Snow-drifts hid the pathway, but he still pressed on
Till his good steed's courage, strength, and speed had flown;
And when midnight's fingers closed the gates of day
He was wandering blindly in the woods astray.
Then Sir Walter humbly bowed his knightly head;
"Dear Lord, send me shelter from the storm," he said.
"Thou whose laws I honor, thou whose power I fear,
Stretch thy hand to aid me, or I perish here.
By thy wondrous mercies to the earth made known,
By the night of beauty which o'er Bethlehem shone,
On this eve of Christmas, Father, do I claim
Refuge, food, and shelter in thy dear Son's name."

While he prayed there glimmered through the frosty
    night,
Close before the wanderer, a welcome ray of light.
At the sight Sir Walter hastened on with speed,
Swifter sped the footsteps of his jaded steed,
Till he reached a cottage standing rude and lone,
Through whose narrow casement the red firelight
    shone;
There in haste dismounting, humbly did he claim
Shelter from the tempest in the Saviour's name.
Open swung the portal, and the knight in need
Found a welcome refuge for himself and steed.

By the glowing hearthside brave Sir Walter stood,
Grateful for the warmth of the blazing wood,
While his boy-host near him sweetly spake and
    smiled
On the way-worn traveller of the forest wild;
For the only dweller in that cottage lone
Was a child whose beauty more than angel's shone.
He with deft white fingers from the weary knight
Loosed the heavy armor shining cold and bright;
From his brow he helped him lift the gold-inlaid
Helmet on which glittered the Cross of the Crusade;
Then bade him sate his hunger with the wine and
    bread
Which on the rude table by the hearth he spread.

Calm and clear and peaceful came the Christmas
    morn,
Jubilant with praises of the Christ new-born;
And Sir Walter, rising, turned to go his way,
But before he parted bent his thanks to say.

Then the boy-host answered in the same sweet voice,
E'en whose lightest whisper made the knight rejoice:
"Thou whose heart ne'er faltered and whose hand ne'er failed
When the Paynim forces thy brave band assailed,
Keep thy heart as spotless and thy faith as pure,
Grounded on God's promise ever safe and sure,
As when, battling bravely for the Holy Shrine,
Thou didst win thy laurels in far Palestine;
Let no wealth or treasure, let no earthly fame,
Be thy star of guiding, but thy Saviour's name—
Talisman of power, when thy life shall cease,
To unlock the portals of his home of peace."

Forth rode good Sir Walter, pondering on each word
Of the child, whose lesson all his being stirred,
When across the silence, borne with joyous swell,
Came the joyous summons of the Christmas bell.
And the opening vista showed a village there,
With the people hastening to the house of prayer:
At its altar kneeling bent the brave knight low,
For in pictured beauty, girt by taper's glow,
Shone the infant Saviour, and the face that smiled
From the breathing canvas was the forest child.

And the story telleth how Sir Walter laid
Down his warlike weapons, and within the shade
Of the great Black Forest dwelt a hermit lone
Where the Christ-Child's beauty first upon him shone,
Keeping his heart spotless, keeping his faith pure,
Trusting in God's promise ever safe and sure.

KING ALFRED AND THE ORPHAN.

OUT from the rosy chambers of the east
    The Morning in her dewy splendor came,
And far along the valleys, blossom-crowned,
    The wild birds hailed her with a glad acclaim.

From the low huts dotting the fallow meads
    The smoke-wreaths slowly rose to greet the sun,
And the first sounds of life by hill and glade
    Proclaimed the duties of the day begun.

But fairest shone the gentle morning's smile
    On the bright scenes round royal Alfred's home,
Where clash of spear on shield, and martial din,
    Challenged the echoes of the azure dome.

Within the palace moved the courtier throng;
    For Alfred held his court at early morn,
With clearer reason to decide each case
    Ere swayed by passions of the noontide born.

So on his throne of power the monarch sate,
    And round him thronged his lords and leaders all—
Brave men who bore the token of each fight
    That freed the Saxons from the Danish thrall.

But on that morning none before him came
    With cause of grievance or to seek redress,
And the king's questioning glances vainly sought
    Amid his thanes the Earl of Holderness.

As o'er its humbler brethren of the wood
    The regal pine its warrior brow uprears,
So Holderness, in proud pre-eminence,
    In field or court stood foremost 'mid his peers.

Of giant form and lion-heart was he,
    His place in battle by his monarch's side,
Where his keen weapon marked his prowess stern
    By its heaped swath of corpses high and wide.

And Alfred loved him for his courage high,
    And his clear mind in council often tried;
But vainly now for many morns his glance
    Sought for that form of warrior strength and pride.

At length unto his lips the question rose,
    His deep voice fraught with anxious tenderness:
" Why from our presence tarries thus so long
    Our well-beloved, the Earl of Holderness?"

Forth from his place amid the courtier crowd
    Strode Wulph, a warrior famed in Alfred's wars;
The storms of battle round his life had raged,
    And left his face seamed deep with many scars.

He cried aloud: "O king! bold warriors meet
    A foe 'gainst whom nor strength nor skill avails—
A foe who enters in where Pleasure dwells,
    And at whose touch her brightest glory pales.

"Before his blow our bravest veiled his crest:
    The great lord earl, my liege, is now no more,
And his good lady Alice, slain by grief,
    Sleeps by his side upon the northern shore.

"To me the news was borne but yesternight,
  And much I grieve to think the great earl dead;
But death is still the birthright of the brave,
  And all his tasks on earth were nobly sped.

"Yet hear me, O my king. The wide domain
  Of Holderness, from Humber to the sea,
Without a lord reverteth to thy hands;
  And, my good liege, I pray thee give it me."

Ere Alfred could reply to his appeal
  Wise Thurstan spoke: "Nay, sire; at thy command
I crossed the seas and to the Danish court
  Bore the commission of thy royal hand,

"And by my wisdom, from experience bought,
  Did more to bridge dread war's volcanic gulf
Than all the hecatombs of foemen slain
  In the fierce battle by the warrior Wulph.

"Give me, as meed of duty nobly done,
  The lands from Humber to the German Sea;
And trust me, sire, no pagan hordes shall dare
  Cross the green border of the earldom free."

Then sturdy Wulph made answer fierce and high,
  And calmer Thurstan to his taunts replied,
While Alfred, sorrowing o'er his subject's death,
  Nor thought nor answer gave to either side,

Though round about him still the tumult grew,
  As friends on either side their counsel lent,
Till from the lower entrance of the hall
  A cry for justice on the air was sent;

And, pressing slowly through the eager throng,
  A woman, worn and aged, made her way,
Leading beside her a fair boy whose face
  Shone in its beauty like a morning's ray.

Leading the child up to the monarch's throne,
  The woman cried : "Behold, to thee I bring
The rightful heir of Holderness, to claim
  The care and the protection of his king.

"Late orphaned by his honored parents' death,
  His claim unto his heritage ignored
By all the neighboring chieftains, whose rude clans
  To waste and pillage o'er his lands are poured ;

The only child, the only hope and joy,
  Of the great earl, thy subject and thy friend—
His claim, the orphan's claim, demands thy care ;
  Give it to him, and Heaven will blessings send."

"His claim, forsooth !" an angry baron cried.
  "What 'gainst our foes can his child-arm avail
When war's dread messenger, with bended bow,
  Rouses the dweller of each Saxon vale?"

Forth from his place close to the nurse's side
  The boy-earl stepped, and back his curls he threw
From his fair brow, and to the baron's face
  Lifted his truthful eyes of azure hue.

And when he spoke his voice was clear and strong
  As though amid his playmates free he trod :
"True, my child-arm as yet can wield no sword,
  But for my country I can pray to God."

Then from his throne the good King Alfred rose
  And clasped the boy's small, white hand in his own,
Saying: "The lands of Holderness belong
  Unto this child, and unto him alone.

"My noble thanes, my gallant warriors all,
  Shall have meet guerdon for each duty done,
But the broad lands from Humber to the sea
  Belong by right unto the great earl's son.

"False were I to the trust my Maker gave
  When in my hands he placed the royal dower,
If to the great and strong I lent my aid
  To crush the weak beneath might's cruel power."

LEGEND OF SAN MIGUEL.

"THE place is desolate," he said,
   "All desolate and drear
From valley unto mountain head;
You mark the ruin Time has spread,
   And Plenty smiles not here.

"The broken walls, the sunken roof,
   The fields where once the maize
In summer flung its silken woof
Of flossy threads—all, all are proof
   Of brighter, happier days:

"Of days when far by hill and stream
   The sounds of life were heard,
When in the autumn's crimson beam
The fruited orchard-boughs would gleam,
   And carolled many a bird;

"When round the Mission Cross arose
   My people's happy home,
And there, at dawn or evening's close,
The chimes' glad, silvery summons rose
   Up to the azure dome;

"And, answering to the merry call
   Of their far-echoing swell,
From lowly hut or pleasant hall
Unto the stately church came all
   Who dwelt at San Miguel.

"Oh! these were days of joy and peace,
  Bright days of hopeful toil,
From which eve brought a glad release,
And every morrow saw increase
  The wealth of herds and soil.

"And yonder, placid, bright, and blue,
  The lovely lake was seen,
From whence the earnest toilers drew
The rippling waves of crystal hue
  To field and orchard green;

"The lake within whose bosom fair—
  Or so our legends told—
Dwelt one whom Neptune's envoys bare
To durance stern, and firmly there
  They made his prison hold;

"A subject of the Sea King's sway
  Condemned to exile here,
Where balmy inland breezes play,
Where then through every winding way
  Wandered the mountain deer.

"And here he dwelt through many years,
  Their number none may know;
His form was such as thrills with fears
The heart when on the gaze uprears
  The cobra's shape of woe.

"Seldom by mortals was he seen,
  And only then by those
Who dared to tread the midnight green
Beside the lake's star-lighted sheen,
  Reckless of terror's throes;

"Though oft throughout the summer day
  Its tranquil breast was stirred,
As when along some sheltered bay
The whistling winds of ocean play,
  Though here no storm was heard.

"And the bright lake divided stood
  From the Salina's flow
By a broad belt of upland good,
Since levelled by that fearful flood
  Of many a year ago

"When up the river's winding course,
  Re-echoing wild and free,
Far louder than the tempest's force
Was heard, in accents stern and hoarse,
  The summons of the sea.

"'Twas then, his term of exile o'er,
  The hour of parting came :
It came amid the sullen roar
Of stormy waves dashed on the shore,
  While the dread lightning's flame

"And the fierce thunder's crashing sound
  Reverberating far,
Shook all the mighty mountains round,
Until the country's widest bound
  Seemed rent by Nature's war.

"Oh! sacredly my people keep
  The memory of that year,
Which marked the wildly rushing sweep
Of torrents from each mountain steep,
  And left this ruin here ;

"When the lake's boundaries gave way,
  And down the valley came,
Its waters in resistless sway,
Bearing upon its onward way
  All that had life or name.

"The soldiers keeping watch that night
  At San Antonio heard
The awful thundering of its might,
And rushing forth in pale affright,
  While awe each bosom stirred,

"Saw, on the river's crest of foam,
  The serpent seaward glide
Down to his own long-wished-for home,
Where, fathoms deep, he loved to roam
  'Neath the Pacific's tide.

"That winter, with its saddening hours,
  Passed slowly, slowly by,
And spring-time came with grass and flowers
To deck the fields and crown the bowers,
  And birds sang clear and high.

"But oh! the ruin far and wide,
  And vanished from our sight
The lake whose waves, a crystal tide,
Had gladdened all the valley side,
  And blessed its verdure bright.

"Now all around is sad and still,
  And seldom sound the chimes
Whose voices rose o'er dale and hill
Like echoes of the heavenly will
  In the dear olden times."

AT THE GENERAL RODEO.

MAY, 185–.

"ARISE, for the day is breaking,
   The timid dawn is here,
The setting stars are rising
   To brighten another sphere.

"Ho, Juan! José! Diego!
   'Tis time to mount and ride
Down through the flower-gemmed vega,
   Over the mountain-side.

"Gather the straying horses,
   Waken the slumbering men;
Lead them out through the morning,
   Some to the distant glen,

"Some to the forest shadows,
   Some to the mountain-side,
Where'er through the grassy pastures
   The cattle wander wide.

"See that no run is slighted,
   Let the widest bounds be sought,
And into the great rodeo
   The scattered herds be brought."

Thus to his men the grave ranchero spoke,
And at his call the lithe vaqueros woke;

Upon the embers broiled their matin cheer,
And quaffed their morning draught of water clear ;
Saddled their well-trained steeds, and o'er the waste
Upon their errands sped in fiery haste.
Swift as an arrow from the bended bow
Along the smooth green vale the coursers go,
Or trace the narrow pathway up each height,
Cross the tall summits, vanish out of sight ;
And soon the startled echoes wake to hear
The wild halloo, the far re-echoing cheer,
And down the hills and o'er the smiling plain
Panting and wild-eyed fly the herds amain.
From every side the living torrents run,
Dappled, or brinded, gleaming white, or dun.
Their snowy horns in the clear sunlight glow
Like foam flung up from surging waves below,
But yet instinctively their course they guide
Where the rodeo-ground stands waste and wide ;
And soon by thousands there they waiting stand
Amid the morning glory of the land,
While all the air is balmy with the sweet
Breath of the flowers crushed by their hurrying feet.

Around them now the arrieros ride,
Sons of the soil, dark-skinned and dusky-eyed.
With eager gaze they scan the moving mass,
As to and fro with tightened rein they pass,
Waiting until their masters' words shall say
Who first shall part their herds upon this day—
Their masters, men of every clime and race :
The Spaniard with his proud and courtly grace ;
Americanos from each State that lends
Stars to the banner o'er our land that bends ;

Blithe sons of Erin, pilgrims from the Rhine,
And they who dwelt in France beneath the vine;
Their homes by Calaveras' distant creek,
Or fertile plains 'neath Santa Anna's peak,
Or where the lake in lonely beauty lies,
Or Gavilan seems lifted to the skies.
They sought their cattle where the bland airs play
Across the fertile vale of San José;
For, all unchecked, the straying herds were free
To roam o'er wind-swept miles of blooming lea.

Now all is ready! See yon rider pass
With tightened rein amid the moving mass,
Daring the lowering fronts, the angry eyes,
And deep-toned bellowings from its midst that rise
Where haughty monarchs of the herds in vain
Essay the freedom of the wild to gain.
With almost human knowledge, human skill,
The well-trained steeds their riders' wish fulfil,
Yet not unscathèd always: Death looks down
Too oft upon the scene with angry frown,
When cattle, tortured by the thirst and heat,
Blinded by dust torn up by myriad feet,
Lashed into fury by the warning cry
Of watchful guards from whom they seek to fly,
Plunge wildly forth, their freedom to regain
In sheltering covert or extended plain.
But happy Fortune seems to-day to bless
The busy toilers with her fond caress.
Fast speed the hours, the work is almost done;
High in the heavens rides the noonday sun.
In many groups the parted cattle stand,
Waiting the glittering knife, the heated brand.

Hither and thither hurrying horsemen ride,
Moving amid the maddened living tide.
But mark how yonder, o'er the grassy mead,
The fierce barroso bull at headlong speed
Flies hillward! From a hundred eager throats
Ring hoarsely out commands and warning notes.
"Hi! Manuel, hi!" The nearest rider turns,
Answering his name. His youthful bosom burns;
He sinks the rowels in his charger's flanks,
And speeds away 'twixt nodding wild-oat ranks
That lift their plumèd crests on either side,
Gemmed with the bright Eschscholtzia's hue of
    pride;
Onward upon his race, unknowing fear,
Hearing afar his comrades' ringing cheer,
Eager to prove with earnest heart and will
His good steed's mettle and his herdsman skill.
Onward he hurries in the headlong race,
And gains upon the object of his chase,
Loosening his good riata as he runs,
Trampling the blossoms wooed by dews and suns.
Nearer, and now aloft the noose is swung;
Nearer, and o'er the shaggy head is flung:
He hears afar a cheer, but hears no more,
For soon, alas! the boy's swift race is o'er.
As the rope tightens, turning to the brunt,
With blazing eyes and lifted tawny front,
And a mad bellow filling earth and air,
The bull turns on his captor fiercely there.
Swift circling round, the youth essays in vain
The unequal strife 'gainst such foe to sustain.
But, fatal moment! when at last, unnerved,
The charger for a moment nearer swerved,

The blazing orbs were veiled, the stout head bent,
And steed and rider crashing earthward sent;
And o'er the twain the bull, in triumph dread,
Shakes from his dripping horns the blood-drops red.
A cry rings out, "Manuel is down!" and then
Swift to the rescue haste the eager men.
One stout-armed giant tosses to the plain
The maddened beast, to rise no more again ;
While others toil to lift with care and speed
From the poor boy the burden of his steed.
Ah! clear as sunlight in the summer skies
They read death written in his glazing eyes,
And hear him falter with pain-laden breath :
"Pray for us at the hour of our death "—
The closing sentence of the sweetest prayer
That keeps man from the demon of despair.
Kneeling beside him, see, one murmurs o'er
The contrite's prayer; the pale lips move once more,
Pleading for pardon. One who sped to bring
Cool water from the nearest bubbling spring
Bathes hand and brow ; all try with friendly art
To turn aside Death's cruel, venomed dart.
But the lids flutter, and with one low moan
His spirit to the judgment-seat has flown.
And men whose lives had known rude border strife,
And all the dangers of wild Western life,
Deemed it no shame that pitying tear-drops rose
And fell above that young life's sudden close ;
And sadly asked they: "Who, alas! will bear
Back to the widow's home her darling heir ?
Who will dare face a stricken mother's woe
Above her son, her only, thus laid low ?"

An aged kinsman of the youth drew near;
On him devolves the task the bravest fear.
Soon from the willow's pliant boughs is made
A litter rude, and pitying hands have laid
Upon it the still body of the boy
That held so late a soul athrill with joy:
And the sad cortége went upon its way,
O'er blooming vales, 'neath forest arches gray,
To the far home where foaming waters made
A murmur round the scenes where once he played.

Then Toil with clarion summons called again
His votaries to their daily round of gain,
To track the herds through many a drear defile,
To watch from eve till dawning's rosy smile,
Counting the hours of guard by stars that glowed
Or paled upon their far celestial road.
But many a year a rugged wayside cross
Told to the wanderers there the widow's loss,
And asked the passer-by to pause and say
One Pater for the spirit passed away.

www.ingramcontent.com/pod-product-compliance
Lightning Source LLC
Chambersburg PA
CBHW051200300426
44116CB00006B/391